Lecture Notes in Computer Scien

Commenced Publication in 1973
Founding and Former Series Editors:
Gerhard Goos, Juris Hartmanis, and Jan van Leeuwen

T0237961

Simone Fischer-Hübner
Costas Lambrinoudakis
Günther Pernul (Eds.)

Trust, Privacy and Security in Digital Business

6th International Conference, TrustBus 2009
Linz, Austria, September 3-4, 2009
Proceedings

 Springer

Volume Editors

Simone Fischer-Hübner
Karlstad University, Department of Computer Science
Universitetsgatan 2, 651 88 Karlstad, Sweden
E-mail: simone.fischer-huebner@kau.se

Costas Lambrinoudakis
University of the Aegean
Laboratory of Information and Communication Systems Security
Department of Information and Communication Systems Engineering
Karlovassi, 83200, Samos, Greece
E-mail: clam@aegean.gr

Günther Pernul
University of Regensburg, Department of Management Information Systems
Universitätsstraße 31, 93053 Regensburg, Germany
E-mail: guenther.pernul@wiwi.uni-regensburg.de

Library of Congress Control Number: 2009932880

CR Subject Classification (1998): K.4.4, H.3.5, E.3, C.2, D.4.6, K.6.5

LNCS Sublibrary: SL 4 – Security and Cryptology

ISSN   0302-9743
ISBN-10 3-642-03747-X Springer Berlin Heidelberg New York
ISBN-13 978-3-642-03747-4 Springer Berlin Heidelberg New York

springer.com

© Springer-Verlag Berlin Heidelberg 2009
Printed in Germany

Typesetting: Camera-ready by author, data conversion by Scientific Publishing Services, Chennai, India
Printed on acid-free paper   SPIN: 12739240   06/3180   5 4 3 2 1 0

Preface

This book presents the proceedings of the 6th International Conference on Trust, Privacy and Security in Digital Business (TrustBus 2009), held in Linz, Austria during September 3–4, 2009. The conference continues from previous events held in Zaragoza (2004), Copenhagen (2005), Krakow (2006), Regensburg (2007) and Turin (2008).

The advances in the information and communication technologies (ICT) have raised new opportunities for the implementation of novel applications and the provision of high-quality services over global networks. The aim is to utilize this 'information society era' for improving the quality of life for all citizens, disseminating knowledge, strengthening social cohesion, generating earnings and finally ensuring that organizations and public bodies remain competitive in the global electronic marketplace. Unfortunately, such a rapid technological evolution cannot be problem free. Concerns are raised regarding the 'lack of trust' in electronic procedures and the extent to which 'information security' and 'user privacy' can be ensured.

TrustBus 2009 brought together academic researchers and industry developers, who discussed the state of the art in technology for establishing trust, privacy and security in digital business. We thank the attendees for coming to Linz to participate and debate the new emerging advances in this area.

The conference program included one keynote presentation, one panel session and six technical papers sessions. The keynote speech entitled "Of Frogs and Herds: Behavioral Economics, Malleable Privacy Valuations, and Context-Dependent Willingness to Divulge Personal Information," was delivered by Alessandro Acquisti from Carnegie Mellon University (USA). The panel session addressed the area of "Security and Privacy Economics," while the reviewed paper sessions covered a broad range of topics, from access control models to security and risk management, and from privacy and identity management to reputation and security measurements. The conference attracted many high-quality submissions, each of which was assigned to four referees for review and the final acceptance rate was 35%.

We would like to express our thanks to the various people who assisted us in organizing the event and formulating the program. We are very grateful to the Program Committee members and the external reviewers, for their timely and rigorous reviews of the papers. Thanks are also due to the DEXA Organizing Committee for supporting our event, and in particular to Gabriela Wagner for her help with the administrative aspects.

Finally we would like to thank all of the authors that submitted papers for the event, and contributed to an interesting set of conference proceedings.

September 2009

Simone Fischer-Hübner
Costas Lambrinoudakis
Günther Pernul

Organization

Program Committee

General Chair

Günther Pernul   University of Regensburg, Germany

Program Committee Co-chairs

Simone Fischer-Hübner   University of Karlstad , Sweden
Costas Lambrinoudakis   University of the Aegean, Greece

International Program Committee Members

Acquisti, Alessandro	Carnegie Mellon University (USA)
Atluri, Vijay	Rutgers University (USA)
Breaux, Travis	North Carolina State University (USA)
Casassa Mont, Marco	HP Labs Bristol (UK)
Chadwick, David	University of Kent (UK)
Clarke, Nathan	University of Plymouth (UK)
Clayton, Richard	University of Cambridge (UK)
Cuppens, Frederic	ENST Bretagne (France)
Damiani, Ernesto	Universitá degli Studi di Milano (Italy)
De Capitani di Vimercati, Sabrina	University of Milan (Italy)
De Meer, Hermann	University of Passau (Germany)
Diaz, Claudia	K.U. Leuven ESAT/COSIC (Belgium)
Eloff, Jan	University of Pretoria (South Africa)
Fernandez-Gago, Carmen	University of Malaga (Spain)
Fernandez, Eduardo B.	Florida Atlantic University (USA)
Foresti, Sara	University of Milan (Italy)
Furnell, Steven	University of Plymouth (UK)
Fuss, Juergen	University of Applied Science in Hagenberg (Austria)
Geneiatakis, Dimitris	University of the Aegean (Greece)
Gonzalez-Nieto, Juan M.	Queensland University of Technology (Australia)

Gritzalis, Dimitris	Athens University of Economics and Business (Greece)
Gritzalis, Stefanos	University of the Aegean (Greece)
Hansen, Marit	Independent Center for Privacy Protection (Germany)
Jøsang, Audun	Oslo University (Norway)
Kalloniatis, Christos	University of the Aegean (Greece)
Karyda, Maria	University of the Aegean (Greece)
Katsikas, Sokratis	University of Piraeus (Greece)
Kesdogan, Dogan	University of Siegen (Germany)
Kokolakis, Spyros	University of the Aegean (Greece)
Lioy, Antonio	Politecnico di Torino (Italy)
Lopez, Javier	University of Malaga (Spain)
Mana Gomez, Antonio	University of Malaga (Spain)
Markowitch, Olivier	Universite Libre de Bruxelles (Belgium)
Martinelli, Fabio	CNR (Italy)
Matyas, Vashek	Masaryk University (Czech Republic)
Mitchell, Chris	Royal Holloway, University of London (UK)
Mouratidis, Haris	University of East London (UK)
Mueller, Peter	IBM Zurich Research Lab. (Switzerland)
Mylopoulos, John	University of Toronto (Canada)
Okamoto, Eiji	University of Tsukuba (Japan)
Olivier, Martin S.	University of Pretoria (South Africa)
Oppliger, Rolf	eSecurity Technologies (Switzerland)
Papadaki, Maria	University of Plymouth (UK)
Patel, Ahmed	Kingston University (UK) - University Kebangsaan (Malaysia)
Pfitzmann, Andreas	Dresden University of Technology (Germany)
Piattini, Mario	University Castilla-La Mancha (Spain)
Pohl, Hartmut	FH Bonn-Rhein-Sieg (Germany)
Posch, Karl	University of Technology Graz (Austria)
Possega, Joachim	University of Passau (Germany)
Priebe, Torsten	Capgemini (Austria)
Quirchmayr, Gerald	University of Vienna (Austria)
Rannenberg, Kai	Goethe University Frankfurt (Germany)
Rudolph, Carsten	Fraunhofer Institute for Secure Informatio Technology (Germany)
Ruland, Christoph	University of Siegen (Germany)
Schaumueller-Bichl, Ingrid	University of Applied Science in Hagenberg (Austria)
Schunter, Matthias	IBM Zurich Research Lab. (Switzerland)
Teufel, Stephanie	University of Fribourg (Switzerland)
Tjoa, A Min	Technical University of Vienna (Austria)
Tomlinson, Allan	Royal Holloway, University of London (UK)

Xenakis, Christos   University of Piraeus (Greece)
Zhou, Jianying   I2R (Singapore)

External Reviewers

Clauß, Sebastian   Dresden University of Technology, Germany
Drogkaris, Prokopis   University of the Aegean, Greece
Fritsch, Lothar   Norsk Regnesentral, Norway
Hazard, Chris   North Carolina State University, USA
Johns, Martin   University of Passau, Germany
Muñoz, Antonio   University of Malaga, Spain
Pöhls, Henrich   University of Passau, Germany
Pujol, Gimena   University of Malaga, Spain
Radmacher, Mike   Goethe University, Germany
Reklitis, Evangelos   University of the Aegean, Greece
Rizomiliotis, Panagiotis   University of the Aegean, Greece
Steinbrecher, Sandra   Dresden University of Technology, Germany
Tsochou,Aggeliki   University of the Aegean, Greece
Weber, Christian   Goethe University, Germany

Table of Contents

Access Control

Authentication and Authorisation

User Profiling and Re-identification: Case of University-Wide Network Analysis

Marek Kumpošt and Vašek Matyáš

Faculty of Informatics, Masaryk University, Brno
{xkumpost,matyas}@fi.muni.cz

Abstract. In this paper we present our methodology for context information processing, modeling users' behaviour and re-identification. Our primary interest is to what extent a user can be re-identified if we have his "user profile" and how much information is required for a successful re-identification. We operate with "user profiles" that reflect user's behaviour in the past. We describe the input date we use for building behavioural characteristics; similarity searching procedure and an evaluation of the re-identification process. We discuss (and provide results of our experiments) how different initial conditions, as well as different approaches used in the similarity searching phase, influence the results and propose the optimal scenario where we obtain the most accurate results. We provide experimental results of re-identification of three protocols (SSH, HTTP and HTTPS).

1   Introduction

The popularity of services (typically web oriented), that serve customized content to users, has grown rapidly during the last decade. Profiles of users of such services correspond to their preferences and interests and are formed progressively as they use the services. The majority of current approaches rely on *context information* – information describing entity (typically user) behaviour within a concrete system.

On one hand, context information is valuable for some profiling techniques that enable the system to serve customized content. On the other hand, context information can be considered as a solid basis for retrieving sensitive information about individuals. Therefore special care has to be taken while analyzing and processing this data.

Some privacy breaches were caused by a successful re-identification of some records from anonymized (search query) database published by AOL [2]. Another attack lead to a successful re-identification of some records from an anonymized Massachusetts hospital database. The re-identification was done by joining the anonymized hospital database with records from a publicly available database of voters [8]. Most recent work focuses on re-identification of movie rating service subscribers [6].

We would like to concentrate on re-identification of entities in the network of computers in order to estimate how much information is needed for a successful re-identification and also how many entities will be re-identified.

S. Fischer-Hübner et al. (Eds.): TrustBus 2009, LNCS 5695, pp. 1–10, 2009.

In this paper we further extend our previous work [4], develop a methodology for representing users' behaviour based on their past activity (i.e. based on all available context information [1]) in the network of computers and evaluate its expressive value (in terms of its ability to pinpoint/re-identify users among others based only on behavioural characteristics). We discuss how this approach performs in searching for similar profiles in order to re-identify users. We study various ways behavioural patterns can be built as well as the influence of different conditions (in terms of input data used) on the quality and stability of the patterns (user profiles). We also evaluate the amount of required information for a successful re-identification.

In section 2 we discuss the input data we use to build profiles and point out issues we had to solve in order to process the data effectively. In section 3 we provide a detailed description of the profiling process and the similarity measure. Section 4 is then dedicated to the evaluation of our similarity searching techniques. We discuss the results of the similarity measure under different initial conditions. We also evaluate the influence of Inverse Document Frequency (IDF) [5] as a tool that improves the model to be more accurate as well as the $d_{(A,B)}$ values and compare these approaches.

2 Input Data and Its Preparation

Efficient profiling cannot be successful with small amount of input data. We have data from the global IP traffic log of our university network (Netflow[1]) This data is utilized to build vectors of behaviour that are used as the input for the profiling. In this paper, the primary focus is on SSH (Secure Shell), HTTPS (Hypertext Transfer Protocol over Secure Socket Layer) and HTTP (Hypertext Transfer Protocol) traffic. The data collection can be considered more or less as "low-level" (when compared, e.g., with [6] who used movie ranking database) information about the users since it provides information about communication flows only – the real content of all data flows is not recorded.

Source IP addresses, destination IP addresses, destination port and the number of connections that were made during a particular period of time (day(s), week(s) or month(s)) is important information from the database. Based on this information, we can create a two-dimensional matrix, where each column is one destination IP address and each row is one source IP address. Every cell (i, j) then contains the number of connections that were initiated from the source IP address i to the destination IP address j. Each row of this matrix reflects the communication pattern of a particular source IP address (we will call it a vector of source IP address behaviour).

3 Behavioural Vectors and User Profiling

In this section we will discuss our proposed methodology for calculating similarities of behavioural vectors. Our review of possible similarity searching approaches

---

[1] http://www.cisco.com/go/netflow

ended up with cosine similarity measure which is very widely used in the area of text mining (information retrieval [3]) and works with vectors. Cosine similarity [7] measures the angle between two vectors (A, B) and the angle expresses the "degree" of similarity.

Output of $\cos(A, B)$ ranges from 0 (vectors are completely unrelated) to 1 (vectors are completely related). This number indicates the similarity of given behavioural vectors. We will denote the result of $\cos(A, B)$ as $sim\_value_{(A,B)}$.

3.1   Use of IDF in the Similarity Measure

Term frequency - inverse document frequency (TF-IDF) [5] is widely used in text mining for calculating the relevance of a term in a collection of documents. We use IDF for calculating the relevance of a given destination IP address with respect to a given set of source IP addresses.

Given the IDF relevance values for destination IP addresses [4] we considered whether this information can also be incorporated in the process of similarity calculation. Having a vector of behaviour it is obvious that some components are more relevant with respect to the actual set of source IP addresses, while some of them not. IDF index is used for expressing this relevancy – the index increases with increasing relevancy. Higher relevancy means that the number of unique visitor of such destination IP address is lower. If we calculate IDF values for all destination IP addresses we obtain a vector which size is the same as for behavioural vectors. We use this IDF vector to balance behavioural vectors – multiplication of all components of all vectors of behaviour with respective IDF values. This helps to strengthen components in behavioural vectors that are of greater relevance. A similar idea but not directly the IDF measure was used by [6] to also strengthen rare attributes in vectors of movie ratings. Authors of [6] used their own proposed approach for strengthening rare attributes.

3.2   Calculating the Similarity of Behavioural Vectors

The similarity searching procedure is done with two input datasets – the training and the testing part. There are some basic set of initial restrictions applied prior to the main similarity searching procedure. At this point we further explore two promising approaches to set the initial restrictions (other approaches are discussed in [4]). We provide an evaluation of either approach in the section 4.

– In the first case, we require only those source IP addresses that initiated at least n communication sessions to any destination IP address and the same rule is applied on the second (testing) set.
– In the second case the minimal number of initiated communication sessions remains the same. When we obtain the results we take the list of destination IP addresses and use it as a the initial restriction to set-up the testing set (the testing set will consists of those source IP addresses that were communication to any destination IP addresses from the given list).

The similarity searching is done in a way that it is firstly computed using just the $\cos(A, B)$ metric and secondly using $\cos(A, B)$ influenced by the IDF vector. For each source IP address from the training set we calculate similarities with all other source IP addresses from the testing set. The output for every source IP address (e.g., A) is a list of candidates (similar source IP addresses from the testing set). Each candidate entity (source IP address B) is characterized by two values – the similarity value (we will denote the similarity value as $sim\_value_{(A,B)}$) between source IP addresses A and B and the number of destination IP addresses that were accessed by both source IP addresses (we will denote this number as d_{comm}).

$$A : \ldots, sim\_value_{(A,B)}(B, d_{comm}), \ldots \tag{1}$$

3.3   Use of the Value d_{comm} in the Similarity Measure

It is not surprising that the number of common destination IP addresses that were visited by both the original source IP address and the one that was marked as similar, will be higher in the case of the "correct" candidate. Therefore we decided to utilize this information in the similarity measure – the value d_{comm} – for every candidate in the list of candidates. This information is used after the similarity values have been computed for all pairs of source IP addresses (from the training and the testing set). That is because we do not have this information before we start the similarity searching procedure. Once we have a list of candidates for a specific source IP address, the recalculation of the similarity value is done in the following way. We find the maximal value from all d_{comm} values and denote this value as d_{max}. Then for every candidate, we calculate

$$d_{(A,B)} = d_{comm}/d_{max} \tag{2}$$

The value $d_{(A,B)}$ ranges from $1/d_{max}$ to 1 (this is the case where $d_{comm} = d_{max}$). Finally we add the value $d_{(A,B)}$ to the respective $sim\_value_{(A,B)}$ and divide the result by number two. The final division is done to keep the result in the (0,1) range (easier for further evaluation) – both the $d_{(A,B)}$ and $sim\_value_{(A,B)}$ range from 0 to 1. To summarize the calculation of the $sim\_value_{(A,B)}$, we provide the following formula:

$$sim\_value_{(A,B)} = \frac{\cos(A, B) + d_{(A,B)}}{2} \tag{3}$$

In the table 1, we provide an overview of how many common attributes (on average) are shared between similar source IP addresses for various protocols (input restriction is the minimal number of required initiated sessions). This means, in other words, how many common destination IP addresses are, on average, needed for a successful re-identification. We provide this type of information for three different similarity calculation approaches – $\cos(A, B)$ values influenced by the IDF and the $d_{(A,B)}$; $\cos(A, B)$ values influenced by the IDF values only; $\cos(A, B)$ values only.

Table 1. Average number of destination IP addresses needed for a successful re-identification

SSH traffic	IDF + $d_{(A,B)}$	1.310	1.224	1.212	1.192	—
	IDF	1.279	1.204	1.205	1.192	—
	$\cos(A, B)$	1.285	1.214	1.220	1.192	—
	input restr.	5	7	10	15	—
HTTPS traffic	IDF + $d_{(A,B)}$	6.097	5.473	5.895	6.446	6.264
	IDF	5.810	5.437	5.929	6.514	6.486
	$\cos(A, B)$	5.781	5.348	5.929	6.502	6.486
	input restr.	3	5	7	9	11
HTTP traffic	IDF + $d_{(A,B)}$	2.227	1.539	1.268	1.204	1.083
	IDF	1.766	1.383	1.272	1.204	1.095
.	$\cos(A, B)$	1.924	1.409	1.292	1.225	1.095
	input restr.	10	20	30	40	50

In all cases, the amount of information needed for a successful re-identification does not significantly changes for different initial restrictions and all three approaches (in absolute numbers) did not need significantly more information for a successful re-identification than the other ones. The "non-decreasing" trend in the case of the HTTPS traffic can be explained by the presence of a TOR[2] node that has been started in the middle of the year and this node accesses significantly higher number of destination IP addresses.

4   Evaluation of the Similarity Measure

In order to evaluate the expressiveness of the similarity measure used in the profiling step we need to design some evaluation criteria. Basic requirements are: to be able to compare the similarity measure with the "ideal" model that would always provide correct answers (in terms of identification based on behaviour characteristics) and the ability to compare results based on various input conditions (e.g. selected communication port, number of distinct source and destination addresses, . . .). We will also evaluate the amount of required information needed for a successful re-identification of entities and compare similarity searching techniques we proposed in the previous section.

First step in our evaluation is to normalize the calculated similarity indexes for each source IP address so that the sum of all indexes equals 1. Second step is to create a vector that describes the "ideal" correct decision that the model should have done. At this point it is necessary to mention that for now, we assume that there is always only one correct answer – for a given source IP address from the set of the training data there is (if exists) only one source IP address from the set of testing data that would match the original source. All other sources from the latter set should be marked 0 by the similarity measurement process.

---

[2] http://www.torproject.org

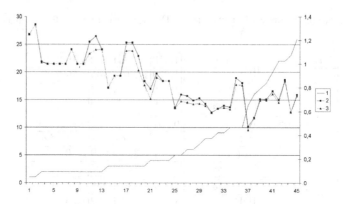

Fig. 1. A graph representing the relation between the behaviour vector dimensions (left Y-axis) and the amount of error (right Y-axis). SSH traffic.

We believe that with the data we have at the moment, this assumption and its application is the only way the model can be reasonably evaluated.

Based on the prediction that we know the correct answer, we can create so called "correction vector" (i.e. the vector representing the ideal similarity) for each source IP address. The vector contains value 1 for the correct answer and 0 for all other, non-similar IP addresses.

To measure the amount of error for a given instance, we calculate the following *error_rates*:

$$error\_rate \ (good \ decision) = |1 - sim\_index|,$$
$$error\_rate \ (bad \ decision) = |0 - sim\_index|.$$

Having this done we calculate a simple sum of all *error_rate* for a given source IP address and this number then represents the actual "amount of error". Boundaries within which this value can fall range from 0 – indicating the ideal correct answer to 2 – indicating the situation where the correct answer was marked as incorrect and some other source IP address was marked as the correct one. Values representing the average amount of error are then used to evaluate correlations with different input settings and conditions.

Impact of the IDF values has been evaluated for the SSH traffic only. But we expect the impact of the IDF in the case of the HTTP or HTTPS traffic to be very similar.

Figure 1 shows the progress of the "amount of error" criterion correlated with the vector dimensions. Line 2 in the graph is without the influence of IDF while line 3 is influenced by these values and line 1 represents the vector dimensions. It is quite clear that the use of IDF values makes certain improvement over values based on original behavioural vectors. Initial conditions were the minimal required number of connections for both the training and the testing sets.

Figure 2 summarizes the influence of different threshold values applied on the similarity index. We started with 0.1 (which means we remove all similarity

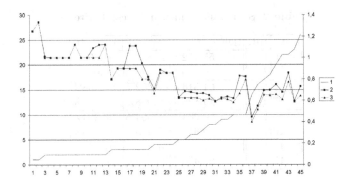

Fig. 2. A graph comparing trends of the "amount of error" (right Y-axis) influenced by a threshold value. Left Y-axis - behavioural vector dimensions.

indexes below this value) and continue by 0.1 steps. With increasing threshold the accuracy of the model increased as well. To make the figure well-arranged, we show the accuracy without any threshold (line 2 in the graph) and with the threshold with the maximal impact in terms of accuracy (line 3 in the graph). We estimated that the optimal value to be applied is around 0.4 (the case of the SSH traffic).

4.1   Evaluation Based on Three Criteria

In order to observe the successfulness of the similarity searching procedure (i.e. the results of the whole re-identification process), we proposed an approach consisting of three criteria. These criteria describe three different types of similarity searching outputs and can be used for comparing all similarity searching approaches we use – $sim\_value_{(A,B)}$ (i.e. with the IDF and $d_{(A,B)}$) values; $sim\_value_{(A,B)}$ only with the IDF values and simple $\cos(A,B)$ (see section 3).

1. We count all cases where the "correct" candidate is the first on the list of candidates.
2. We count all cases where the "correct" candidate is in the list of candidate, but the candidate is not the first on the list. We also estimate the average *distance* of the "correct" candidate from the first candidate on the list.
3. We count all cases where the "correct" candidate is not in the testing set. We can call these occurrences as false positives.

We provide the results (regarding the three criteria listed above) of the similarity searching approaches in tables 2, 3 and 4. Numbers in tables represent percentages from the whole set of source IP addresses (input restriction is in the first column in all tables – the minimal required number of initiated communication sessions).

Results regarding the last criteria, and the average distance from the first candidate in case of the second criteria:

Table 2. SSH traffic – first and second criteria

restr.	crit.	IDF + $d_{(A,B)}$	IDF	$\cos(A,B)$
5	1	55.452%	53.828%	54.060%
5	2	16.705%	18.329%	18.097%
7	1	61.514%	60.252%	60.568%
7	2	14.826%	16.088%	15.773%
10	1	60.204%	59.694%	60.204%
10	2	20.918%	21.429%	20.918%
15	1	57.265%	57.265%	57.265%
15	2	26.496%	26.496%	26.496%

Table 3. HTTPS traffic – first and second criteria

restr.	crit.	IDF + $d_{(A,B)}$	IDF	$\cos(A,B)$
3	1	11.806%	11.806%	11.806%
3	2	29.514%	29.514%	29.514%
5	1	17.103%	15.862%	15.862%
5	2	22.483%	23.724%	23.724%
7	1	19.955%	19.274%	19.274%
7	2	17.914%	18.594%	18.594%
9	1	22.924%	22.259%	21.927%
9	2	15.615%	16.279%	16.611%
11	1	26.561%	25.636%	25.662%
11	2	12.192%	13.702%	13.716%

Table 4. HTTP traffic – first and second criteria

restr.	crit.	IDF + $d_{(A,B)}$	IDF	$\cos(A,B)$
10	1	16.029%	10.483%	13.228%
10	2	21.765%	26.622%	23.877%
20	1	17.357%	13.412%	14.596%
20	2	11.637%	15.582%	14.398%
30	1	18.584%	16.372%	18.142%
30	2	8.407%	10.619%	8.850%
40	1	23.571%	22.143%	22.857%
40	2	5.714%	7.143%	6.429%
50	1	21.348%	20.225%	20.225%
50	2	4.494%	3.371%	3.371%

- HTTPS traffic: amount of false positives – 59.8%; distance from the first candidate, if the "correct" candidate is not the first, but is in the list of candidates – 0.13 (the similarity value ranges from 0 to 2).
- SSH traffic: amount of false positives – 21.3%; distance from the first candidate – 0.02.
- HTTP traffic: amount of false positives – 67.9%; distance from the first candidate – 0.19.

We can see that in all cases the use of both the IDF and the $d_{(A,B)}$ values provide the best results in terms of successfully re-identified entities. Re-identification is better as we apply more strict input restriction rules – this trend is natural because with more strict input restriction rules the number of source IP addresses in both the training and the testing set is decreasing. Regarding the second criteria, i.e., the "correct" candidate is on the list of candidates but the candidate is not at the first place – again the IDF with the $d_{(A,B)}$ produce the best results as the number of such entities is lower than in the case of IDF or $\cos(A,B)$ only.

If we consider the re-identification ratio only, then the best results are achieved with the SSH traffic data (tab. 2). As we expected, SSH users behave significantly more consistent than in the other two scenarios. Number of successfully re-identified entities in the case of the HTTP and the HTTPS traffic is almost the same. In case of the HTTP traffic there is a higher number of false positives. But this reflects our assumption that the behavioural characteristics of HTTP users will be the most variable.

Entities in the set of the second criteria cannot be directly re-identified but based on the distance of the similarity values, the anonymity of these entities is greatly reduced. The amount of false positives is quite high in case of the HTTP and HTTPS traffic. The main reason for this result is the usage of wireless connection with laptops. Students can connect almost everywhere in the university and assigned IP addresses will not always be the same.

Regarding the amount of information required for a successful re-identification, the results are: SSH traffic – 1.2 common destination IP addresses; HTTPS traffic – 6 common dest. IP addresses and HTTP traffic – 3.2. If we compare our results to [6] than the amount of common attributes needed for re-identification is (on average) lower ([6] needed an a priori knowledge between 3-8 attributes). We think that the lower amount of information required is caused by even more sparse data we worked with.

5   Conclusion

This paper looked into the issue of profiling and re-identification based on user past activity in a network. Our experiments with profiling have been based on real data that is collected regularly in a large university network with thousands of connected users. Such database allows for building long-term behavioural characteristics that we use at the only identifying information of a user.

The main contribution of this paper is our proposed similarity searching methodology. We proposed two improvements of the original cosine similarity measure in order to make the re-identification process to perform better. We use inverse document frequency and $d_{(A,B)}$ values to strengthen rare attributes in the behavioural vectors. We showed how this knowledge influences the similarity searching procedure and provided some results of our experiments.

The final part of our paper is dedicated to the evaluation of the similarity measure. This step is natural in order to asses the expressiveness of the measure. We designed our own evaluation approach, where we can observe the actual "amount of error" of a given instance and observe the model performance under different circumstances. Based on our experiments, we confirmed our initial assumption that the use of IDF makes the model more accurate and we can do even better by setting reasonable thresholds.

In order to evaluate the actual number of successfully re-identified entities, we defined three criteria and perform an evaluation in accordance with these criteria. We showed that even with a little knowledge about an entity it is still possible to re-identify it in the testing set.

For the following work, we plan to continue evaluating the model under different initial conditions. Namely the impact of the IDF values in the case of the HTTP or HTTPS traffic. We also want to estimate the confidence of user profiles (using e.g. confidence intervals, error distributions and probabilities of errors) and their stability in time. The main issue here is the durability of the user profiles and the accuracy of the re-identification based on these old user profiles.

References

1. Cvrček, D., Kumpošt, M., Matyáš, V.: A privacy classification model based on linkability valuation. In: Security and Embedded Systems. NATO Security through Science Series, D: Information and Communication Security, vol. 2, pp. 91–98. Kluwer Academic Publishers, Dordrecht (2006)
2. Hansen, S.: AOL removes search data on vast group of web users. New York Times (October 2006)
3. Korfhage, R.R.: Information storage and retrieval. John Wiley & Sons Inc., New York (1997)
4. Kumpošt, M.: Data preparation for user profiling from traffic log. In: Proceedings of The International Conference on Emerging Security Information, Systems, and Technologies (SECURWARE 2007), vol. 0, pp. 89–94. IEEE Computer Society Press, Los Alamitos (2007)
5. Lee, J.-W., Baik, D.-K.: A model for extracting keywords of document using term frequency and distribution. In: Gelbukh, A. (ed.) CICLing 2004. LNCS, vol. 2945, pp. 437–440. Springer, Heidelberg (2004)
6. Narayanan, A., Shmatikov, V.: Robust de-anonymization of large sparse datasets. IEEE Symposium on Security and Privacy 0, 111–125 (2008)
7. Salton, G.: Automatic text processing: the transformation, analysis, and retrieval of information by computer. Addison-Wesley Longman Publishing Co. Inc., Boston (1989)
8. Sweeney, L.: Weaving technology and policy together to maintain confidentiality. Journal of Law, Medicine and Ethics 25 (1997)

Search Engines: Gateway to a New "Panopticon"?*

Eleni Kosta[1], Christos Kalloniatis[2], Lilian Mitrou[3], and Evangelia Kavakli[2]

[1] Interdisciplinary Centre for Law & ICT (ICRI)
Kathtolieke Universiteit Leuven
Sint-Michielsstraat 6, 3000, Leuven, Belgium
eleni.kosta@law.kuleuven.be
[2] Cultural Informatics Laboratory
Department of Cultural Technology and Communication
University of the Aegean, Harilaou Trikoupi & Faonos Str., 81100 Mytilene, Greece
{ch.kalloniatis,kavakli}@ct.aegean.gr
[3] Information and Communication Systems Security Laboratory
Department of Information and Communications Systems Engineering
University of the Aegean, 83200, Samos, Greece
L.Mitrou@aegean.gr

Abstract. Nowadays, Internet users are depending on various search engines in order to be able to find requested information on the Web. Although most users feel that they are and remain anonymous when they place their search queries, reality proves otherwise. The increasing importance of search engines for the location of the desired information on the Internet usually leads to considerable inroads into the privacy of users. The scope of this paper is to study the main privacy issues with regard to search engines, such as the anonymisation of search logs and their retention period, and to examine the applicability of the European data protection legislation to non-EU search engine providers. Ixquick, a privacy-friendly meta search engine will be presented as an alternative to privacy intrusive existing practices of search engines.

Keywords: search engines, privacy, cookies, search logs.

1 Introduction

Many people, nowadays, spend a lot of time online typing search queries either for private or professional use. Are you looking for a nice Italian restaurant in the city centre? Do you suffer from diabetes? Are you missing out important data for your report? Who won the Oscar Awards? The first thing a vast amount of people do in order to get the information they are looking for easily and fast is to search for available information on the Internet, using their favourite search engine. Search engines have become an indispensable tool in everyday life, serving as the gateway to important information for

---

* The research leading to these results has received partially funding from the European Community's Seventh Framework Programme (FP7/2007-2011) under the PICOS project (Grant Agreement n° 215056).

S. Fischer-Hübner et al. (Eds.): TrustBus 2009, LNCS 5695, pp. 11–21, 2009.

the users. In January 2009 there were more than 9.4 billion queries, initiated in the U.S. alone. Globally, Google holds the lion's share in online searches, as 62.8% of the aforementioned search queries were conducted by it. Google was followed by Yahoo! with 16.2%, MSN/Windows Live search with 11.2% and AOL with 4% [1].

However, the increasing importance of search engines as a tool for finding information is not free of further implications. The search engines typically keep logs of users' search queries, along with a number of search parameters, matching the search terms with the IP address allocated to the user's computer, the date and time of the search, the web browser used and the cookie identifier, as well as the results of the search, the advertising that has been displayed with the outcome of a specific search and the user clicks [2]. The period for which these data are retained differs among the various search,engines. In all cases, however, based on the richness of the information they have about their users, the providers of search engines have the capability to draw up detailed profiles of the interests, thoughts and activities of their users. Their retention policy in combination with their increasing importance result in considerable threats to the privacy of users of search engines [3].

The Norwegian *Datatilsynet* (the national Data Inspectorate of Norway) was the first European authority to question the retention policies of search engines, and more specifically of Google, an initiative that has lead to ongoing discussions at European level between the Article 29 Working Party[1] and leading search engine providers, i.e. Google, Microsoft, Yahoo! and Ixquick, on various topics related to privacy and search engines [4]. The major issues of the debate focus on the applicability of the European legislation to search engine providers, the retention period of the search logs and the anonymisation of the search logs.

2 Anonymity on the Internet and the Role of Search Engines

Back in 1993, Peter Steiner published a very famous cartoon in The New Yorker magazine with the title: "on the Internet, nobody knows you're a dog" [5]. This line meant to be one of the most famous quotes that have been linked to the Internet and represented the value of anonymity, which at least in the advent of the Internet, was inherent with the notion of Internet and Cyberspace. Since then, however, some 15 years have passed and the Internet landscape has changed dramatically.

In June 2007 Privacy International prepared a consultation report on privacy practices of key internet based companies. Search engines occupied a "prominent" role in this report, which classified companies, into six categories, ranking from privacy-friendly and privacy enhancing to comprehensive consumer surveillance & entrenched hostility to privacy [6]. Major search engines, such as Google, Microsoft, Yahoo! and AOL, were examined in the study. All of them scored very low in the protection of privacy: Microsoft was ranked orange, meaning that there are serious

---

[1] Under Article 29 of the Data Protection Directive, a Working Party on the Protection of Individuals with regard to the Processing of Personal Data is established, made up of the Data Protection Commissioners from the Member States together with a representative of the European Commission. The Working Party is independent and acts in an advisory capacity. The Working Party seeks to harmonize the application of data protection rules throughout the EU, and publishes opinions and recommendations on various data protection topics.

lapses in its privacy practices, Yahoo! and AOL got a red evaluation of "substantial threat", while Google managed to get the lowest black ranking, characterized as "hostile to privacy" [6].

Nowadays, many users still believe that they are anonymous when using the internet, although practice has shown otherwise. In August 2006, the US based search engine AOL released a file containing more than 20 million search queries from approximately 657.000 users for research purposes. The AOL user name was replaced by an *anonymous* user ID and the data were sequentially arranged. The data set included {AnonID, Query, QueryTime, ItemRank, ClickURL} [7].

Table 1. Example of AOL published search logs

AnonID	Query	QueryTime	ItemRank	ClickURL
1337	searchtec	2006-03-22 17:58:46	1	http://www.searchtec.com
1337	fiserv	2006-03-24 14:05:01	3	http://www.fiservlendingsolutions.com
1337	integrated loan services	2006-03-29 17:12:27	1	http://www.ils.com

AOL withdrew the file after complaints of users, but even after the removal copies continued to circulate online. In a short period after the publication of the file, the New York Times could suss out that for instance AOL searcher number 4417749 corresponded to Mrs Thelma Arnold, a 62-year-old widow, as she conducted hundreds of searches over a three-month period on her personal interests, her friends' medical ailments and her dogs [8].

Nevertheless, the majority of Internet users are still not aware of the extent to and the purposes for which their data are being used. People make hundreds of search queries every month on their private and professional interests and there is a tendency to make so called vanity searches, i.e. searching information about themselves. The status of the current surveillance on the Internet has been compared with the Panopticon prison model of Jeremy Bentham [9], which enables continual watching, while the prisoners are not able to see *if* and *when* they are watched. This new online "Panopticon" represents the situation when Internet users give out too much information about themselves, thus allowing others to "view" them, not knowing however *when* they are being watched or *what* will happen with the information they gave away [9]. Under –even potential– surveillance users may shape and steer their behaviour accordingly and adapt their choices to mainstream expectations[2] [10].

---

[2] The so-called "chilling effect" refers to the concern that constitutionally protected freedom of information will be inhibited by the potential for individuals and authorities to engage in forms of *post hoc* surveillance of search data and may refrain users from searching, receiving and imparting information.

3 Search Engines Scrutinised under European Legislation

The increasing power of the search engines to draw up profiles of the network activities of their users, as well as the possibility that they will be used for "data mining" raise concerns with regard to the privacy of the Internet users [11]. The International Working Group on Data Protection in Telecommunications (IWGDPT), as well as the 28th International Data Protection and Privacy Commissioner's Conference adopted specific positions on privacy protection and search engines [3].

The Article 29 Working Party recognizing the importance of search engines as information retrieval technologies and the significant privacy concerns relating to them published an opinion on data protection issues related to search engines and is engaged into discussions with major search engine operators [4]. Given that Google occupies the largest share in online searches and has received criticism on its online practices, the Article 29 Working Party has exchanged interesting correspondence with the Global Privacy Counsel of Google, Peter Fleischer.

3.1 Applicability of European Data Protection Legislation to Search Engine Providers Established Outside the EU

The AOL case illustrated clearly that the users' information contained in search logs can lead to the identification of individuals and shall therefore be considered as personal data under relevant European legislation. Before examining in detail, however, some specific data protection issues arising with regard to search engines, it is important to clarify the conditions under which the European legislation applies to search engine providers that are established outside the EU[3], such as Google, Yahoo! and Microsoft.

The Data Protection Directive (hereafter Directive) [12] applies to providers who have their place of establishment outside of the EU in two exceptional situations: 1) in case the processing of personal data is carried out in the context of the activities of an establishment of the provider within the EU; and 2) in case equipment based within the EU is used for the processing of data outside of it. It is essential therefore to examine if and when the search engine providers fall under the scope of these provisions.[4]

3.1.1 The Processing of Personal Data Is Carried Out in the Context of the Activities of an Establishment within the EU

"Establishment" refers to the effective and real exercise of activity through stable arrangements, regardless its legal form as branch or subsidiary [12]. The establishment should be interpreted broadly, including establishments, which are not necessarily permanent [13].

---

[3] Actually the Directive refers not to the EU but to the European Economic Area (EEA). For the convenience of the reader, however, we refer to EU instead of EEA.

[4] For the analysis that will follow, it is helpful to clarify that according to the European data protection legislation "data controller", is the person or the authority, which alone or jointly with others "determines the purposes and means of the processing of personal data" [12].

European Data Protection Authorities and the Article 29 Working Party have been "quite imaginative in finding that there is some sort of connection between the processing and the establishment" [13]. The Article 29 Working Party described three situations under which the establishment of the search engine providers in the EU will play a relevant role in the specific data processing operation, namely when:

- "an establishment is responsible for relations with users of the search engine in a particular jurisdiction;
- a search engine provider establishes an office in a Member State [...] that is involved in the selling of targeted advertisements to the inhabitants of that state;
- the establishment of a search engine provider complies with court orders and/or law enforcement requests by the competent authorities of a Member State with regard to user data." [14].

In its response to the Article 29 Working Party, Google has questioned the validity of the abovementioned interpretation and claimed that it does not process personal data in the context of the activities of its European branches and therefore there is no ground for the applicability of EU law [15]. Google added that its commercial operations in Europe, such as the practice of selling targeted advertising, do not entail the processing of user data and that in any case it is the Google Inc, i.e. the parent company situated in USA, which takes all the relevant decisions regarding the purpose and means of the data processing activities and acts as "data controller" in terms of the European data protection legislation [15]. Actually, the applicability of EU law, even if the EU regulator has no jurisdiction over the parent entity, remains a controversial issue.

3.1.2 Equipment Based within the EU Is Used for the Processing of Data

According to the Article 29 Working Party even the installation of cookies to the terminal equipment of European users from a provider established outside the EU is considered as use of equipment and invokes the European data protection legislation [16]. The collection of personal data by means of cookies enables the controller to "link up all information he has collected during previous sessions with information he collects during subsequent sessions. In this way, it is possible to create quite detailed user profiles." [16].

The use of cookies, which track activity on a computer's Internet browser, has been standard practice of various search engines.[5] They store information about the end-user and enable in this way a relationship between the server and end-user. Of course, cookies don't always necessarily identify a person by name, which is the case for instance when more people use the same web browser to make a search query without subscribing to the service [17].

This approach of the Article 29 Working Party to consider the use of cookies as use of equipment has however been criticised as "unconvincing", especially by providers established outside the EU [15]. It has also been characterised as "regulatory overreaching" in an online environment, in the sense of "a situation in which rules are

---

[5] Cookies are packets of information transmitted from a server to the web browser of users and are transmitted back to the server every time the user accesses a server's page using the same browser.

expressed so generally and non-discriminatingly that they apply *prima facie* to a large range of activities without having much of a realistic chance of being enforced" [18]. The position of the Article 29 Working Party can thus be questioned or endorsed, according to the position one takes on this matter [13][6].

3.2 Anonymisation of Search Logs

Search log files contain information regarding the server logs and the data on the content offered (links and advertisements resulting from the query) as well as data on the subsequent user navigation (clicks) [14]. The server logs typically include the web request of the user, the Internet Protocol address, the browser type, the browser language, the date and time of the user request and one or more cookies that may uniquely identify the user browser. An example of a typical log entry where the user searches at Google for "cars" is the following: "123.45.67.89 - 25/Mar/2003 10:15:32 - http://www.google.com/search?q=cars - Firefox 1.0.7; Windows NT 5.1 - 740674ce2123e969" [19].

The Article 29 Working Party considers log files to be the most important category of data processed by search engines, as they reveal a lot of information for the user [14]. In respect of the privacy of the internet users, the user data related to their searches should not be kept for a period longer than is necessary for the purposes for which the data were collected or for which they are further processed[7]. The Article 29 Working Party considers *six months* as a reasonable retention period for the search logs and the related user data and requests explicit justification for periods exceeding the six months. After the said period the data should be *deleted* or *anonymised*, in a way that will not allow the identification of the individual users. In the aftermath of the AOL search data scandal, the Article 29 Working Party requested that anonymisation should be completely irreversible. Any combination of the search log data with data owned by other providers should be excluded and in cases the search history of a user is so detailed that can lead to his indirect identification, parts of the search history should be removed [14]. Notwithstanding the fact that such a request of full anonymisation of the data is absolutely compliant to the data protection legislation, it is still questionable if combination of data available at different sources (providers) will *never* lead to a potential identification of an internet user.

3.2.1 Why Are Search Logs Needed?

Search engines claim that search logs are necessary data for various purposes and their retention for a certain period of time is essential. Most search engines operate on a pay-per-valid-click business model for personalised advertising. Although such a purpose can be justified as legitimate right of the search engine provider in order to increase its revenue, it is questionable if it legitimises the processing of search logs of unregistered users [14].

In fact, the information related to the kind of queries people make and of the answer they choose to click on is useful for the optimisation of the services offered. However it is not obvious why the content of the search query needs to be attributed

---

[6] We would like to point out that it is out of the scope of this paper to take a specific position.
[7] Art. 6(1)(e) Data Protection Directive.

to an identified user. Analysis of the search logs is also used for ensuring the system security and fraud prevention. As legitimate as these reasons may be, the search engine provider should keep the data in a way that can lead to the identification of the internet users for the shortest possible period and provide sufficient justification for it [14]. Google claims that the retention of search information is needed for auditing and evidentiary purposes, in order to prove the correctness of the billing data, as advertisers are only charged for valid clicks [15]. The Article 29 Working Party argued though that the information that does not relate to the choices made by the user, such as the advertising that was not clicked on, should not be retained [14]. Additionally search engine providers assert that the retention of search logs is needed for auditing purposes and for compliance with legal obligations imposed by specific legislation, such as the Sarbanes-Oxley Act [20].

The retention of such data and their use for unspecified and secondary purposes may interfere with fundamental rights and freedoms of individuals. Google, in contrast to other major search engines companies (Yahoo!, Microsoft, AOL), refused to comply with US Government subpoena to provide all URLs indexed in their search engines and their search term queries used between 1 June 2005 and 31 July 2005. Some months later the District Court granted the modified governmental request for a random sample of 50.000 URLs from Google's query log [21]. In the European Union, the adoption of the Data Retention Directive [22] was followed by unclarity in the field of search engine providers, as to whether they fall under the scope of application of this Directive and would therefore need to retain specific categories of data for law enforcement purposes. It was clarified by the Article 29 Working Party that the Directive addresses only "providers of publicly available electronic communications networks and services" and clearly excludes the retention of data related to the content of electronic communications.[8] Therefore it does not apply to search engine providers [14].

3.2.2 Search Engines Current Retention Time

Notwithstanding the validity of all the arguments on the actual necessity for retention of the search logs, there is no clear justification for a specific retention period. As a result, the retention periods are not unified among the various search engine providers. The Article 29 Working Party has defined six months as a reasonable retention period for the search logs and the related user data, requiring their deletion or anonymisation after the end of this period.

In September 2008, Google announced that it would reduce its data retention period from 18 to nine months, following long negotiations with the Article 29 Working Party. A few months later, in December 2008, Yahoo! announced that it dropped the retention period for the data collected from its search engine from 13 months to 90 days. Under this new policy, Yahoo will delete the last octet of the IP address associated with a search query and that it will also hide cookie data related to each search log and strip out any personal identifiable information like a name, phone etc. from the query itself [23]. However this initiative of Yahoo! did not seem to convince the privacy advocates, who were still asking for full deletion of the IP address. It was even compared to the use of "a butter knife as a paper shredder" [24].

---

[8] Art 1(2) and 5(2) Data Retention Directive.

Microsoft decided in July 2007 for a retention period of 18 months, with full dele-tion of "the IP address and all other cross-session identifiers, such as cookie IDs or other machine identifiers, from the search terms" [25]. In December 2008 Microsoft announced its further intention to drop its data logging plan to six months if its com-petitors did the same. However, Microsoft was not ready to receive the big reduction step followed by Yahoo!.

The pressure imposed on search engine providers by the Article 29 Working Party as well as the competition among them seems to be resulting in reductions in the re-tention periods of the major search engine providers. Although Google in its response to the Opinion of the Article 29 Working Party provided a long list of reasons, why the retention of search logs is necessary [15], it did not manage to convincingly prove why a nine-month retention period is absolutely necessary, instead of the six-month one proposed by the European advisory body. The limitation of the retention period of search data from Yahoo!, the second largest search engine provider, to 90 days and the proposal of Microsoft for a unified six-month retention period weaken signifi-cantly the arguments of Google. It is worthy to mention that some providers, fearing the unfair competitive advantage of their competitors which failed to adopt equivalent privacy policies, called for a common industry standard that would include, among other features, truly efficient anonymisation and a maximum retention period of six months [4].

3.3 Ixquick: An Alternative Privacy Friendly Option?

Ixquick is a search engine different from the traditional ones. Ixquick is actually a meta search engine, meaning that it searches several other search engines, such as Yahoo!, Google and ask.com to combine results and pick out the most relevant ones. Ixquick looks at the top ten of the results of the other search engines. "Every result generated that is in the top ten will get one star. So if a result is in five search results in the top ten it will get five stars. Based on the stars, the user will get an optimal result, with high relevance" [26].

One main argument of search engine providers for retaining user information re-garding their searches is that their business model requires the retention of specific information to support charges to advertisers. The revenue model of Ixuick is based on the number of hits times the advertising benefits, which is highly correlated to the search queries done through the site, without revealing though the search query and the IP address of the user.

In June 2006 Ixquick started to delete its users' privacy data within 48 hours and it abolished the use of unique ID cookies. Ixquick uses two anonymous cookies instead: an anonymous "preferences" cookie, which is used to remember the search engine settings for the next visit, which expires after 90 days; and a session-only "exclude repetitive results" cookie to prevent showing duplicate search results when you per-form a follow up search with the same search term. The second cookie expires imme-diately at the end of the session. Ixquick only logs data for maintenance purposes like tracking site performance and statistics, while all other data, like the anonymous search queries, are deleted from the log files within a maximum of 48 hours, often sooner. Since January 2009 Ixquick does not even record the IP addresses of its users at all, while in the past it used to retain them for 48 hours [27].

In July 2008 Ixquick was awarded the first European Privacy Seal, which was developed in the context of the EuroPriSe European project funded by the European Commission under the eTEN programme. Meanwhile Ixquick decided not to record the IP addresses of its users, an initiative that called for a rectification of the privacy seal; according to the new evaluation the underlying technical solution of Ixquick was checked and the data minimization of the search engine was rated "excellent" [28].

4 Concluding Remarks

The increasing use of search engines has taken a central position in the everyday life of the Internet user, bringing with it both promise and peril. The capacity of the search engines to collect information about the personal preferences of their users and to combine them with identification information they have at their disposal has raised significant concerns on dangers for privacy they entail. The search engines collect information not only on the search queries of the internet users, their time and data, but also on the user preferences (such as browser type and language), on the content offered (links and advertisements resulting from the query), as well as data on the subsequent user navigation (clicks). Given that the major search engine providers are established outside the European Union, it is very interesting to examine how the European legislation can react to this new phenomenon. A crucial issue to this point is first of all when and if the European data protection legal framework can be applied to search engine providers outside the EU. The anonymisation of search logs and their retention period in a way that allows the identification of the internet users are the main topics discussed. The meta search engine Ixquick gained the first privacy seal and has managed to prove that a search engine can still function successfully and make revenues even when it does not retain personalised information about its users. It remains to be seen if the new privacy-friendly business model presented by Ixquick will be further followed by the major search engine providers, inaugurating a new era of internet searching.

References

1. Nielsen Online: Press release, U.S. search share rankings (January 2009), http://www.nielsen-online.com/pr/pr_090211.pdf
2. Spanish Data Protection Agency (Agencia Española de Protección de Datos): Statement on Internet Search Engines, (January 12, 2007), http://tinyurl.com/dkopph
3. 28th International Data Protection and Privacy Commissioners' Conference: Resolution on Privacy Protection and Search Engines, November 02-03, 2006, London United Kingdom (2006)
4. Article 29 Working Party (Press Release): Search Engines, Brussels (February 12, 2009), http://ec.europa.eu/justice_home/fsj/privacy/news/docs/pr_12_02_09_en.pdf
5. Steiner, P.: On the internet, nobody knows you're a dog. The New Yorker 69(20), 61 (1993)

6. Privacy International: A Race to the Bottom: Privacy Ranking of Internet Service Companies – A consultation report (June 9, 2007),
   `http://www.privacyinternational.org/`
   `article.shtml?cmd[347]=x-347-553961`
7. Pass, G., Chowdhury, A., Torgeson, C.: A Picture of Search. In: The First International Conference on Scalable Information Systems, Hong Kong (June 2006)
8. Barbaro, M., Zeller Jr., T.: A Face Is Exposed for AOL Searcher No. 4417749. The New York Times (August 9, 2006)
9. Rochford, M.: Designing for the social: avoiding anti-social networks. Presentation given at IA Summit, 14.04.2008 and UPA London, 24.04.2008 (2008),
   `http://www.slideshare.net/rochford/`
   `designing-for-the-social-avoiding-antisocial-networks`
10. Wood, D.: A report on the Surveillance Society for the (UK) Information Commissioner. In: Surveillance Studies Network (September 2006)
11. International Working Group on Data Protection in Telecommunications: Common Position on Privacy Protection and Search Engines first adopted at the 23rd Meeting in Hong Kong SAR, China (April 15, 1998); Revised and updated at the 39th meeting, Washington D.C (April 6-7, 2006)
12. Directive 1995/46/EC of the European Parliament and of the Council of 24 October 1995 on the protection of individuals with regard to the processing of personal data and on the free movement of such data, O.J. L 281/31(November 11, 1995)
13. Kuner, C.: European Data Protection Law – Corporate Compliance and Regulation, 2nd edn. Oxford University Press, Oxford (2007)
14. Article 29 Data Protection Working Party: Opinion on data protection issues related to search engines, WP 148 (April 4, 2008)
15. Fleischer, P.: Response to the Article 29 Working Party opinion on data protection issues related to search engines (September 8, 2008)
16. Article 29 Data Protection Working Party: Working document on determining the international application of EU data protection law to personal data processing on the Internet by non-EU based web sites, WP56 (May 30, 2002)
17. Glasner, J.: What search sites know about you,
   `http://www.wired.com/politics/security/news/2005/04/67062`
18. Bygrave, L.: Determining Applicable Law pursuant to European Data Protection Legislation. Computer Law & Security Report 16, 252–257 (2000)
19. Google Privacy Glossary,
   `http://www.google.com/intl/en/privacy_glossary.html`
20. Church, P., Kon, G.M.: Google at the heart of data protection storm. CLSR 23, 461–465 (2007)
21. Fry, J.: Google's Privacy Responsibilities at Home and Abroad. Journal of Librarianship and Information Science 38(3), 135 (2006)
22. Directive 2006/24/EC of the European Parliament and of the Council of 15 March 2006 on the retention of data generated or processed in connection with the provision of publicly available electronic communications services or of public communications networks and amending Directive 2002/58/EC, O.J. L105/54 (April 13, 2006)
23. Helft M/: Yahoo limits retention of search data, NY Times.com (December 17, 2008),
   `http://www.nytimes.com/2008/12/18/technology/internet/`
   `18yahoo.html?_r=1&ref=technology`

24. Rottenberg, M.: Executive Director of the Electronic Privacy Information Center (EPIC), as quoted in Singel, R.: Yahoo to Anonymize User Data After 90 Days (February 17, 2008), http://blog.wired.com/business/2008/12/yahoo-to-anonym.html

25. Microsoft's Privacy Principles for Live Search and Online Ad Targeting (July 23, 2007), http://tinyurl.com/ck9zq7

26. Personal communication with John Borking, on the report he prepared with Robert-Jan Dijkman on Ixquick (January 20, 2008)

27. Ixquick's Privacy Q&A, http://www.ixquick.com/uk/protect_privacy.html#q

28. Borking Consultancy: Ixquick Evaluation Short Public Report (Recertification) (January 27, 2009), http://tinyurl.com/bo7b43

Supporting Local Aliases as Usable Presentation of Secure Pseudonyms

Elke Franz[1] and Katja Liesebach[2]

[1] Dresden University of Technology, Dresden, Germany
elke.franz@tu-dresden.de
[2] Goethe University Frankfurt, Frankfurt am Main, Germany
katja.liesebach@m-chair.net

Abstract. Privacy-Enhancing Identity Management (PIM) enables users to control which personal data they provide to whom by partitioning this information into subsets called partial identities. Since these partial identities should not be linkable except by their owner, randomly generated pseudonyms that are unique are used as their identifiers instead of real names. Randomly generated pseudonyms do not leak any information about the corresponding user, but their handling is not easy for human beings. Users should therefore be enabled to assign local aliases according to their individual preferences to such pseudonyms to allow for a better recognizability in interaction scenarios. However, the use of local aliases requires a reasonable support to ensure both privacy and usability.

This paper introduces an architecture that enables users to manage local aliases in a reasonable and usable way. Possible solutions for alias assignment, alias improvement, and replacement between aliases and pseudonyms are discussed. The suggested approach was realized within a collaborative eLearning environment but is also applicable for other collaborative applications.

1 Introduction

Complex collaborative environments comprise a variety of scenarios that clearly imply risks to user's privacy: While acting in different scenarios, users might deliver various personal data. Additional information can be divulged in communications with other users. Moreover, even information describing actions performed might allow for drawing conclusions about the user, e.g., about habits or interests. Recent studies show that users are concerned about privacy issues (e.g., [6,8]). Hence, supporting privacy in such environments is of growing importance.

Despite the potential risks to privacy, acting anonymously is not always possible and beneficial. Thus, recognition is essential within collaborative scenarios to allow for a reasonable working or if users want to establish reputation.

To maintain privacy even if person-related data needs to be provided, users should be enabled to control which data they deliver to whom considering the current situation. This goal can be achieved by partitioning person-related data

S. Fischer-Hübner et al. (Eds.): TrustBus 2009, LNCS 5695, pp. 22–31, 2009.

into subsets called partial identities (pIDs). User centric Privacy-Enhancing Identity Management (PIM) provides the necessary techniques for such a partitioning [4,5]. Basically, pIDs should not be linkable except by their owner; it should neither be possible for any other person to link a pID to the user's real identity nor to link different pIDs of one and the same user. Thus, pseudonyms are used as identifiers for the pIDs instead of real names [12]. Although pseudonyms cannot guarantee unlinkability comprehensively [10,11,13], they obviously strongly influence unlinkability and, hence, we focus on them within this paper. To allow for recognizing pIDs, pseudonyms must be unique within their scope.

We consider a pseudonym as secure if it does not threaten unlinkability. From point of view of an observer, assigning a pseudonym to each user must be possible with equal probability. These requirements can be fulfilled best by randomly generated pseudonyms that do not encode any information about their holders [2]. Using an arbitrary number of pIDs within a complex collaborative environment is reasonable and recommendable as well to prevent the above mentioned privacy risks [1]. However, handling and managing randomly looking pseudonyms are not easy for human beings: Users cannot remember these pseudonyms easily or recognize already known pseudonyms of other users in highly dynamic situations like a chat. Hence, a usable solution should enable users to assign some shorthand semantics to pseudonyms according to their individual preferences. Within this paper, we focus on aliases as textual representation of pseudonyms. We assume in the following that these aliases are assigned and used solely locally since they would threaten unlinkability [2].

A reasonable support of local aliases is necessary in order to achieve user acceptance. The contribution of this paper is to introduce an architecture that enables users to comprehensively manage their locally assigned aliases in a usable way. We point out relevant tasks and discuss possible solutions.

After introducing the suggested architecture in Section 2, the required components are described in Section 3 and Section 4. Summary and outlook conclude the paper in Section 5.

2   Fundamentals

Generally, two basic requirements need to be fulfilled: (R1) Any data leaving users' clients may only include the secure, randomly looking pseudonym as identifiers for a pID; i.e., aliases must not leave users' clients. (R2) For representing information about pIDs to the user, only locally assigned aliases are used as identifiers.

Supporting alias management has to consider all scenarios in which pseudonyms or aliases are used within the application and information about pIDs shall be represented to users. Pseudonyms are important for any communication, for addressing users as well as for referring to users. Moreover, any text generated within the application might contain a reference to a pID. Pseudonyms can also occur as part of meta data assigned to any data created within the application, e.g., to give a hint about the owner of data.

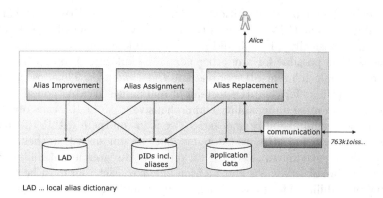

Fig. 1. Suggested architecture

Managing local aliases basically requires three components (Fig. 1). The *Alias Assignment* component assists the user in assigning aliases to own pseudonyms as well as to pseudonyms of other users. Possible aliases are contained in a local alias dictionary (LAD); assigned aliases are stored as attribute of the pIDs.

During communication and collaboration processes, a user might get further information about other users due to made observations or experiences. Consequently, *Alias Improvement* might become necessarily or desired over time. A user should have the possibility to manually reassign new aliases to already existent pseudonym/alias mappings of other users to increase recognizability. Since alias improvement takes place locally, only replacement and representation of pseudonyms by reassigned aliases on user's client are affected. Due to usability aspects and to avoid disorientation of users, the conducted improvement should be stored within a respective history and the according alias should be marked as 'improved', as well. To allow for an easy handling of current aliases and for representing information about possibly former aliases, only pseudonyms should be stored as part of application data.

Alias Replacement is an especially important component since it has to enforce the requirements (R1) and (R2). Replacement has to deal with possible errors resulting from ambiguities and typos.

One might additionally consider to remove aliases, e.g., if the pseudonym is no longer used. The alias used so far could be stored again in the LAD and possibly be used for another pseudonym. However, we do not consider such removal: Later, information about the formerly used pseudonym or the communication partner might be of interest and the alias would be necessary to support recognition. Moreover, an alias used again for a different pseudonym might confuse the user who possibly remembers the former assignment, too.

In order to demonstrate the applicability of the described ideas, the privacy-enhanced eLearning environment BluES'n[1], which offers a variety of complex

---

[1] *BluES like universal eEducation System privacy-enhanced*;
http://blues-portal.de/bluesn.html

and collaborative scenarios, was extended by the introduced alias management concepts. BluES'n especially aims at supporting collaborative working and at providing its users a flexible working environment that can be adapted to their individual needs [3]. Users act under different pIDs addressed by randomly generated pseudonyms; hence, supporting users in assigning aliases to own pseudonyms and pseudonyms of other users and in managing these aliases is an important issue.

3   Alias Assignment

3.1   Local Alias Dictionary (LAD)

The LAD contains a list of possible aliases for assigning them to own pIDs and to pIDs of other users. In general, four different approaches regarding the management of user's LAD can be distinguished.

Solution 1: The client-side PIM is delivered together with a default LAD for all of its users. Although users are not confronted with LAD generation, the approach might not meet their expectations due to users' varying interests and preferences as well as cultural and regional differences. Since the user does not have any possibility to enhance his own LAD, he might feel restricted in his individuality and thus the acceptance of the application itself could be affected.

Solution 2: The server-side PIM offers a set of LADs; users can download favored dictionaries. Comparable to the first alternative, again the availability of LADs corresponding to user's interests and needs is requisite.

Solution 3: The user is responsible for generating his own LADs consisting of aliases corresponding to his own preferences. Ideally, this time-consuming process has to take place before starting to work within the application.

Solution 4: The alias assignment component dynamically generates the LAD entries while the user is working within the application: It asks the user to assign an according alias whenever a formerly unknown pID appears. This approach is time-consuming especially within a complex collaborative application, since the user is disturbed every time a new pID appears.

With respect to flexibility and usability aspects, we suggest a hybrid approach of the first and third variant enhanced by the possibility to support users in generating and improving their LADs. Users are provided a default LAD on their PIM client; besides, they can also generate further LADs according to their preferences and needs. At any time, they can choose an alias from a dictionary or assign an arbitrary alias which is inserted into their default LAD as well. The use of a default LAD provided to any user does not threaten privacy since the assignment and use of aliases remains locally.

3.2   Assigning Aliases

Assigning aliases to pseudonyms based on user's indicated LAD can be done either automatically or manually. With respect to own pseudonyms, manually assigning

an appropriate alias implicates a higher degree of user's recognizability and individuality. In contrast, manual assignment of aliases to pseudonyms of other users
might be time-consuming especially in complex collaborative environments, where
the number of currently available pIDs addressed by pseudonyms fluctuates.

4   Alias Replacement

4.1   Important Issues for the Replacement Process

Replacement between aliases and pseudonyms and vice versa has to be reasonably supported by the system to ensure that only secure pseudonyms leave the
users' client and that only aliases as usable representation of the secure pseudonyms are presented to users. Due to the use of local aliases, one and the same
pID will be represented differently on different clients (Fig. 2).

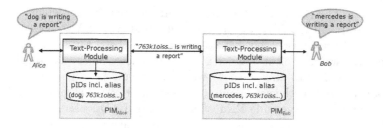

Fig. 2. Representing pIDs on different clients

A usable replacement should be performed mostly automatically to minimize
disturbances of users during their work within the application. Saddling users
with manual replacement would increase the risk of possible errors and, furthermore, significantly decrease the acceptance of local alias management at all. Of
course, automatic replacement will not be possible in any case since we have to
treat different types of errors what may demand user interactions.

A necessary prerequisite for replacement is that there is already an alias assigned to a pseudonym. Otherwise, alias assignment as described in Section 3
needs to be done. Replacement contains the following three tasks:

1. decide, whether a string represents an alias or pseudonym,
2. replace the alias/pseudonyms by the corresponding pseudonym/alias, and
3. represent the result of replacement.

The first task is simple if a pID is explicitly addressed, e.g., in case of writing
an email to another user. An alias of the other user has to be given as recipient
of the message, and an own alias as sender. Implicit addressing is more difficult
to handle; this case occurs any time the user wants to refer to a pID at another
place, e.g., in the content of the message itself. The decision step identifies an
additional task that needs to be realized: Supporting users in selecting pIDs

referenced by aliases. There are various possible solutions which differ in usability as well as possible errors that have to be treated.

The subsequent replacement simply uses the alias/pseudonym mapping and, hence, needs not to be discussed further.

The third task comprises both presenting the alias to the user in the user interface and including the pseudonym instead of the alias before data is internally stored or leaves the client. For both directions of replacement, ambiguity issues have to be considered, i.e., it must be clear within the system whether a character string represents a pseudonym or alias, respectively, or not. Again, an explicit needed reference to a pID establishes the simple case while implicit references require handling possible ambiguity errors.

4.2   Replacing Aliases by Pseudonyms

Support users in selecting aliases

Generally, there are two possible approaches for selecting an alias: (1) presenting a list of assigned aliases from which the user can select, and (2) let the user type in the alias.

If the first approach is realized, a decision whether a string represents an alias is not necessary at all, hence, replacement can be done without further steps. An important advantage is that typo errors regarding the alias are impossible. However, another source of errors is the possibility that the user forgets to select the alias from the list, e.g., in a chat discussion when he wants to write an answer quickly and types in the alias directly. Without any further measure, such errors would remain undetected. The solution is usable regarding the fact that the user does not have to remember existing aliases. However, opening the list and selecting an alias from this list are additional steps to be performed by the user.

If the second approach is realized, we have to handle possible typo errors. Deciding whether a string represents an alias cannot be done automatically; an additional disadvantage is that users have to remember the text strings they have assigned to pseudonyms as aliases. But in situations where users want to write undisturbed and are sure about the alias they want to use, they might prefer this solution since it allows faster working.

To conclude, there is a need for a combined approach for a practical solution including the possibility to select aliases from a list as well as the possibility to handle aliases directly typed in by users.

Decision about alias considering ambiguity errors

If the user has typed in the alias, we need further functionality that searches for possible aliases. Thereby, we have to cope with possible *ambiguity errors*, i.e., problems to distinguish aliases and non-aliases. Since aliases should be usable, it is very likely that users chose usual words as aliases. An unsolved ambiguity problem might imply that an alias is not interpreted as alias and, consequently, is not replaced by a pseudonym. Especially in case of communication, this can cause confusion. Consider, e.g., user A wants to tell user B that a third user C, known to A and B as pID_C with the pseudonym $pID_C.ps^2$, is a good programmer. A has assigned the alias "dog" to pID_C while B has assigned the alias "mercedes". Now A writes the message "dog is a good programmer" and sends it to B. If the alias is not correctly identified, the original message would be delivered to B who cannot understand the meaning of the message.

For making a decision whether a word is an alias or not, there are at least the following three possibilities:

Solution 1: The user actively highlights words he intends to use as an alias by putting the alias in a specific format, e.g., in a tag-form like:
<al> *alias* **</al>**.
In the example described above, A would have to type:
"**<al>** dog **</al>** is a good programmer".
The advantage of the solution is that making a decision simply requires to search for such tags. The disadvantage is that using this format requires additional steps. Moreover, we also have to deal with possible errors – users could forget the tags, they could write the tags erroneously, and, further, the alias could contain typos. Hence, an additional error handling would be required in any case.

Solution 2: The *Alias Replacement* analyzes the semantic of the sentence and determines whether a word is used as an alias or not. However, this alternative is complicated and almost impossible to solve completely. Let's consider another example message that needs to be analyzed: "dog said that he hates dog". What the actually meant might be: "$pID_C.ps$ said that he hates dog". But it might also be: "dog said that he hates $pID_C.ps$" (because C is a hunter).

Solution 3: The replacement component searches for each appearance of words in text typed by a user which are known as assigned aliases. Afterward the replacement component asks the user to explicitly determine whether a detected word should be treated as alias or not. This verification process might take place on-the-fly, i.e., the user is asked right after typing a potential alias.

The advantages of this solution in comparison to the former solutions are that the user does not have to learn any specific format, and that the solution can be quite easily implemented. The drawback is the fact that the user is disturbed by a question every time he types in an alias. However, this fact can be utilized to handle typo errors.

Considering the advantages and disadvantages of these solutions, we suggest a hybrid approach including solution 1 and solution 3. While solution 3 seems to be most suitable for a practical realization, some users might prefer solution 1 since they can actively highlight aliases and do not have to rely on a correct analysis by the system.

Handling typo errors

If the user types in aliases, we have to cope with possible *typo errors.* Generally, there are three different types of errors which have to be handled:

---

[2] Actually, there would be a random number instead of $pID_C.ps$ what is omitted here due to simplicity.

(1) *Typos from non-alias word to alias*: The incorrectly typed word corresponds to an assigned alias.
(2) *Typos from alias to non-alias word*: The incorrectly typed alias is not recognized by the replacement component and hence would not be translated into a pseudonym.
(3) *Typos from alias to alias*: Finally, an alias could be changed into another alias if the two aliases are not too different. Such errors are especially hard to detect for other users since their locally assigned aliases might be absolutely different from each other.

The replacement component should be able to detect such typos. A function to calculate the similarity between strings is necessary, e.g., the Levenshtein distance [9]. The Levenshtein algorithm computes the least number of edit operations that are necessary to modify one string into another one. Based on such a difference, a threshold can be defined to determine whether two strings are considered to be similar or not; in the former case, a possible correction is considered. Particularly, the *Alias Replacement* checks the similarity between a word written by the user and the assigned aliases.

Automatically correct detected typos would again demand analyzing the semantic of the text written by the user in order to find out whether an alias could be meant. Thus, we suggest realizing user-aided correction. Based on evaluating the similarity measure, the *Alias Replacement* detects potential aliases in a message and asks the user to decide whether an alias is meant or not.

Regarding the typo errors we want to consider, this approach provides the following possibilities for error correction:

– *Typos from non-alias to alias:* Since the *Alias Replacement* detects a potential alias, it initiates a user action anyway. The user gets informed that he has input an alias and can correct the word accordingly.
– *Typos from alias to non-alias word:* Since the similarity is checked, the Alias Replacement can detect up to a certain number of errors potential aliases. The user is notified that the word is similar to an alias and gets the possibility to correct the word.
– *Typos from alias to alias:* The user gets the usual notification and, thus, he can check the alias used in the text and correct it.

Representing the pseudonym
There is only a need for a specific representation if the reference to a pID is not explicitly required. Using a specific format to represent pseudonyms prevents that the *Alias Replacement* has to decide whether a randomly looking string represents a pseudonym or not. Thus, the explicit highlighting of pseudonyms, which is not acceptable for aliases, is reasonable in this case: The task to include, e.g., specific tags like

    <ps> *pseudonym* **</ps>**

is performed by the system, and as a result, interpreting pseudonyms can be done automatically by the system.

4.3 Replacing Pseudonyms by Aliases

Decision about pseudonym considering ambiguity errors
Due to the specific representation of pseudonyms as suggested before, they can be interpreted easily. We do not have to deal with ambiguity errors since now we can assume that pseudonyms either appear at specified positions or are marked by means of specific tags.

A possible source of errors could be wrong pseudonyms. They might result from accidental errors of the stored data, e.g., if some bits of pseudonyms stored in the pID data base are flipped, or transmission errors. Another reason are intended attacks to modify the data. We do not consider corruption of pseudonyms since we assume the integration of suitable methods to prevent or detect them.

Representing the alias
If the alias is used to implicitly address a pID, possible ambiguity problems have to be prevented: While presenting the text in the user interface, the user should be able to distinguish between aliases and non-aliases.

For example, displaying the internal message "$pID_C.ps$ said that he hates dog" is difficult if the user has assigned the alias "dog" to pID_C: After replacing the pseudonym, the message is "dog said that he hates dog". Consequently, the user interface has to provide possibilities to present aliases in a specific format so that they can be easily recognized as aliases, e.g., enclose the aliases in specific signs, or set them in a style not used for another purpose.

5   Summary and Outlook

Within this paper, we introduced an architecture that provides to users a reasonable and usable support for managing local aliases as representation of secure pseudonyms. A general pseudonym/alias mapping was integrated into the example environment BluES'n. By means of this approach the user is supported in handling and managing his own pseudonyms as well as pseudonyms of other users in a comprehensible and usable way. Additionally, a first automatic analysis and replacement of pseudonyms appearing in commonly used content by aliases takes place in communication and cooperation processes. For example, a replacement within a chat session takes place in case of addressing the communication partner directly by means of his locally assigned alias. The *Alias Replacement* component of BluES'n checks whether the typed in text corresponds to an existent alias/pseudonym mapping while a user writes a message. If such a mapping exists, the user is asked on-the-fly whether the word should be marked as alias. Since Levenshtein distance is computed additionally, the user is also presented a list of possibly matching aliases.

The implementation demonstrates the feasibility of the suggestion to use locally assigned aliases as usable presentation of secure, randomly looking pseudonyms [2]. The suggested approach is also applicable for other collaborative environments such as Instant Messaging that comprises a lot of interactions between users [7].

Future work will focus on considering additional contextual information for dynamically assigning aliases to pseudonyms. This implies the availability of respective mechanisms for monitoring and deriving application context information and creating appropriate aliases. Additionally, there is also a need to improve handling aliases over a longer period: The user might learn a lot of pseudonyms and, consequently, needs a long list of aliases. Archiving aliases might become helpful in such cases. Finally, a comprehensive user evaluation of the introduced pseudonym/alias mapping in real-life scenarios could reveal to what degree users understand and accept the introduced concept.

Acknowledgments. We like to thank Mike Bergmann, Alexander Böttcher, and Hai Duy Nguyen for fruitful discussions, and all in the BluES'n project involved people for their support and encouragement.

References

1. Borcea, K., et al.: Intra-Application Partitioning of Personal Data. In: Proc. of PEP, Edinburgh, UK, pp. 67–74 (2005)
2. Borcea, K., Franz, E., Pfitzmann, A.: Usable Presentation of Secure Pseudonyms. In: Proc. of DIM 2005, Alexandria, Virginia, USA (November 2005)
3. Borcea-Pfitzmann, K., Liesebach, K.: The Concept of Workspaces – Re-defined for eLearning. Advanced Technology for Learning (ATL) International Journal, Special Issue on Technology for Collaborative Learning 4(1) (2007)
4. Clauß, S., et al.: Privacy Enhancing Identity Management: Protection Against Re-identification and Profiling. In: Proc. of DIM 2005, Alexandria, Virginia, USA (November 2005)
5. Clauß, S., Pfitzmann, A., Hansen, M., Herreweghen, E.V.: Privacy-Enhancing Identity Management. The IPTS Report 67, 8–16 (2002),
   http://www.jrc.es/pages/iptsreport/vol67/english/IPT2E676.html
6. Eurobarometer. Flash Eurobarometer, Citizens' perceptions, N225 (2008)
7. Franz, E., Groba, C., Springer, T., Bergmann, M.: A Comprehensive Approach for Context-dependent Privacy Management. In: Proc. of ARES 2008, Barcelona (2008)
8. Kobsa, A.: Privacy-enhanced web personalization. In: Brusilovsky, P., Kobsa, A., Nejdl, W. (eds.) Adaptive Web 2007. LNCS, vol. 4321, pp. 628–670. Springer, Heidelberg (2007)
9. Levenshtein algorithm website, http://www.levenshtein.net
10. Narayanan, A., Shmatikov, V.: De-anonymizing Social Networks. To appear at IEEE Security & Privacy 2009 (2009),
    http://randomwalker.info/social-networks/
11. Novak, J., Raghavan, P., Tomkins, A.: Anti-Aliasing on the Web. In: Proceedings of the 13th Int. Conference on the World Wide Web, pp. 30–39 (2004)
12. Pfitzmann, A., Hansen, M.: Anonymity, unlinkability, undetectability, unobservability, pseudonymity, and identity management – a consolidated proposal for terminology, v0.31, http://dud.inf.tu-dresden.de/Anon_Terminology.shtml
13. Rao, J.R., Rohatgi, P.: Can Pseudonymity Really Guarantee Privacy? In: Proc. of the 9th USENIX Security Symposium, August 2000, pp. 85–96 (2000)

A Privacy-Preserving Platform for User-Centric Quantitative Benchmarking

Dominik Herrmann, Florian Scheuer, Philipp Feustel,
Thomas Nowey, and Hannes Federrath

University of Regensburg, 93040 Regensburg, Germany
http://www-sec.uni-regensburg.de/

Abstract. We propose a centralised platform for quantitative bench-marking of key performance indicators (KPI) among mutually distrust-ful organisations. Our platform offers users the opportunity to request an ad-hoc benchmarking for a specific KPI within a peer group of their choice. Architecture and protocol are designed to provide anonymity to its users and to hide the sensitive KPI values from other clients and the central server. To this end, we integrate user-centric peer group forma-tion, exchangeable secure multi-party computation protocols, short-lived ephemeral key pairs as pseudonyms, and attribute certificates. We show by empirical evaluation of a prototype that the performance is acceptable for reasonably sized peer groups.

1 Introduction

During financial crisis banks have an increased need to take their bearings on the market. The comparison of own key performance indicators (KPI) to competitors' ones or to the overall baseline within the industry is a promising approach. Relevant KPIs may be for instance the proportion of subprimes in the asset portfolio or the return per worker in segment. Such benchmarks are tradition-ally calculated by a trusted third party (TTP) – which inevitably learns the KPI values in the process.

Benchmarking becomes non-trivial, though, when competitors are mutually distrustful or unwilling to hand over their KPI values to a TTP. Although the application of *secure multi-party computation* (SMC) protocols is a frequently cited solution, significant results can only be obtained if users can ensure com-parability of their KPIs. An intuitive solution for this task is *user-controlled peer-group formation,* i. e. the initiator of a benchmarking may specify concrete selection criteria all participants have to meet (cf. Table 1).

To the best of our knowledge there is currently no practical solution with acceptable security properties for this challenge. In this paper we present a plat-form that allows privacy-preserving comparison of KPIs over the Internet – not relying on a TTP at all. It integrates user-controlled peer group formation with exchangeable SMC protocols and offers its users practical anonymity. We discuss the requirements and the attacker model addressed by the platform, outline the

S. Fischer-Hübner et al. (Eds.): TrustBus 2009, LNCS 5695, pp. 32–41, 2009.

Table 1. Example of selection attributes, attribute values of an individual user i, and selection criteria used for peer-group formation of benchmarking b

Selection attribute s_j	Attribute values $a_j^{(i)}$	Selection criteria $c_j^{(b)}$	a_j matches c_j
Location (country)	Germany	Germany	true
Business area	financial services	financial services	true
Sales in 1000 US\$	517,000	$100 < x \leq 1000$	false

architecture and protocols employed and evaluate the performance of a proto-typical implementation.

2   Related Work

There have been a couple of initiatives to develop Internet-based benchmarking systems (cf. [1,2]). However they neglect important privacy issues. Those issues can be tackled with SMC protocols. Numerous variants have been proposed in the last decades, among them generic ones [3,4,5,6] as well as protocols tailored for specific scenarios [7,8,9].

The work by Kerschbaum et al. [10,11,12] is especially focused on privacy-preserving benchmarking between (mutually distrustful) organisations. Their concept of peer-group formation using adapted k-means clustering is fundamen-tally different from our user-controlled approach, though. While Kerschbaum's proposal in [12] only allows users to be part of one peer group at a given time, we enable participation in various peer groups. Furthermore, our approach offers more privacy to the users, which may increase adoptability. Finally, while Ker-schbaum et al. advocate an SMC protocol based on homomorphic encryption for their benchmarking platform, we additionally consider a secret sharing scheme from [3].

Catrina et al. [13] advocate the involvement of a central service provider that does not take part in benchmarking computations, but only offers communi-cations services to the clients. Furthermore, they suggest that clients delegate work to multiple identical service providers to distribute trust among them and to reduce the risk of compromise.

3   Architecture Overview

Many SMC protocols (e. g. [3]) rely on fully meshed peer-to-peer communica-tions. Catrina et al. [13] argue that this network topology is not suitable in a real-world setting, though. They advocate the involvement of a central ser-vice provider (SP) that reduces complexity, acting as a communication mediator for the clients (star topology). We have designed our platform following this reasoning. However, in contrast to their proposal to employ multiple identical

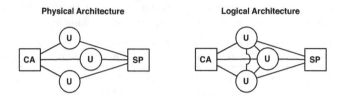

Fig. 1. Involved parties: users (U), service provider (SP), certification authority (CA)

service providers, we include a certification authority (CA) in our architecture. We believe that users are more likely to trust a dedicated CA than multiple (possibly relatively unknown) service providers (cf. Kerschbaum's argumentation in the introduction of [11]).

Figure 1 shows the physical and logical architecture of the platform. Clients do not communicate directly with each other, but only via the public SP. The SP stores incoming messages temporarily, and the clients poll the SP to retrieve new messages in regular intervals. For addressing a specific recipient, clients use public key certificates as pseudonyms. Moreover, the SP allows clients to request new benchmarkings or discover currently running ones as well as to retrieve the results of past ones. The CA issues certificates used for various purposes.

4   Requirements and Attacker Model

Table 2 contains the set of functional and non-functional requirements which are addressed by our privacy-preserving benchmarking platform.

Our attacker model is based on the definitions for multilateral security [14]. We differentiate between the group of *all users of the platform (users)* and the (usually smaller) group of *participating users (participants)* of an ongoing benchmarking. Following classical SMC research principles [15], we limit our attacker model to participants who are semi-honest ("honest but curious") for now: they follow the protocol and always tell the truth[1]. However, they may try to learn other participants' KPI values or identities. Multiple participants may collude to achieve this goal. We leave malicious participants, who inject or forge messages, for future work.

Furthermore, we limit ourselves to SPs and CAs who carry out their duties honestly. While the CA is considered trustworthy the SP may maliciously try to gain information about the benchmarkings. The last group we consider are outsiders who are not using the platform. They may either passively or actively try to gain knowledge about running benchmarkings, the identity of participants or their KPI values. To this end, they may record network traffic or even maliciously inject messages.

---

[1] For sake of brevity we neglect free-riding and truth-telling issues in this paper. Refer to Ziv's model [16] for a detailed treatment of these issues. In future research, we will look into incentives that encourage truth-telling.

Table 2. The benchmarking platform addresses functional (F) and non-functional, i. e. security (S) and usability (U), requirements

#	Description
F1	**User-driven Initiation.** Each user of the platform can initiate a benchmarking of a particular KPI whenever need arises.
F2	**User-controlled Peer Group Formation.** An accurate definition of the peer group is a prerequisite to gain useful insights from the benchmarking. The initiator must be able to control the peer-group formation process on a per-benchmarking level so that the participants meet certain criteria. The criteria should be specified with real-world attributes to facilitate intuitive classification.
F3	**Support for Various Statistics.** The platform must support the calculation of various statistics (e. g. mean, median and variance) for different KPI data types. Apart from integer and real values, benchmarking of categorical values may also be of interest.
S1	**Anonymity of Users.** The identity of the users must remain private. Other parties (including the platform provider) may neither learn who is participating in a benchmarking nor whether a particular organisation is participating.
S2	**Confidentiality of KPIs.** As KPI values may contain sensitive information about a user's organisation, they must not be revealed to third parties (including the platform provider). The platform has to ensure that the benchmarking results are aggregated in a fashion that prohibits the recovery of individual KPI values.
S3	**Confidentiality of Selection Attributes.** If other parties learned the selection attributes of a participant, they could deduce the identity of a participant, either with context knowledge or by an intersection attack (cf. Sect. 5.2). Therefore, the values of selection attributes used during peer-group formation must not be revealed to other parties (including the service provider).
S4	**Enforced Peer Group Formation.** The platform has to enforce the peer-group formation as requested by the initiator. Users who do not meet the requested criteria may not join a benchmarking.
U1	**Off-the-Shelf Technologies.** The platform should utilise existing technologies and communications infrastructure, i. e. the Internet, to lower entry barriers for users and platform providers.
U2	**Polling.** The platform should not require its users to run servers which require inbound connections. Instead, the client software should use polling to retrieve new messages in short intervals.
U3	**Near-time Availability of Results.** Benchmarking results have to be available within a short time to enable users to set up multiple consecutive benchmarkings over various KPIs and peer groups to gain information exploratively. Results should be made available to the other participants as an incentive to participate. They schould be archived and published on the platform.
U4	**Scalability.** The system is supposed to scale with increasing numbers of participants and benchmarkings.

5   Addressing Core Requirements

5.1   Secure Multi-party Computation of Mean Value

Our benchmarking platform is independent of the SMC protocols. For evaluation purposes we have implemented two popular SMC protocols prototypically (results are provided in Sect. 7). Both of them facilitate the distributed computation of the sum of multiple values. The arithmetic mean of the values is easily found by dividing the sum by the number of participants. Of course, more advanced protocols addressing other statistics can be implemented in the future.

SumSecureSplit. The first one is an extension to Atallah's Secure Split Protocol (cf. [3] for a detailed explanation of that building block). The Secure Split protocol allows a group of m participants P_j, $1 \leq j \leq m$, who provide private numeric inputs $x^{(j)}$, to securely share these values among themselves. As output of the protocol each participant obtains m blinded values $z^{(j)}$ such that $\sum_{j=1}^{m} x^{(j)} = \sum_{j=1}^{m} z^{(j)}$. In addition to Atallah's specification, our scheme requires each participant P_j to send his value $z^{(j)}$ to all the other participants, enabling each of them to compute the final result $z = \sum_{j=1}^{m} z^{(j)}$. The presented protocol uses a collusion threshold $k = m - 1$ for best privacy protection.

SumHomomorphic. The second protocol employs a homomorphic cryptosystem with an additive property $E_{\text{hPub}}(\sum_{j=1}^{m} x^{(j)}) = \prod_{j=1}^{m} E(x^{(j)})$ [17]. Using a shared homomorphic key pair $K_{\text{h}} = (K_{\text{hPub}}, K_{\text{hSec}})$ participants $P_j, 1 < j < m$ submit their encrypted private numeric inputs $E_{\text{hPub}}(x^{(j)})$ to a party unaware of K_{hSec} (the SP), which will execute the multiplication and distribute the still encrypted result to the participants afterwards. Finally they gain the result $\sum_{j=1}^{m} x^{(j)}$ by decrypting the received result with K_{hSec}.

5.2   Preserving User's Anonymity

Users should connect to the server through an anonymisation service (like Tor or JonDonym)[2] to protect their IP addresses. On the platform, they are addressed with a pseudonym, which cannot be linked to their identity. Our protocol uses public key certificates as pseudonyms. However, this scheme is not sufficient: it is conceivable that the set of selection attribute values may uniquely identify a participant, i. e. when only one organisation exists in the world which matches those criteria. Our protocol ensures that neither the service provider nor other clients learn the selection attribute values.

If other participants can observe that a single client (identified by a static pseudonym) takes part in consecutive benchmarkings, they can mount an intersection attack by slightly varying the selection criteria and observing whether the targeted client takes part in the benchmarking or not. In order to protect clients from intersection attacks, clients use a new pseudonym *(ephemeral public key certificate)* for every benchmarking.

---

[2] cf. http://www.torproject.org/ and http://www.jondonym.de/, respectively

5.3   Enforcing Peer-Group Formation

Given our set of requirements, the SP cannot enforce peer-group formation on its own, because it must not learn the selection attribute values (cf. requirement S3). We assume that – as a trusted party – the CA may learn these values and is able to validate their correctness, though. Therefore, the client has to present the selection attribute values to the CA in order to receive an *attribute certificate* containing them.

In order to participate in a benchmarking a client has to forward the list of requested selection criteria together with its own attribute certificate to the CA. The CA checks whether the client's attributes match the requirement and creates a *participation certificate*, which includes the current pseudonym of the client and the satisfied selection criteria, on success. The client has to present the participation certificate as a means of authorisation to the SP. In order to maintain unlinkability (cf. Sect. 5.2), the client must request a fresh participation certificate for each benchmarking – even if it contains the same statement.

6   Protocol

The protocol proceeds in four phases. Figure 2 outlines the involvement of the various parties in each phase. We assume that all connections between clients, SP and CA are encrypted using TLS to protect against attacks from outsiders. For practical purposes the SP offers a predefined list of selection attributes S_{global} and KPIs X_{global} for various subject areas to choose from. The following sections outline the building blocks of the communication protocol.

Registration at the CA. In *phase 1* a user i creates a permanent key pair $K_{\text{perm}}^{(i)} = (k_{\text{pPub}}^{(i)}, k_{\text{pSec}}^{(i)})$. Then, he registers at the CA providing $k_{\text{pPub}}^{(i)}$, his real-world identity, and a list of j selection attributes $\mathbf{s}_{\text{client}}^{(i)} = (s_1, \ldots, s_j)$ with their corresponding attribute values $\mathbf{a}_{\text{client}}^{(i)} = (a_1^{(i)}, \ldots, a_j^{(i)})$ which shall be used during peer-group formation. If the verification of the supplied data succeeds the CA will sign the user's long-lasting public key $k_{\text{pPub}}^{(i)}$ for future authentication. The user also receives an attribute certificate $\text{Cert}_{\text{attributes}}^{(i)} = (k_{\text{pPub}}^{(i)}, \mathbf{s}_{\text{client}}^{(i)}, \mathbf{a}_{\text{client}}^{(i)})$, which ties the validated selection attribute values $\mathbf{a}_{\text{client}}^{(i)}$ to his identity represented

			User	SP	CA
Phase 1	Registration		←		→
Phase 2	Peer-Group-Formation		←	→	→
Phase 3	Statistics	SumSecureSplit	↻		
	Computation	SumHomomorphic	←	→	→
Phase 4	Result Announcement		←	→	

Fig. 2. Involvement of parties in the course of the protocol

by $k_{\text{pPub}}^{(i)}$. Once the registration is completed, a user can either initiate a new benchmarking or participate in a pending one.

Creating Ephemeral Key Pairs. In *phases 2–3* users are identified by ephemeral public-key certificates. $K_{\text{perm}}^{(i)}$ cannot be used for communication with the SP or other clients in order to maintain unlinkability. Whenever a user i wants to set up or participate in a benchmarking, he creates a short-lived (ephemeral) key pair $K_{\text{eph}}^{(i)} = (k_{\text{ePub}}^{(i)}, k_{\text{eSec}}^{(i)})$, which is exclusively used for one benchmarking and cannot be linked to $K_{\text{perm}}^{(i)}$.

Benchmarking Setup. When a new benchmarking is set up *phase 2* is entered. A user i can issue an ad-hoc request for a new benchmarking b of a specific KPI $x \in X_{\text{global}}$ at any time. Therefore, he requests the CA to sign an ephemeral public key $k_{\text{ePub}}^{(i)}$ after having authenticated with $k_{\text{pPub}}^{(i)}$. Then, the user sends a benchmarking request $\text{BR} = (k_{\text{ePub}}^{(i,b)}, x, t, s_{\text{req}}, c_{\text{req}})$ to the SP. The BR includes a vector of selection attributes s_{req} and the requested criteria c_{req}. The initiator is willing to wait for participants until deadline t. The SP validates the signature on $k_{\text{ePub}}^{(i)}$ and adds the request to the list of benchmarking announcements on success. All clients (including the initiator) can now indicate their interest to participate. When the deadline expires, the announcement will be removed from the list and the computation starts.

Joining a Benchmarking. If user i wants to participate in a pending benchmarking b from the list of announcements, he will create a new ephemeral key pair $K_{\text{eph}}^{(i)}$. Then, he presents $k_{\text{ePub}}^{(i)}$, $\text{Cert}_{\text{attributes}}^{(i)}$, $s_{\text{req}}^{(b)}$ and $c_{\text{req}}^{(b)}$ to the CA and requests it to sign $k_{\text{ePub}}^{(i)}$ and to issue a participation certificate $\text{Cert}_{\text{p}}^{(i,b)} = (k_{\text{ePub}}^{(i)}, s_{\text{req}}^{(b)}, c_{\text{req}}^{(b)})$. The CA will only comply, if $a_{\text{client}}^{(i)}$ matches the criteria specified by $s_{\text{req}}^{(b)}$ and $c_{\text{req}}^{(b)}$. After that, the client sends a *participation request* $\text{PR} = (\text{Cert}_{\text{p}}^{(i,b)}, b)$ to the server. The server validates PR and checks that $s_{\text{req}}^{(b)}$ and $c_{\text{req}}^{(b)}$ contained in $\text{Cert}_{\text{p}}^{(i,b)}$ are identical to the corresponding fields in BR. On success it will add the signed $k_{\text{ePub}}^{(i)}$ to the list of participants. Once the deadline t is reached, the server checks whether the security requirements are met, i.e. a certain minimum number of clients are willing to participate. It proceeds by publishing the list of participants $\text{PL}^{(b)} = k_{\text{ePub}}^{(\cdot)}$, which contains a list of their signed ephemeral public keys.

Participating in a Benchmarking. In *phase 3* the distributed computation takes place. All n participants of benchmarking b retrieve $\text{PL}^{(b)}$ from the server and validate the signatures of the contained $k_{\text{ePub}}^{(\cdot)}$ to prevent the SP from maliciously injecting participants. On success they proceed with the actual SMC protocol, which is not shown here in detail for conciseness. Each message m exchanged between two clients is signed and encrypted using the ephemeral keys before transmission: $m' = \text{enc}_{k_{\text{ePub}}^{(j)}}(m, \text{sig}_{k_{\text{eSec}}^{(i)}}(m))$. When the SMC protocol terminates, all clients submit their final result values to the SP, which announces them publicly *(phase 4)*. The SP may use a majority vote in case the reported values are not identical.

7   Performance Evaluation

We implemented the platform prototypically in Java SE 5 on Linux. All messages were encoded in XML and transmitted over TLS-secured sockets. Clients applied end-to-end encryption to all messages exchanged between each other using 1024 bit RSA keys. The JVMs of the CA and the SP were running on off-the-shelf hardware (2 cores, 2.20 GHz, 3 GB RAM), the clients were instantiated on a Dual Xeon 2.13 GHz machine with 2 GB of RAM and connected with 100 MBit/s.

As a comparison with existing SMC-based platforms [11,8] is difficult due to differing assumptions, we limited our evaluation to the SMC protocols we implemented so far, *SumHomomorphic* and *SumSecureSplit*, for varying numbers of users (10, 20, 40, 80). In each run all users registered in the first 60 seconds. Afterwards 10 benchmarkings with 10 selection criteria each were executed in sequence. Each time users had 60 seconds to join the benchmarking and to form the peer group. Clients were configured to use a polling interval of 7 seconds. On average the statistics computation was finished within 8 seconds *(SumHomomorphic)* or 17 seconds *(SumSecureSplit)*, respectively.

According to our results both SMC protocols offer satisfactory performance for peer groups of reasonable size. Figure 3 indicates that *SumSecureSplit* induces more traffic than *SumHomomorphic*. As illustrated in Fig. 4 the traffic for the one-time registration is insignificant – in stark contrast to the peer-group formation. While the proportion of the SMC protocol increases rapidly with the number of users for *SumSecureSplit*, this is not an issue for *SumHomomorphic*. This finding is not surprising as *SumHomomorphic* has been designed with a client-server architecture in mind and does not rely on extensive peer-to-peer communications [11].

The CPU load of both SMC protocols is noncritical as seen in Fig. 5. The servers are idle, waiting for requests most of the time. Considering the distributed computation of the *SumSecureSplit* protocol the load of the SMC component is

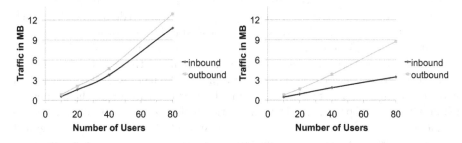

Fig. 3. Server-side traffic for *SumSecureSplit* (left) and *SumHomomorphic* (right)

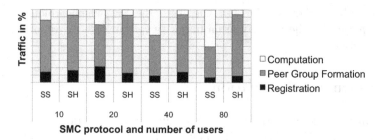

Fig. 4. Server-side traffic allocation for various protocol phases using *SumSecureSplit* (SS) and *SumHomomorphic* (SH)

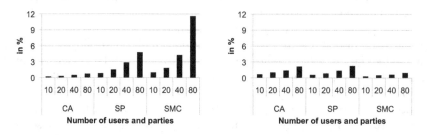

Fig. 5. Average CPU load for CA, SP and its SMC component for *SumSecureSplit* (left) and *SumHomomorphic* (right)

surprisingly high, though. This can be ascribed to the extensive processing of client-client-messages at the server.

8   Conclusion and Future Work

We presented a centralised privacy-preserving platform for benchmarking of numeric values which is the first one to integrate intuitive, user-controlled peer-group formation with flexibly exchangeable SMC protocols. Users are free to initiate and participate in benchmarkings, while the employed SMC protocols ensure that sensitive KPI values are not disclosed at any time. Furthermore, we have demonstrated how ephemeral key pairs can be used to foil intersection attacks targeting users' anonymity. Another novel concept in our work concerns the architecture of the platform: in addition to a central service provider we deploy a dedicated CA, which ensures appropriate separation of duties. The evaluation of a prototypical implementation using off-the-shelf technologies yielded promising results. The calculation of the arithmetic mean of a set of secret KPI values with the help of two classical SMC protocols performs fast enough for practical purposes. Following up from here the modular concept of the platform allows us to easily assess the properties of many more SMC protocols addressing various other statistics in a common environment. Furthermore, the platform will allow us to study countermeasures against iterative intersection attacks, which exploit our peer-group formation scheme to identify certain participants with unique selection attribute values.

References

1. Bogetoft, P., Nielsen, K.: Internet Based Benchmarking. Technical report, Dept. of Economics, The Royal Veterinary and Agricultural University, Denmark (2002)
2. Crotts, J., Pan, B., Dimitry, C., Goldman, H.: A Case Study on Developing an Internet-Based Competitive Analysis and Benchmarking Tool for Hospitality Industry. In: Proc. Conference of Travel and Tourism Research Association (2006)
3. Atallah, M., Bykova, M., Li, J., Frikken, K., Topkara, M.: Private collaborative forecasting and benchmarking. In: Proc. 2004 ACM workshop on Privacy in the Electronic Society, pp. 103–114. ACM, New York (2004)
4. Yao, A.: Protocols for Secure Computations. In: Proc. 23rd annual IEEE Symposium on Foundations of Computer Science, pp. 160–164 (1982)
5. Malkhi, D., Nisan, N., Pinkas, B., Sella, Y.: Fairplay – a Secure Two-Party Computation System. In: Proc. 13th USENIX Security Symposium, pp. 287–302 (2004)
6. Liu, W., Luo, S.S., Chen, P.: A Study of Secure Multi-party Ranking Problem. In: 8th ACIS International Conference on Software Engineering, Artificial Intelligence, Networking, and Parallel/Distributed Computing, pp. 727–732 (2007)
7. Bogetoft, P., Damgård, I.B., Jakobsen, T., Nielsen, K., Pagter, J.I., Toft, T.: A practical implementation of secure auctions based on multiparty integer computation. In: Di Crescenzo, G., Rubin, A. (eds.) FC 2006. LNCS, vol. 4107, pp. 142–147. Springer, Heidelberg (2006)
8. Bogetoft, P., Christensen, D.L., Damgard, I., Geisler, M., Jakobsen, T., Krøigaard, M., Nielsen, J.D., Nielsen, J.B., Nielsen, K., Pagter, J., Schwartzbach, M., Toft, T.: Multiparty Computation Goes Live. Cryptology ePrint Archive, Report 2008/068 (2008)
9. Feigenbaum, J., Pinkas, B., Ryger, R., Saint-Jean, F.: Secure Computation of Surveys. In: Proc. EU Workshop on Secure Multiparty Protocols (2004)
10. Kerschbaum, F., Terzidis, O.: Filtering for private collaborative benchmarking. In: Müller, G. (ed.) ETRICS 2006. LNCS, vol. 3995, pp. 409–422. Springer, Heidelberg (2006)
11. Kerschbaum, F.: Practical Privacy-Preserving Benchmarking. In: Jajodia, S., Samarati, P., Cimato, S. (eds.) Proc. IFIP TC-11 23rd International Information Security Conference. IFIP, vol. 278, pp. 17–31. Springer, Heidelberg (2008)
12. Kerschbaum, F.: Building A Privacy-Preserving Benchmarking Enterprise System. Enterprise Information Systems 2(4) (2008)
13. Catrina, O., Kerschbaum, F.: Fostering the Uptake of Secure Multiparty Computation in E-Commerce. In: Proc. Third International Conference on Availability, Reliability and Security, pp. 693–700 (2008)
14. Rannenberg, K., Pfitzmann, A., Müller, G.: In: Multilateral Security in Communications, vol. 3, pp. 21–29. Addison-Wesley, Reading (1999)
15. Canetti, R., Lindell, Y., Ostrovsky, R., Sahai, A.: Universally Composable Two-Party and Multi-Party Secure Computation. In: Proc. 34th annual ACM symposium on Theory of Computing, pp. 494–503. ACM, New York (2002)
16. Ziv, A.: Information Sharing in Oligopoly: the Truth-Telling Problem. RAND Journal of Economics 24(3), 455–465 (1993)
17. Paillier, P.: Public-key cryptosystems based on composite degree residuosity classes. In: Stern, J. (ed.) EUROCRYPT 1999. LNCS, vol. 1592, pp. 223–238. Springer, Heidelberg (1999)

An Anonymous Credit Card System

Elli Androulaki and Steven Bellovin

Columbia University
{elli,smb}@cs.columbia.edu

Abstract. Credit cards have many important benefits; however, these same benefits often carry with them many privacy concerns. In particular, the need for users
to be able to monitor their own transactions, as well as bank's need to justify its
payment requests from cardholders, entitle the latter to maintain a detailed log
of all transactions its credit card customers were involved in. A bank can thus
build a profile of each cardholder even without the latter's consent. In this paper,
we present a practical and accountable anonymous credit system based on ecash,
with a privacy preserving mechanism for error correction and expense-reporting.

1 Introduction

Motivation: Credit Cards vs. Consumer's Privacy. Credit cards have many useful
properties. Apart permitting delayed payment, they provide users with logs of their own
transactions, receipts, and the opportunity to challenge and correct erroneous charges.
However, these same benefits are a privacy risk: banks can use the same information to
build and sell profiles of their customers. We need a system that preserves the benefits
of credit cards without violating users' privacy.

In the context of e-commerce, privacy of an entity is being able to transact with other
entities without any unauthorized outsider being able to acquire any transaction-related
information. In addition, no party should be able to build profiles of any other party based
on purchases without the latter's consent. Being closely related to their owners'identities,
credit cards' extended use constitutes a serious threat to consumers' privacy: *Frequent
occurrences of credit card losses, credit card number based-impersonation attacks as
well as human nature errors, i.e. overcharge of a client, make it necessary for cardholders to be able to monitor their own transaction activity and for merchants to provide banks with detailed description of each credit card transaction. Under the umbrella
of the need of immediate charge justification/correction, each bank, which is no more
trusted than the people operating it, acquires a global view of its customers' transaction activity.* None of the currently deployed credit card systems offer consumer's privacy towards banks. Given the fact that the percentage of credit card-based purchases
is increasing, a deployable privacy preserving credit card system has become quite important. This is the problem we have solved.

Privacy Preserving Payment Mechanisms. A very detailed report on the state of the
art of electronic payment systems was first done by Asokan e.t.l. in [AJSW99]. [K99]
and [BBG+00] are credit card related protocols securing or blinding credit card information from third parties or merchant respectively but *not towards banks.* Credit Cards

S. Fischer-Hübner et al. (Eds.): TrustBus 2009, LNCS 5695, pp. 42–51, 2009.

providing cardholder anonymity even towards the banks were introduced in 1994 by Low etl. [LPM94]. However, their scheme involves many trusted parties and offers no expense report or error correction service. Current schemes have some of the privacy problems mentioned earlier:

Ecash. Ecash [CHL05, DCN90] is a substitute of money on the Internet which cannot be faked, copied or spent more than once. It is known to provide absolute anonymity, namely no one can relate a particular ecash coin (ecoin) with its owner. One would argue that ecash could solve the problem we described before. Consumers can indeed buy anonymous ecoins from a bank/mint and use them in their online transactions. [B95] is a ecash based electronic payment system taking in consideration real world system threats. However, ecash is a prepayment based — as opposed to the most popular credit based — scheme, and used strictly for online transactions; additionally, the complete anonymity it guarantees gives no opportunities for error correction or expense reporting.

Anonymous Debit Cards(ADCs). Anonymous Debit Cards are prepaid ecash -based cards, which are recharged by cardholders and used to pay for goods anonymously. However, their use is very limited; among the reasons are the lack of error correction and proof of purchase mechanisms; additionally, they operate in a debit rather than a credit fashion, i.e. the amount of money paid by it, is subtracted from one's account, when the card is initially obtained.

Our Contribution. In this paper we introduce a privacy-preserving credit card mechanism which can be applied in current credit card systems. In particular, we present a realizable protocol to support "credit card"-based online and offline transactions, in which banks, unless authorized by the cardholder, do not acquire any knowledge of their customers' transactions. At the same time, cardholders are provided with detailed reports regarding their purchases and may participate on any type of merchant credit card offers. For the purposes of our system, we made use of a combination of two types of the compact ecash [CHL05] scheme for payments, and a combination of blind [CL02] and plain digital signatures for the rest of our system's operations.

In the following sections we will briefly present our system's main functions. For space reasons, we have put the more detailed presentation of all the services provided by our scheme in [AB09].

2   System Architecture

A typical credit card mechanism consists of cardholders (consumers), merchants (sellers), Card Issuing Banks, Acquiring Banks and Credit Card Associations.

When eligible to receive a credit card, a consumer applies to a *Card Issuing Bank* she maintains an account with. The *Card Issuing Bank* bills the *cardholders* for payment and bears the risk of fraudulent use of the card. On the other hand, *Merchants*, who are eligible to receive credit card payments, are in agreement with an *Acquiring Bank* authorized to receive payments on their behalf. Banks are organized in *Credit Card*

Associations (such as Visa® or Master Card®) that set the transaction rules between *Card Issuing* and *Acquiring Banks*.

For convenience, in the following sections, we will refer to a merchant as 'he', to a client as 'she' and to any type of Bank as 'it'. In addition, we will use the following acronyms: CIB for Card Issuing Bank, AB for Acquiring Bank, ACCA for our Anonymous Credit Card Association and ACC for Anonymous Credit Card.

As we aim to create a realizable system, we assume that our adversary has all the powers and motives real Banks/merchants/cardholders or groups of them would have. In addition, we assume that all parties have as main objective to increase their profit and would not act against it. More specifically:

a. All of banks are "honest but curious": they are trusted to do their functional operations correctly, but they may collude with each other or with merchants and combine the information they possess to track their customers' activities.

b. Merchants are mostly interested in receiving their payment. However, they may try to "deceive" a cardholder into making her pay more. For advertising purposes, merchants may be motivated — if cost effective — to collaborate with banks to profile their customers. In offline transactions the merchant knows the customer's face. However, any attempt to identify a customer manually (i.e. by comparing pictures online) is not cost effective and is thus highly unlikely.

c. Cardholders may try to "cheat", i.e. not to pay a merchant, to forge an ACC, or perhaps to frame another customer by accusing her of having cheated.

3 Requirements

Privacy and the rest of our system requirements will be presented in this section. For simplicity (and since we assumed collaboration between banks), we will refer to all of them as a united organization, a general Bank.

Privacy. Given a simple (online) cardholder-merchant transaction, no unauthorized third party — including the bank — should be able to gain any information regarding that particular transaction or link it to a particular cardholder even with merchant's collaboration (We call this *Customer Anonymity w.r.t bank and the merchant*). In addition, linking different ACC-based transactions as having been done by the same cardholder should be impossible (*Transaction Unlinkability*). However, we require that the privacy provided in our system is *conditional*: guaranteed for honest cardholders, but immediately revoked for dishonest ones.

As mentioned before, one of our fundamental requirements is the system's **Deployability**, i.e. our protocols should be usable with the current credit card systems' architecture as described in the previous section. **Credit Card Unforgeability** and **non-Transferability** are also required; our cards should not be forgeable or usable by any third party. It should be possible for cardholders to track their transactions (**Expense Report Service**) and provide an undeniable proof of any mischarge (**Error Correction Service**) without endangering their privacy. Privacy-preserving **Loss Recovery** of the card and **Special** payment rate **offers** should be supported.

4 Anonymous Credit Card System

A credit mechanism can be viewed as a long term loan. The cardholder is credited the amount she borrows to transact, while credit limit L_{credit} is the highest loan balance that is authorized. To avoid charges for a more than she has spent, the customer is required — at the end of each month — to provide undeniable proof of the amount of money she has spent within that month. In this section we will provide a brief presentation (see [AB09] for more details) of the most important services of our system: ACC payment, Merchant payment, Loss recovery, and Expense report service.

Payments are realized through the use of two types of ecash -wallets presented at [CHL05] withdrawn at the *ACC Issue* procedure: the payment wallet W_p, which — if spent more than its value — reveals the cardholder's identity and the identity wallet W_{id}, which — if overspent — reveals the entire transaction activity of the double-spender. The two wallets have an equal number of electronic coins (ecoins), which is proportional to the cardholder's credit limit L_{credit}. To enforce different privacy levels, various combinations of these wallets' spendings are used in the *ACC-payment procedure*, where the product value is spent from both wallets; in *ACC-loss recovery*, where only W_p is used; and in *ACC-monthly payment calculation*, where only W_{id} is used. To get paid, merchants simply deposit the ecash they receive, while blind signature schemes [JLO97, LR98, O06] are used for the different types of market offers.

In what follows we will use $[B]Sig_C(Msg)$ ($[B]Sig_C^H(Msg)$) to denote the [blind] signature of C on Msg (H(Msg)) and $\{Msg\}_K$ to denote encryption of Msg under key K. For efficiency, every asymmetric encryption is inducted to a symmetric one: $\{Msg\}_{PK}$ denotes $\{K\}_{PK}\|\{Msg\}_K$ for a random K.

Setup. CIBs maintain a large database consisting of their customers' account information: D_{debit}, for customers' debit accounts, D_{credit} for credit accounts, D_{anon}, for temporary anonymous accounts used only in online ACC transactions, and D_{hist} which is used as a log of D_{credit} and D_{anon}. ABs, which may or may not be CIBs, are linked to merchants' debit accounts.

In addition to the signature key pair (pk_B^s, sk_B^s) which identifies it, each CIB carries out the appropriate setup process to support the two compact ecash schemes in [CHL05]. The ACCA chooses and publishes (online) transaction-related hashes (H_{ot}) H_t and H_r.

Merchants and Cardholders are identified by the signature keys they use when opening an account with a bank B. Each party collaborates with B to issue a digital signature key-pair (pk_x^s, sk_x^s), where $x = M$ or C. Each merchant M also obtains a validity certificate $Cred_M = Sig_B(pk_M^s)$. Customer's C signature key-pair, (pk_C^s, sk_C^s), is strongly connected with her transaction activity; a part of it is revealed when C misbehaves.[1]

ACC Issue. (Cardholder C–CIB CIB interaction) A CIB CIB and its customer C collaborate so that the latter can withdraw from the L_{credit}-size payment W_p and identity W_{id} wallets. It is a typical withdrawal of the two ecash schemes in [CHL05], for which

---

[1] In reality, there are two key-pairs issued by C; each is indicative of C and corresponds to the two ecash schemes in [CHL05]; for simplicity, we will refer to both as (pk_C^s, sk_C^s).

C provides her sk_C^s-related password, $pass_{pin}$. Public information regarding the banks participating in ACCA (params) is also stored in ACC.

C also chooses a set of passwords: a backup $pass_e$ password, from which her backup encryption key pair (pk_C^e, sk_C^e) is derived, and $pass_e^t$, $pass_e^w$, $pass_e^c$ — which correspond to three encryption key-pairs (pk_C^{et}, sk_C^{et}), (pk_C^{ew}, sk_C^{ew}), and (pk_C^{ec}, sk_C^{ec}) that serve for encryption of transaction, wallet and coupon part of the card, as we will describe later on. C also agrees on two hashes, H_K and H_{CB}, with B.

Offline Payment. (ACC–merchant machine interaction) Merchant M provides $Cred_M$ to the cardholder C, who checks its validity using params. M provides C with $(Cred_M, T_{det}, Sig_M^{H_t}\{T_{det}\})$, where T_{det} is the transaction information, including *price* and *date*. C enters her $pass_e^w$ to have her W_p and W_{id} wallets decrypted, verifies the product information and inserts her $pass_{pin}$ to spend *price* value from both wallets. Let W_p' and W_{id}' be the remaining wallets. C is immediately provided a printed transaction record. A merchant-signed receipt, $Rec_T = Sig_M^{H_r}(Cred_M, T_{det} - fin)$, and T_{det} are encrypted with $pass_e^t$ (pk_C^{et}) into $E_{T_{det}}$ and stored in the ACC. C also uses her $pass_e^w$ (pk_C^{ew}) to encrypt W_p' and W_{id}' into $E_{W_{p,id}}$.

To receive his payment, M deposits to his AB (AB) the ecoins he has received from his customers. In particular, AB contacts each customer's CIB to validate each pair of payment-identity ecoins deposited by M. If everything is fine, both banks make the required transfers to M's account. On the other hand, if a cardholder C tries to use her ACC to spend more than L_{credit} value, i.e. if a double-spending occurs, the owner of the card is identified through the ecash anonymity revocability properties. If the latter is the case, all the ecoins the dishonest C withdrew are blacklisted.

Online Payment is performed in two stages:

Anonymous Account Setup. (ACC–ATM interaction) Cardholder C spends to her CIB (CIB) M_{ot} value from her $\overline{W}_p$, W_{id} wallets, where M_{ot} is the amount to be spent online. To refer to M_{ot}, C chooses m, R_{ot}, hashes H_{ot} and H_α and a pseudonym key-pair (pk_C^P, sk_C^P). C computes $A_C^m = H_{ot}^{(m)}(R_{ot})$ and sends to CIB the message:

$$\{A_C^m, m, H_{ot}, H_\alpha, pk_C^P\}.$$

CIB updates D_{anon} with

$$\alpha_C(m) = \{A_C^m, H_{ot}, M_{ot}, m, H_\alpha, pk_C^P\}$$

and sends a confirmation to C $Rec_{\alpha_C(m)} = Sig_{CIB_{ot}}(H^r(\alpha_C(m)), date)$. A_C^m will be the initial number of the anonymous account created and m is the upper bound of the number of transactions C can participate in using the online account she created.

Transaction Payment. (Cardholder C–gateway G online interaction) The cardholder C provides the merchant's (M) website or the gateway G behind it with:

$$Info_{CIB} = \{\{Cred_M, T_{det}, A_C^{m-1}\}_{K_\alpha}, A_C^m\}_{\{pk_{CIB}^e}$$

where $Cred_M$ is M's credential, T_{det} the transaction details and $K_\alpha = H_\alpha(A_C^m))$ is a key derived from C-chosen H_α and A_C^m. Both A_C^{m-1} and K_α are used for authentication purposes; the owner of A_C^m account is the only one who knows H_{ot}, H_α and A_C^m's pre-image. G sends $\mathsf{Info_{CIB}}$, $\mathsf{Cred_M}$ and T_{det} to C's CIB (CIB) for it to check the A_C^m's validity and balance. CIB sends G either a payment check $\mathsf{Paym_{CIB \to AB}}$ for merchant's AB (AB) or a signed rejection message $\mathsf{Rej_{CIB}}$ in case of error. All messages are signed and contain T_{det} and timestamps to avoid confusion and replay attacks. G forwards $\mathsf{Paym_{CIB \to AB}}$ to AB and acknowledges CIB with

$$\mathsf{Rec_T} = \mathsf{Sig}_\mathsf{G}^{H_r}(\mathsf{Cred_M}, T_{det} - fin)$$

CIB updates D_{hist} with $\mathsf{Rec_T}$ and substitutes $\alpha_C(m)$ D_{anon}entry with $\alpha_C(m-1)$, where the M_{ot} is reduced by *price* or not depending on whether CIB accepted or rejected the request. To close the entry in D_{anon}, C, in an ACC-ATM interaction, demonstrates knowledge of $\mathsf{Rec}_{\alpha_C(m)}$ and her ACC context is updated accordingly.

ACC BackUp - Loss Recovery. (Cardholder C–CIB CIB in-person interaction)
ACC BackUp. Cardholder C generates a random number N_b and sends to her CIB CIB

$$\{N_b\}_{pk_\mathsf{C}^e}\text{——}\{ACCcontent\text{——}date - time\}_K$$

where *ACContent* is the content of the ACC, $date - time$ is the backup timestamp and $K = H_K(N_b, pass_{pin})$ is a symmetric encryption key, which only C may derive given N_b. *BackUp* is hashed and signed by both parties for integrity purposes into $BackUp_x = Sig_x^{H_{CB}}(BackUp)$, $x = \{C, B\}$. CIB updates D_{hist}.
Loss Recovery. Cardholder C is provided by her CIB CIB with the most recent BackUp of her ACC, $BackUp$. C verifies that $BackUp$ matches the most recent $BackUp_B$ of her and spends to the latter the $BackUp$'s remaining payment wallet (W_p'). CIB credits C's entry in D_{credit} for the amount spent till $BackUp$ was taken ($\mathsf{L_{credit}} - |W_p'|$, where $|W_p'|$ are the remaining value (ecoins)of W_p'. When merchants' deposit ends, CIB updates C's credit entry with any double-spent payment-ecoin indicating C's pk_C. In this way, we cover the case where $BackUp$ is not up-to-date with the most recent transactions of C without sk_C being revoked. Based on current D_{credit} Centry, CIB and C collaborate to issue an ACC with the new or different credit limit.

Monthly Payment Calculation. (Cardholder C–CIB in-person interaction) Cardholder C proves to CIB the amount of money she has spent throughout the past month month. To calculate C's monthly payment, C's CIB, CIB, applies the formula used in current Credit Card Systems on C's overall credits.

After decrypting (via $pass_e^w$) the remaining of her W_{id} wallet (W_{id}'), C interacts with CIB to spend it entirely. The amount of ecoins spent by C through the past month is $\mathsf{L_{credit}} - |W_i d'|$ and CIBcan now estimate the monthly payment for C. If C is still eligible for an ACC, she interacts with CIB to issue a new W_{id} and additional W_p according to C's new credit limit. Any attempt on C's part to lie for the remaining W_{id} wallet, e.g., by presenting a former version of her ACC, would reveal sk_C^s since a part of W_{id} will be spent twice.

Expense Report. For offline transactions or for online transactions of deactivated anonymous accounts, C decrypts $E_{T_{det}^i}$ parts of her ACC to obtain the detailed chain of her transactions. For online transactions referring to active anonymous accounts, C in an ACC-ATM interaction with CIB, sends through her sends a $\mathsf{Info_{CIB}}$ message with expense report request message instead of T_{det}. CIB sends back the corresponding report and updates D_{anon} accordingly. See [AB09] for more details.

Error Correction. (Cardholder C–ACCA/Merchant in-person interaction) If an error has occurred, e.g., a mischarge by M, C contacts the ACCA and provides it with $\mathsf{Rec_T}$. ACCA contacts M, who may accept ($\mathsf{Ref_M}$) or reject ($\mathsf{Rej_M}$) the refund-request (see [AB09]). If M accepts, the ACCA sends $\mathsf{Ref_M}$ to M's AB, AB, to verify M's account balance. AB provides ACCA the actual payment, which is forwarded to C's CIB CIB. C deposits to CIB an ACCA-issued digital check, $\mathsf{RefCoup_{ACCA\to C}}$, to receive the payments in the form of wallets. In case of purchase cancellation, if M accepts the return of the product, it provides C with $\mathsf{Ref_M}$, which C deposits to her CIB.

ACC Promotion Offers. These offers involve discounts or better credit card interest rates, when a carholder makes many purchases from particular merchants. This option is supported by our system through the use of blind coupons only offer-eligible merchants may issue. However, as it does not constitute a core attribute of a credit card system and because of space limitations, we will not elaborate on it here. See [AB09] for details.

5 Other System Considerations

We will now outline particular system issues. See [AB09] for a full discussion.

Cardholder Anonymity - Transaction Unlinkability. Both of them are satisfied through ecash anonymity and unlinkability properties [CHL05]. As every payment procedure (including the anonymous account setup) consists of two typical ecash spending procedures from the W_p and W_{id} wallets, they thus cannot be linked to the cardholder C who used the ACC or to any other transaction from the same wallets (ACC). However, the anonymity provided is conditional: if C tries to spend more ecoins than her $\mathsf{L_{credit}}$, i.e., the initial amount of ecoins in each wallet, or lie at the monthly payment calculation procedure for the amount she has spent, a part of W_{id} will inevitably be double-spent, and — through anonymity revocability and traceability property of the W_{id} ecash scheme [CHL05] — sk_C^s will be revealed; all the ecoins withdrawn by C will then be traced.

There are two cases in which we accept a small breach in a cardholder's anonymity or transaction unlinkability: (a) in *Loss Recovery* and (b) in *Online Payment*. In the Loss Recovery process — an unusual situation — when the most recent $BackUp$ is not up-to-date, a cardholder C inevitably doublespends a part of her W_p wallet: to the merchants she interacted and to her CIB, CIB. pk_C^s is then revealed and CIB knows whom C interacted with. However, this anonymity breach becomes less important since we require that backups are taken regularly. In the *Online Payment* case, CIB can obviously trace what type of transactions a particular anonymous account is involved in through D_{hist}. However, thanks to the unlinkability property of the ecash spent at the anonymous account setup phase, linking that profile to a particular identity is impossible. In any case, the cardholder may open as many anonymous accounts she wishes, in order to avoid transaction linkability.

Security of Online Transactions. Customer C authentication is achieved via (a) the $pass_{pin}$ C enters to setup the A_C^m anonymous account and through (b) demonstration of knowledge of H_{ot}, H_α and A_C^m's pre-image w.r.t. H_{ot}. On the other hand, the signed endorsement $Rec_{A_C^m}$ provided by C's CIB, CIB, at the $\alpha_C(m)$ setup phase prevents CIB from cheating. As T_{det} and $Cred_M$ are part of $Info_{CIB}$, i.e., encrypted with K_α, a key only CIB and C may derive, G cannot lie about the price of C's intended purchase (*price*) or M. In addition, as timestamps are included in every message and account numbers change in every authorized request, replay attacks or offline account guessing attacks cannot succeed.

On the other hand, C cannot use the same account for purchases of value more than M_{ot}: if she tries to spend the same part of her wallets in offline purchases, her identity will be revoked while if the account balance is less than *price*, she will receive a CIB signed rejection message. In addition to the measures mentioned before, we assume that there is an upper bound for M_{ot} and that the latter is spent within a particular time interval to reduce the amount of transaction-wise information bound to each anonymous account.

Authorized Anonymity Revocation. This is the case where a cardholder C is a suspect of a offense and a judge requests a detailed description of that C's ACC related transactions. In our system, this can be achieved only with C's consent.

a. Cis asked to provide sk_C^s for all her transactions to be revealed, which we want to avoid. *b.* Cis asked to enter her $pass_e^t$ to decrypt the transaction related part of her ACC and "spend" the rest of her W_p to CIB. Transaction details of each transaction are signed by a merchant or C's CIB (CIB) — in the case of Anonymous Account Setup — and, thus, cannot be forged. To check for any deceptive deletion of a transaction on cardholder's side, CIB may use D_{hist} to check whether the overall amount spent matches the aggregated amount in the backed-up transaction details.

ACC Unforgeability is satisfied through the Correctness and Unforgeability properties of the underlying ecash schemes. **ACC non-Transferability** is also satisfied since sk_C^s is required for the card to be used in both offline and online purchases.

Bank Dishonesty. $BackUp_{pB}$ is used to avoid any attempt of a CIB to trick a cardholder into tracing more of the latter's transactions: Assuming the CIB provided a less recent backup, then a bigger part of W_p would be double-spent and more merchants would be directly linked to the cardholder. $BackUp_{pB}$ will act as an undeniable proof of the date and integrity of the backup kept.

ACC Organization. ACCs' content is organized as $\{E_{T^1}, \ldots, E_{T^\ell}, padding, E_{W'_{p,id}}\}$, where E_{T^1} is the encryption of the i-th transaction performed by an ACC and ℓ is the number of transactions the performed through that particular ACC. We use *padding* to avoid any information leakage regarding ℓ. This modular form of encryption is necessary for each of the procedures mentioned before to be able to be executed individually.

Computing power. Credit card customers in our system often lack in computing sophistication: not all of them have or know how to install software able to encrypt or decrypt text or verify the hashes used in our system. A solution on this problem would be for the CIBs to provide their customers with special machines dealing with card encryption/decryption issues. The extra cost of these devices may be viewed by the cardholder as an extra price for her privacy.

6 Conclusion

In this paper, we addressed e-commerce Context Privacy. In particular, we presented a deployable credit card system which guarantees cardholder anonymity and transaction unlinkability, even towards to Credit Card Associations or Card Issuing Banks. At the same time, we have preserved many of the essential benefits of credit cards. In special circumstances the transactions of a party may be revealed but only with that party's consent. Undeniably, there are still issues to be dealt, such as password loss recovery and operational transparency with respect to cardholders. However, we do believe that this paper is a good start for privacy in current credit card systems.

Acknowledgments

The authors would like to thank Moti Yung and the anonymous referees for their valuable comments and suggestions and Google Inc. for subsidizing this work.

References

[AB09]   Androulaki, E., Bellovin, S.: Anonymous credit cards. Technical Report cucs-010-09. Columbia University, New York, USA (2009)
[AJSW99]   Asokan, N., Janson, P., Steiner, M., Waidner, M.: State of the art in electronic payment systems. IEEE Computer 30, 28–35 (1999)
[B95]   Brands, S.: Electronic cash on the internet. In: Proceedings of the Symposium on the Network and Distributed System Security (1995)
[BBG+00]   Bellare, M., Bellare, M., Garay, J., Hauser, R., Krawczyk, H., Herzberg, A., Tsudik, G., van Herreweghen, E., Krawczyk, H., Steiner, M., Tsudik, G., Herreweghen, E.V., Waidner, M.: Design, implementation and deployment of the ikp secure electronic payment system. IEEE Journal on Selected Areas in Communications 18, 611–627 (2000)
[CHL05]   Camenisch, J.L., Hohenberger, S., Lysyanskaya, A.: Compact E-cash. In: Cramer, R. (ed.) EUROCRYPT 2005. LNCS, vol. 3494, pp. 302–321. Springer, Heidelberg (2005)
[CL02]   Camenisch, J.L., Lysyanskaya, A.: A signature scheme with efficient protocols. In: Cimato, S., Galdi, C., Persiano, G. (eds.) SCN 2002. LNCS, vol. 2576, pp. 268–289. Springer, Heidelberg (2003)
[DCN90]   Chaum, A.F.D., Naor, M.: Untraceable Electronic Cash (1990)
[JLO97]   Juels, A., Luby, M., Ostrovsky, R.: Security of blind digital signatures. In: Kaliski Jr., B.S. (ed.) CRYPTO 1997. LNCS, vol. 1294, pp. 150–164. Springer, Heidelberg (1997)

[K99]   Krawczyk, H.: Blinding of credit card numbers in the SET protocol. In: Franklin,
          M.K. (ed.) FC 1999. LNCS, vol. 1648, pp. 17–28. Springer, Heidelberg (1999)
[LPM94]   Low, S.H., Paul, S., Maxemchuk, N.F.: Anonymous credit cards. In: CCS 1994: Pro-
          ceedings of the 2nd ACM Conference on Computer and communications security,
          pp. 108–117. ACM, New York (1994)
[LR98]   Lysyanskaya, A., Ramzan, Z.: Group blind digital signatures: A scalable solution to
          electronic cash. In: Hirschfeld, R. (ed.) FC 1998. LNCS, vol. 1465, pp. 184–197.
          Springer, Heidelberg (1998)
[O06]   Okamoto, T.: Efficient blind and partially blind signatures without random oracles.
          In: Halevi, S., Rabin, T. (eds.) TCC 2006. LNCS, vol. 3876, pp. 80–99. Springer,
          Heidelberg (2006)

A Cluster-Based Framework for the Security of Medical Sensor Environments

Eleni Klaoudatou, Elisavet Konstantinou, Georgios Kambourakis,
and Stefanos Gritzalis

Laboratory of Information and Communication Systems Security
Department of Information and Communication Systems Engineering
University of the Aegean, Karlovassi, GR-83200 Samos, Greece
{eklad,ekonstantinou,gkamb,sgritz}@aegean.gr

Abstract. The adoption of Wireless Sensor Networks (WSNs) in the healthcare sector poses many security issues, mainly because medical information is considered particularly sensitive. The security mechanisms employed are expected to be more efficient in terms of energy consumption and scalability in order to cope with the constrained capabilities of WSNs and patients' mobility. Towards this goal, cluster-based medical WSNs can substantially improve efficiency and scalability. In this context, we have proposed a general framework for cluster-based medical environments on top of which security mechanisms can rely. This framework fully covers the varying needs of both in-hospital environments and environments formed ad hoc for medical emergencies. In this paper, we further elaborate on the security of our proposed solution. We specifically focus on key establishment mechanisms and investigate the group key agreement protocols that can best fit in our framework. Keywords: Wireless Sensor Networks; Security; Medical Environments; Clustering; Group key management.

Keywords: Wireless Sensor Networks; Security; Medical Environments; Clustering; Group key management.

1 Introduction

One of the most promising contributions of Wireless Sensor Networks (WSN) is their adoption in the healthcare sector. Their use can improve the quality of medical care provided and facilitate patients' every day living. However, the adoption of WSNs in the healthcare sector also introduces many security issues and challenges mostly because medical services and the associated to them information are considered particularly sensitive. In general, every information system deployed in medical premises must comply with the following security requirements: confidentiality, integrity, availability, authentication, privacy, non-repudiation, authorization and accountability.

The mechanisms employed in medical WSNs should also consider patients' mobility without compromising the needs for security and efficiency. In order to provide the necessary security in such networks, we must rely on key establishment and management mechanisms which will guarantee the secure communication between the nodes. The choice of a key establishment protocol for the creation of a shared, secret

S. Fischer-Hübner et al. (Eds.): TrustBus 2009, LNCS 5695, pp. 52–62, 2009.

key must be done very carefully, taking into consideration all possible limitations of medical WSNs, e.g. nodes mobility, frequent topology changes and scalability needs. In particular, group key management mainly includes activities for the establishment and maintenance of a group key. Potentially, group key establishment is more suitable than pairwise key establishment as devices do not waste energy every time they need to communicate with another device by establishing a new shared secret key. Most of the traditional group key management protocols cannot cope with the dynamic nature and limitations of medical WSNs. However, key management protocols that are based on a cluster formation of the nodes have been proved to be more efficient and scalable especially when they are applied on WSNs. Clearly, these protocols can be envisioned in medical environments providing the most efficient solutions. In this context, many modern applications for medical environments assume a cluster-based sensor network (e.g. [1-3]) but they do not specifically focus: (a) on how clustering is applied and (b) how key management mechanisms can fit and be particularly effective on top of the clustered network.

In our previous work [4], we proposed a general framework for cluster-based medical environments on top of which security mechanisms can rely. This framework fully covers the varying needs of both intra-hospital environments and environments formed ad hoc for medical emergencies but it can be realized for hybrid scenarios as well. Despite the scalability of this framework, a question that remains unanswered is which key management protocols can be applied over it. Group key Agreement (GKA) protocols which do not require the presence of central entities seem to be more suitable for our framework. In this paper we elaborate on the most important cluster-based GKA protocols and we discuss which of them can be custom-tailored and thus profitable to medical applications. The performance of each examined GKA protocol is theoretically investigated as well.

The rest of this paper is organized as follows: Section 2 describes related work. Section 3 presents a short analysis of our two scenarios for sensor clustering in medical environments. Section 4 examines existing authenticated GKA mechanisms that can fit in our framework. Section 5 concludes the paper and gives pointers to future work.

2 Related Work

Clustering has been used in medical environments in various applications and for many purposes [1-3], [5-8]. In [1] clusters are formed ad hoc to accommodate emergency situations. In [2] the authors have applied their location-aware group membership middleware in an e-care scenario where cluster heads are responsible to send user information to every group the user joins. In medical environments, location awareness can help in tracking the nearest specialist to the location of the patient. In [5] clusters are created based on an infrastructure that uses the base station to elect the leaders of the clusters. In [6] a 3G telemedicine application is proposed based on energy-efficiency mechanisms in large-scale and a multi-class admission mechanism. It uses super-sensors as cluster-heads to query sensors for medical data and perform data aggregation, filtering and compression, and forward them towards the medical center. Clustering is based on the Zone Routing Protocol (ZRP). For security purposes, the authors of [3] assume that every patient forms a different cluster and the cluster coordinator is a special entity called PSP (Patient Security Processor) that not only relays data to the gateway but is also responsible for the distribution of the symmetric key needed for encryption. Moreover, [7] and [8] describe two mechanisms for cluster-based key management for medical applications. The first one proposes a re-keying mechanism for tree-based networks while the latter proposes a cluster-based group key management mechanism for wireless networks. They apply this mechanism in a medical environment and use a bottom-up approach to specify and distribute group keys.

Compared to previous work, our framework [4], described shortly in the next section, has the advantage that is not case-oriented and can be applied in any cluster-based medical environment. The flexibility of this framework allows the efficient application of various security mechanisms which can cover all the security requirements of medical environments.

3 A Cluster-Based Framework for Medical Environments

WSNs can be deployed in several medical environments, like intra-hospital or medical emergencies. For this reason, our framework is comprised of two different scenarios based on the nature of the medical environment. Scenario I copes with medical environments which have a fixed infrastructure while scenario II considers infrastructureless environments. In both cases, a number of wireless sensors are implanted on every patient's body in order to collect and transfer real time vital sign data to a central database.

For the first scenario we consider a hierarchical network with Cluster-Heads (CH). This scenario is more suitable for environments where we can afford some more powerful nodes, which can play the role of CH, like intra-hospital environments. Consequently, we consider that CHs are fixed and energy consumption is not a key issue for them. The hospital sensor network can be decomposed to several clusters, based on their geographical location. For example, we can realize one cluster per one or more neighbouring rooms and one or more clusters for the external area of the hospital. This grouping scheme minimizes frequent topology changes each time a patient roams within the boundaries of her cluster. Clusters' number and size may vary according to the size of the hospital premises, the different units and the number of sensors as well as the number of fixed-nodes or CH available and their level of wireless coverage. For this scenario we assume that Cluster Members (CM) communicate with their CH every time they need to transfer data and that communication between each node and the CH is typically one-hop. As a result, the sensors used in this scenario do not need to have special processing capabilities and can be very cheap. The CH collects medical data from all nodes and forwards them towards the central database. Additionally, the CH can perform aggregation and filtering of the collected data. This method eliminates even more the amount of data in transit improving resource utilization too.

For the second scenario we assume that there aren't any powerful nodes to act as CHs. This architecture is more suitable for medical environments where there is no full coverage or no fixed infrastructure at all, as is the case of medical emergencies.

According to this scenario, sensors can be dynamically grouped into clusters which can be overlapping or not. Every time a node has some information to transmit, the node closer to the gateway (best path) is selected as the Cluster Leader (CL). The CL can either forward the data directly to the gateway, if it is located nearby, or forward the data via the CLs of adjacent clusters located near the gateway. To do so the CL must implement a multi-hop routing scheme. Communication between each node and the CL might also be multi-hop. Having in mind that the sensors' location may change very often, the CL responsibility will be automatically assigned to the node that is located closest to the gateway or to the CLs of neighbouring clusters located near the gateway. This means that all nodes should be able to potentially become CLs. As a result, nodes need to have some computing power and capabilities and therefore be more expensive than the ones employed in the first scenario.

A detailed description of the proposed framework can be found in [4]. Since nodes that belong to a cluster need to communicate securely there is also a need for a key management mechanism. In this paper, we mainly focus on GKA protocols that can best fit to our framework. In the following section we investigate GKA protocols that can best match with our scenarios and we evaluate their performance.

4 Authenticated Group Key Agreement Protocols

By nature WSNs are vulnerable to a number of threats already identified in several works, e.g. [9-11]. Every security solution adopted for the protection against these threats requires the employment and management of cryptographic keys. Group-key agreement protocols are considered to be more efficient than centralized key establishment schemes for WSN because devices do not waste energy every time they wish to communicate with another device by establishing a new shared secret key. However, most of the proposed GKA protocols offer protection only from passive attacks and an intruder can easily realize a man-in-the-middle attack during the key-agreement phase, to gain all the information needed for the keys. We therefore focus on authenticated GKA protocols where every node is authenticated in order to ensure that only valid group members participate in the key setup phase.

Clearly, GKA protocols that are based on cluster-based formation of the network nodes are more suitable for our framework (both for scenario I and II). In most of the cluster-based key agreement schemes proposed so far, a general key agreement protocol is applied in every cluster and then the clusters' keys are used by the same or another key agreement mechanism to form the final group key. Protocols that are relying on clustering are [12-20]. These recent works consider different cluster sizes and they are based on either two-party key agreement protocols, (like Diffie-Hellman protocol) or on other GKA protocols (like the well known protocol of Burmester and Desmedt (BD) [21]). The cluster-based protocol described in [12] uses virtual nodes and backbone nodes in addition to the real ones and requires many rounds (linear to the number of the nodes). The ID-AGKA protocol given in [13] has an extra communication overhead caused by the fact that each node must communicate with the Key Generation Centre (KGC) in every round. The protocol described in [14], considers clusters of arbitrary sizes and executes the Diffie-Hellman agreement between every two nodes in a cluster. A very recent work [15] presents a clique-based GKA which uses the efficient BD protocol [21] within every clique. A clique is actually a cluster where each member can communicate in one-hop with every other member of the cluster. This is clearly a restriction for the clustering formation procedure. Another GKA protocol that is based on the communication efficiency of the BD protocol is [16]. In this work, the nodes are separated in clusters of specific size, then the CLs are organized in clusters of the same size and so on until a final root cluster is constructed. The protocol is energy efficient but this particular clustering formation of the nodes can be restrictive in a more general framework like ours.

The protocols described in [17-20] are more general and we will, therefore, examine their applicability in our two scenarios. The first two ([17] and [18]) are well suited for hierarchical networks while the other two ([19] and [20]) can be used in an ad hoc infrastructureless network. Their detailed description and the way they can be applied in our framework follow in the next subsections. We also evaluate the computational and communication cost of each solution in a comparative analysis. After the execution of each protocol, every node will have at its disposal several keys which can be used from the group members in order to communicate with each other securely.

4.1 Authenticated GKA Protocols for Scenario I

The GKA protocols presented in [17] and [18] are well suited for hierarchical networks and therefore can be applied in scenario I of our framework. We present here the main features of each protocol followed by a comparative evaluation in terms of computational and communication costs.

The protocol proposed in [17] is a password based GKA Protocol, for hierarchical wireless networks. Three main entities exist in the network, the main controller C (highest layer), various subgroup controllers (S_i) and several members (M). The protocol assumes that each subgroup member holds a password and a pairwise secret key shared with the subgroup controller S_i. Also the subgroup controller holds a password and a pairwise secret key which are shared with the main controller. Note that both the pairwise secret and the password are securely pre-loaded in the devices.

We can distinguish 3 phases for the establishment of a common group key. During Phase 1, S_i interacts with the subgroup members to compute the subgroup key K_i. In Phase 2, S_i interacts with the controller C to obtain the final group key K. Finally, in Phase 3, the group key K is sent downward securely by the controller to the subgroup controllers which are responsible to securely send the K to their members. Key confirmation messages are also sent together to verify and confirm the subgroup key K_i and final group key K. Clearly, this mechanism can fit into scenario I of our framework, where a hierarchical WSN is configured, i.e. if we consider that the main controller is the BS, the several subgroup controllers are the CHs of various clusters formed with several members each.

The authors in [18] propose an Identity-Based (ID-Based) scheme for secure communication in a hierarchical cluster-based ad hoc network. The scheme consists of two phases, Authentication and Communication phase. For the needs of our study, we will focus on the authentication phase. The protocol assumes that there is a Trusted Authority (TA) which is responsible for generating and issuing the secret information to the nodes and also that all CHs in the system are trusted entities. During the system setup phase, the TA generates a pair of {public, private} keys, which are then used to compute a secret key K_i for each cluster member and a secret key CK_j for each CH. Then, the TA sends these keys to the corresponding nodes, along with the result of a public one-way hash function, and a number N, which is the product of four relatively prime numbers.

The first phase of the authentication procedure begins when a node joins a cluster and has to be authenticated by the CH. The node therefore generates an authentication token and sends it to the CH along with its ID and a timestamp. During the second phase, the CH checks the validity of the message sent by the node and if it succeeds it accepts the join request for the node. After that the CH computes a secret key K_{MH}, using the group key GK_j. This key is sent to the node along with the ID of the CH. In the third phase, the cluster-member checks the validity of K_{MH} and GK_j in order to prove that the ID of the cluster head (i.e., the $CHID_j$) is legal. Finally, those keys can be used by the CM as the secret key shared between him the CH and the group key.

In order to have a comparative evaluation of the two examined mechanisms, we can make the following assumptions. The TA in [18] performs similar functions to the controller in [17], therefore the role controller in the comparative tables 1 and 2 stands for both entities. The CH in [18] performs similar function to the S_i in [17] therefore we will adopt the description CH for both entities, as it is closest to our framework. Summarizing, we consider a WSN group of nodes comprised by: One controller, N nodes and n_c clusters. Finally, the symbol n_j signifies the number of members in the *j-th* cluster (or subgroup) and symbols CH_j and $CM_{i,j}$ signify the CH of the *j-th* cluster and the *i-th* CM of *j-th* cluster, accordingly. Table 1 shows a comparative analysis of the two mechanisms discussed, in terms of computational and communication costs. Additionally, Table 2 presents the prerequisites, i.e., the number of keys that need to be stored and the number of keys available after the execution of each protocol.

Table 1. Comparative Analysis of the two Mechanisms for Scenario I

Protocol		Mod. Exp.	Messages Sent	Messages Received
[17]	C	$2n_c+2$	2	n_c
	CH_j	$2n_j+5$	3	n_j+2
	$CM_{i,j}$	3	1	2
[18]	C	$N+1$	$N+1$	0
	CH_j	n_j	$2n_j$	n_j+2
	$CM_{i,j}$	1	1	5

Table 2. Prerequisites – Keys Stored – Keys Created (Scenario I)

Protocol	Prerequisites	Keys stored	Keys created
[17]	password shared with S_i and C ($pw_{i,j}$) password shared with the controller (pw_i) pairwise secret key between $CM_{i,j}$ and S_i ($K_{i,j}$) pairwise secret key between S_i and C(K_i)	K_i, $K_{i,j}$	subgroup key K_i final group key K
[18]	secret key for node i (K_i) a secret key for $CHID_j$ (CK_j)	K_i, CK_j	a group key GK_j K_{MH} (CM-to-CH)

The results of Table 1 show that protocol [18] has a lower communication and computation cost per node. However, this is something we should expect since the protocol is not contributory (i.e. not all the members contribute to the creation of the group key) and therefore the load of computation and communication operations is shifted to the hierarchically higher members, namely the CHs and the Controller. The protocol described in [17] on the other hand, is contributory which means that computation and communication operations are distributed to all nodes. Moreover, protocol [18] also calculates various Hash functions and performs some extra symmetric operations which are not included in our evaluation.

4.2 Authenticated GKA Protocols for Scenario II

The protocols described in [19] and [20] are well suited for our second scenario. This is because they can be applied in dynamic networks comprised of nodes with similar capabilities. Here, we present the main features and a comparative evaluation of these two protocols.

The protocol described in [19] is an authenticated group-key agreement protocol for ad hoc networks and it is based on hierarchical authentication. The protocol is ID-based and uses pairwise keys for entity authentication. It comprises of two phases: (1) organization of the nodes into clusters and (2) generation of the group session key. For the needs or our study we will focus on the latter phase. The protocol assumes that each node is equipped with a secret Group Identity Key (KIG), a one-way hash function H() and a local identifier (ID). Also, every node is able to compute its weight. This weight is a numerical quantity that expresses the node's current status in terms of node's mobility, battery power level, distance from the other nodes, and values related to the surrounding environment (terrain, temperature, battery power, etc). Moreover, the protocol assumes that identities are publicly available. A TA is also needed during the setup phase to generate the private keys for every node.

We can distinguish 3 different phases of the protocol, for the construction and distribution of the final group key. During the first phase, which is also the setup phase, every node computes the pairwise shared secret key using the secret key and the hash of the ID of the other node. This pairwise secret key is used by each member for the authentication phase. Therefore, this phase does not require communication between members. In the second phase, a mutual authentication procedure takes place between members that belong to the same cluster (inner-cluster authentication). The result of this phase is that every node within the cluster is authenticated with the others and with the CL and that each cluster holds a cluster session key. During the third phase, the protocol is repeated with the upper level clusters, considering that the CLs that participated in the previous phase are now the children for their one level hierarchically higher CL. The CL in the lower level has to decrypt every message he receives from upper levels to first check the identity of the transmitter and then forward the message to his children (re-)encrypted using the cluster session key he shares with them. This procedure repeats until the root level is reached.

This mechanism blends with scenario II of our framework, if we consider that every node authenticates its neighbour and the neighbour his next node and so on until they reach the CL. This is useful for our scenario since communication between the CM and the CL might not always be one-hop. Due to the infrastructure-less form of the WSN in scenario II, the frequent changes of the cluster structure do not introduce significant additional cost, since every node that joins a cluster has only to obtain from the CL the local parameters of the new cluster and the cluster session key. On the other hand, the number of rounds increases along with the number of hierarchical levels.

The protocol described in [20] is a cluster-based GKA protocol based on Joux's tripartite key agreement protocol [22] and comes in two versions, namely contributory and non-contributory. Although in the current version of the protocol nodes are not authenticated during the key agreement phase, authors state that the protocol can easily provide members' authentication. This can be achieved by substituting Joux's tripartite key agreement protocol with an authenticated version of it, like those described in [23] or [24]. For the needs of our study we will examine an authenticated version of this protocol, using the ID-based tripartite authenticated key agreement protocol from [24]. The protocol assumes clusters consisted of either two or three members each. The authenticated version of the protocol also assumes that a Key Generation Center (KGC) exists and participates in the generation of the public/private keys for each member. However, this operation is held once, during the setup phase and thus can be considered as an offline procedure.

The protocol is consisted of 3 main phases following the setup phase. During the setup phase every node has to obtain a long term private key from the KGC. In order to do so, every node sends its long-term public key to the KGC, calculated based on its Identity (ID). The KGC calculates and sends back the private key. During the first phase of the authentication procedure every member computes two elliptic curve points Pi and Ti and sends them towards the other members of its cluster. Nodes in the lower levels belong to only one cluster, but nodes in upper levels belong to two clusters and therefore will have to send those points to a greater number of nodes (actually, this number depends on the size of the clusters the nodes belong to). During the second phase an AuthCreateClusterKey procedure is executed simultaneously in every cluster. Every member first verifies the other members of the same cluster and if verification succeeds, each member calculates the common secret key $K_{cluster}$. By the end of this phase every group member shares a secret key with the nodes of the clusters it belongs to. Finally, in the third phase of the protocol, the root key (K_{root}) is sent downwards to the members of the lower levels, one level at a time, by encrypting the key with the session key of every level. This phase takes as many steps as the height of the tallest branch of the cluster-based structure.

In order to have a comparative evaluation of the two mechanisms we can make the following assumptions. Since both protocols are based on elliptic curve cryptography, we will calculate the number of scalar multiplications and pairings that each entity has to perform. Both protocols assume a tree-based structure where nodes in the lower levels belong to only one cluster and nodes in the upper level (who are actually the CLs of previous levels) belong to at least 2 clusters. Therefore, every node in the lower level will be called a leaf node and their CLs that belong in the upper level structure will be called intermediate nodes.

Table 3 shows a comparative analysis of the two mechanisms discussed, in terms of computational and communication costs. In order to be able to evaluate the protocol in [19] we make the assumption that each cluster is consisted of 4 members. This is an assumption the authors also make while describing the protocol. We have also

Table 3. Comparative Analysis of the Two Mechanisms for Scenario II

Protocol		Scalar multiplications (SM) and Pairings (P)	Messages Sent		Messages Received	
			other rounds	last round (root key)	other rounds	last round (root key)
[19]	intermediate nodes	6 (SM) + 6 (P)	3+1	1	2+1	1
	leaves	3 (SM) + 3 (P)	1	0	1	1
[20]	intermediate nodes	7 (SM) + 10 (P)	4	1	4	1
	leaves	5 (SM) + 5 (P)	2	0	2	1

Table 4. Prerequisites-Keys Stored – Keys Created (Scenario II)

Protocol	Prerequisites	Keys stored	Keys created
[19]	- a TA to calculate the private keys - private key - 1 hash function	master key S	- a pairwise key shared between two members - a cluster session key - a root key
[20]	- a KGC for the setup phase - a public/private key pair for every node - 2 hash functions - a cluster of 2 or 3 members each	public/private key of each member	- a shared cluster key for every cluster - a root Key (K_{root})

calculated the communication cost of the final phase which includes the distribution of the root key in a separate column of the table, in order to keep the calculations as independent from the number of levels as possible. Table 4 presents the prerequisites of every protocol, the number of keys that need to be stored in each node and the number of keys available after the execution of the protocol.

Based on the results of Table 3 we can see that protocol [19] has a lower communication and computation cost per node. However, the protocol in [19] requires a larger number of rounds and more memory in every node for the key storage, i.e., a key must be kept for every pair of nodes which belong to the same cluster. Moreover, it requires the presence of some sort of TA during the setup phase.

5   Conclusion and Future Work

In the previous sections we examined several authenticated GKA protocols that can be custom-tailored to our scenarios. The main issue here is whether these protocols can be implemented by limited-resources devices. In order to deal with this, we must first take a look at the capabilities of the sensors usually employed in medical implementations. Most of the well-known medical sensors implementations use Crossbow's Mica, Mica2, MicaZ and Telos motes and Tmote Sky by Texas Instruments. The Mica2 sensor is build upon ATmega128L processor and Chipcon IEEE 802.15.4 compliant radio interface whereas Tmote Sky is build upon Texas Instrument's

MSP430F1611 microcontroller and Chipcon's CC2420 radio interface. Their memory ranges between 4-10 KB RAM and the maximum data rate of the radio interface is 250 Kbps. Based on the performance measurements presented in [25], a Mica2 mote consumes 30.02mJ for a prime field point multiplication and 423.87mJ for a pairing. The energy consumption for a prime field point multiplication and a pairing performed by Tmote Sky is 7.95mJ and 130.49mA accordingly. We therefore believe that the examined GKA protocols are viable and attractive for medical sensor environments since every node is able to perform ECC scalar multiplications, exponentiations and pairings [26].

For security sensitive environments, as is the case of medical environments, the employment of only a group-key management mechanism is not enough in order to provide data confidentiality and integrity. The fact that data aggregation and filtering procedures are performed at intermediate nodes implies that such nodes access and process data from every patient. This might lead to a privacy threat. Therefore, secure aggregation/filtering mechanisms need to be employed, in order to ensure data integrity and confidentiality and perhaps privacy. For future work we plan to also examine how secure aggregation mechanisms can blend with our framework.

References

1. Dembeyiotis, S., Konnis, G., Koutsouris, D.: A Novel Communications Network for the Provision of Medical Care in Disaster and Emergency Situations. In: 24th EMBS/IEEE, San Francisco (2004)
2. Bottazzi, D., Corradi, A., Montanari, R.: AGAPE: a location-aware group membership middleware for pervasive computing environments. In: 8th IEEE International Symposium on Computers and Communication, pp. 1185–1192. IEEE CS Press, Turkey (2003)
3. Misic, J., Misic, V.B.: Implementation of security policy for clinical information systems over wireless sensor networks. Ad Hoc Networks 5(1), 134–144 (2007)
4. Klaoudatou, E., Konstantinou, E., Kambourakis, G., Gritzalis, S.: Clustering Oriented Architectures in Medical Sensor Environments. In: International Workshop on Security and Privacy in e-Health, March 2008, pp. 929–934. IEEE CS Press, Barcelona (2008)
5. Schwiebert, L., Gupta, S.S., Weinmann, J.: Challenges in Wireless Networks of Biomedical Sensors. In: SIGMOBILE 2001, pp. 151–165 (2001)
6. Hu, F., Kumar, S.: QoS considerations in wireless sensor networks for telemedicine. In: SPIE ITCOM Conference, Orlando, FL (2003)
7. Hu, F., Tillett, J., Ziobro, J., Sharma, N.K.: Secure Tree-Zone-Based Wireless Sensor Networks for Telemedicine Applications. IEEE GLOBECOM, 345–349 (2003)
8. Chen, Y.J., Wang, Y.L., Wu, X.P., Le, P.D.: The Design of Cluster-based Group Key Management System in Wireless Networks. In: International Conference on Communication Technology (2006)
9. Karlof, C., Wagner, D.: Secure Routing in Wireless Sensor Networks: Attacks and Countermeasures. Ad Hoc Network Journal, special issue on sensor network applications and protocols (2002)
10. Raymond, D.R., Midkiff, S.F.: Denial-of-Service in Wireless Sensor Networks: Attacks and Defenses. IEEE Pervasive Computing 7(1), 74–81 (2008)

11. Kambourakis, G., Klaoudatou, E., Gritzalis, S.: Securing Medical Sensor Environments: The Codeblue framework case. In: 2nd International Conference on Availability, Reliability, and Security - 1st International Symposium on Frontiers in Availability, Reliability and Security, April 2007, pp. 637–643. IEEE CS Press, Austria (2007)
12. Shi, H., He, M., Qin, Z.: Authenticated and communication efficient group key agreement for clustered ad hoc networks. In: Pointcheval, D., Mu, Y., Chen, K. (eds.) CANS 2006. LNCS, vol. 4301, pp. 73–89. Springer, Heidelberg (2006)
13. Yao, G., Ren, K., Bao, F., Deng, R.H., Feng, D.: Making the key agreement protocol in mobile ad hoc network more efficient. In: Zhou, J., Yung, M., Han, Y. (eds.) ACNS 2003. LNCS, vol. 2846, pp. 343–356. Springer, Heidelberg (2003)
14. Chen, Y., Zhao, M., Zheng, S., Wang, Z.: An Efficient and Secure Group Key Agreement Using in the Group Communication of Mobile Ad-hoc Networks. In: IEEE CIS 2006, pp. 1136–1142. IEEE CS Press, Los Alamitos (2006)
15. Hietalahti, M.: A clustering-based group key agreement protocol for ad-hoc networks. Electronic Notes in Theoretical Computer Science 192, 43–53 (2008)
16. Teo, J.C.M., Tan, C.H.: Energy-Efficient and Scalable Group Key Agreement for Large Ad Hoc Networks. In: 2nd ACM international workshop on Performance evaluation of wireless ad hoc, sensor, and ubiquitous networks, pp. 114–121 (2005)
17. Teo, J.C., Tan, C.H.: Denial-of-service resilience password-based group key agreement for wireless networks. In: 3rd ACM Workshop on QoS and Security For Wireless and Mobile Networks, Crete Island, Greece, pp. 136–143. ACM Press, New York (2007)
18. Lee, J., Chang, C.: Secure communications for cluster-based ad hoc networks using node identities. Journal of Network and Computer Applications 30(4), 1377–1396 (2007)
19. Abdel-Hafez, A., Miri, A., Oronzo-Barbosa, L.: Authenticated Group Key Agreement Protocols for Ad hoc Wireless Networks. International Journal of Network Security 4(1), 90–98 (2007)
20. Konstantinou, E.: Cluster-based Group Key Agreement for Wireless Ad Hoc Networks. In: ARES 2008, pp. 550–557. IEEE Press, Los Alamitos (2008)
21. Burmester, M., Desmedt, Y.G.: A secure and efficient conference key distribution system. In: De Santis, A. (ed.) EUROCRYPT 1994. LNCS, vol. 950, pp. 275–286. Springer, Heidelberg (1995)
22. Joux, A.: A one round protocol for tripartite Diffie-Hellman. In: Bosma, W. (ed.) ANTS 2000. LNCS, vol. 1838, pp. 385–394. Springer, Heidelberg (2000)
23. Al-Riyami, S.S., Paterson, K.G.: Authenticated three party key agreement protocols from pairings. In: Paterson, K.G. (ed.) Cryptography and Coding 2003. LNCS, vol. 2898, pp. 332–359. Springer, Heidelberg (2003)
24. Zhang, F., Liu, S., Kim, K.: D-based one round authenticated tripartite key agreement protocol with pairings (2002), http://eprint.iacr.org
25. Szczechowiak, P., Oliveira, L.B., Scott, M., Collier, M., Dahab, R.: NanoECC: Testing the limits of elliptic curve cryptography in sensor networks. In: Verdone, R. (ed.) EWSN 2008. LNCS, vol. 4913, pp. 305–320. Springer, Heidelberg (2008)
26. Roman, R., Alcaraz, C., Lopez, J.: A survey of cryptographic primitives and implementations for hardware-constrained sensor network nodes. Mobile Networks Applications 12(4), 231–244 (2007)

Formal Specification and Automatic Analysis of Business Processes under Authorization Constraints: An Action-Based Approach*

Alessandro Armando, Enrico Giunchiglia, and Serena Elisa Ponta

DIST – Università di Genova, Italy
{armando,enrico,serena.ponta}@dist.unige.it

Abstract. We present an approach to the formal specification and automatic analysis of business processes under authorization constraints based on the action language $\mathcal{C}$. The use of $\mathcal{C}$ allows for a natural and concise modeling of the business process and the associated security policy and for the automatic analysis of the resulting specification by using the Causal Calculator (CCALC). Our approach improves upon previous work by greatly simplifying the specification step while retaining the ability to perform a fully automatic analysis. To illustrate the effectiveness of the approach we describe its application to a version of a business process taken from the banking domain and use CCALC to determine resource allocation plans complying with the security policy.

1 Introduction

Business processes are sets of coordinated activities subject to an access control policy stating which agent can access which resource. The specification of the policy is usually given in terms of a basic access control model (e.g. the RBAC model) possibly enriched with features providing the flexibility required by the application domain (e.g. delegation) and mechanisms that are necessary to meet mandatory regulations (e.g. separation of duty constraints). The complexity of the resulting system is usually so big that the ability to verify even basic properties such as the executability of the process w.r.t. the available resources cannot be done by manual inspection only. In previous works [1,2] it has been shown that model checking can be profitably used for the automatic analysis of business processes. Yet their applicability to business processes of real-world complexity is problematic as state-of-the-art model checkers—being geared to the analysis of hardware designs—require the system to be modeled as the composition of independent (yet interacting) sub-components. On the contrary business processes and the associated security policies are best viewed as a collection of actions whose execution must satisfy a given workflow pattern and a set of access control rules.

---

* This work was partially supported by the FP7-ICT-2007-1 Project no. 216471, "AVANTSSAR: Automated Validation of Trust and Security of Service-oriented Architectures" (www.avantssar.eu).

S. Fischer-Hübner et al. (Eds.): TrustBus 2009, LNCS 5695, pp. 63–72, 2009.

In this paper we present an approach to the formal specification and automatic analysis of business processes under authorization constraints based on the action language $\mathcal{C}$ [3]. The use of $\mathcal{C}$ allows for a natural and concise modeling of the business process and the associated security policy as well as for the automatic analysis of the resulting specification by using the Causal Calculator (CCALC) [4]. To illustrate the effectiveness of the approach we have applied it against a version of the Loan Origination Process (LOP) that features an RBAC access control model extended with delegation and separation of duty constraints. By using CCALC we have faced the problem of finding if there exists a resource allocation plan for the business process.

The rest of the paper is structured as follows. In the next section we provide a brief introduction to business processes under authorization constraints by describing our case study which will be used throughout the paper. In Section 3 we present the action language $\mathcal{C}$. In Section 4 we show how a business process under authorization constraints can be expressed in $\mathcal{C}$. In Section 5 we describe the analysis of the LOP carried out with CCALC. In Section 6 we discuss the related work and we conclude in Section 7 with some final remarks.

2   Business Processes under Authorization Constraints

Let us consider the Loan Origination Process (LOP) graphically presented in Figure 1. The workflow of the process is represented by means of an extended Petri net. Next to the basic concepts of Petri nets [5], i.e places, transitions, and arcs, an extended Petri net considers conditional arcs between places and transitions. Places from which arcs run to a transition are called the input places of the transition; places to which arcs run from a transition are called the output places of the transition. A transition of an extended Petri net can *fire* if there is a token in every input place of the transition and the conditions associated with the arcs between the input places and the transition hold.

Informally, the process starts with the input of the customer's data (inputCustData). Afterwards a contract for the current customer is prepared (prepareContract) while the customer's rating evaluation takes place concurrently. By means of the rating evaluation the bank establishes if the customer is suitable to receive the loan. To this aim, the execution may follow different paths: if the risk associated with the loan is low (lowRisk), then an internal rating suffices (intRating); otherwise the internal rating is followed by the evaluation of an external rating (extRating). The lowRisk condition denotes a situation in which the internal rating is ok and the amount of the loan is not high. The external rating is carried out by means of credit information stored and safeguarded by a Credit Bureau (CB), a third-party financial institution. As soon as it is ascertained that the external rating is needed, a request to obtain the credit information about the current customer is sent to a CB (invoke creditBureau). By using this information, the external rating evaluation is performed by executing the task extRating. Notice that the invocation of the CB and the execution of the task extRating are performed by the same agent. In case there is a forbidden access to the information sent from the CB to the bank, i.e. an agent different from the one who sent the request has accessed the information exchanged, then the execution of the task is prevented and the rating evaluation is interrupted. In case of interruption, the director of the bank has to reinvoke the CB and to execute the task extRating for the rating evaluation to be successfully completed. The loan request must then be approved (approve) by the bank. Subsequently, if the customer and the bank have reached an agreement, the contract is signed (sign). Notice that the execution of a task may affect the state of the process, e.g the task approve modifies the state of the execution by issuing a statement asserting if the proposed product is suitable or not for the customer.

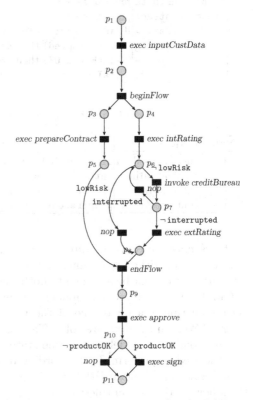

Fig. 1. Extended Petri net for the LOP

An agent can execute a task only if she has the required permissions. As it is common in the business domain, the access control policy of the LOP relies on an access control model based on RBAC [6] enhanced with delegations and separation of duty constraints. According to the RBAC model, to perform a task an agent must be assigned to a role enabled to execute the task and the agents must be also active in that role. The roles used in our case study are given in Table 1 w.r.t. the tasks they are enabled to execute. Roles can be organized hierarchically. In our case study, a director is more senior than a manager and a supervisor is more senior than a postprocessor. Senior roles inherit the permission to perform tasks assigned to more junior roles. As a consequence, an agent can execute a task if her role *(i)* is directly assigned the required permissions or *(ii)* is more senior than a role owning such permissions. The permission assignment relation in Table 1 associates each task of the LOP with the most junior role entitled to execute it. Notice also that the invocation of the CB does not appear in Table 1 as this activity has to be executed by the same agent of the task extRating and, as a consequence, uses its permission assignment. We consider a static assignment of agents to roles subject to the following constraints:

Table 1. Permission assignment for the LOP

Task	Role
inputCustData	preprocessor
prepareContract	postprocessor
intRating	if (isIndustrial) then postprocessor else preprocessor
extRating	if (interrupted) then director else supervisor
approve	if (intRatingOK) then manager else director
sign	if (isIndustrial) then director else manager

Table 2. SoD Constraints of the LOP

Name	Object	Critical Tasks
C1	customer's data	inputCustData, prepareContract, intRating, extRating
C2	internal rating	intRating, approve
C3	external rating	extRating, approve
C4	contract	prepareContract, approve, sign

(i) there must be only one director, *(ii)* the director must not be assigned to any other role, *(iii)* an agent must not be assigned to roles hierarchically related, e.g. an agent cannot be assigned to both roles supervisor and postprocessor.

Our RBAC access control model is enhanced with delegation as follows. A delegation rule is a quadruple of the form: $\langle Condition, ARole, DRole, Task \rangle$, where $ARole$ and $DRole$ are roles, $Task$ is a task, and $Condition$ is the applicability condition. A delegation rule states that if $Condition$ holds and $ARole$ is authorized to perform $Task$ according to the permission assignment relation, then $ARole$ can delegate $DRole$ to execute $Task$. In our case study we consider the following delegation rules:

- D1: $\langle \neg \text{highValue}, \text{supervisor}, \text{postprocessor}, \text{extRating} \rangle$,
- D2: $\langle \text{intRatingOK}, \text{director}, \text{supervisor}, \text{sign} \rangle$.

Finally, the RBAC access control model of our case study is enhanced with a mechanism that is necessary to meet separation of duty constraints. Separation of Duty (SoD) constraints are used for internal control and amounts to requiring that some critical tasks are executed by different agents. (See [1] for a survey on SoD properties.) In this paper we focus on a relaxed form of *object-based SoD* properties according to which an agent can access the same object through different roles as long as she does not perform all the tasks accessing that object. For each object involved in the LOP we define a set of critical tasks, i.e. all and only the tasks accessing to the same object. We then assume that the process implements a mechanism that prevents an agent from executing all the critical tasks for each object. The SoD constraints enforced by the presented mechanism in our case study are given in Table 2.

3   The Action Language $\mathcal{C}$

Action languages are high level formalisms for expressing *actions* and how they affect the world described with a set of atoms called *fluents*. Thus, the signature σ of the language is partitioned into the *fluent symbols* σ^{fl} and the *action symbols* σ^{act}. Intuitively, *actions* are a subset of the interpretations of σ^{act} while *states* are a subset of the interpretations of σ^{fl}. A formula of σ is a propositional combination of atoms. Each action language differs from the other for the constructs used to characterize how actions affect states.

$\mathcal{C}$ is an expressive propositional action language allowing for two kinds of propositions: *static laws* of the form

$$\textbf{caused } F \textbf{ if } G \tag{1}$$

and *dynamic laws* of the form

$$\textbf{caused } F \textbf{ if } G \textbf{ after } H, \tag{2}$$

where F, G, H are formulas of σ such that F and G do not contain action symbols. In a proposition of either kind, the formula F will be called its *head*.

An *action description* is a set of propositions. Consider an action description D. A *state* is an interpretation of σ^{fl} that satisfies $G \supset F$ for every static law (1) in D. A *transition* is any triple $\langle s, a, s' \rangle$ where s, s' are states and a is an action; s is the *initial* state of the transition, and s' is its *resulting* state. A formula F is *caused* in a transition $\langle s, a, s' \rangle$ if it is

- the head of a static law (1) from D such that s' satisfies G, or
- the head of a dynamic law (2) from D such that s' satisfies G and $s \cup a$ satisfies H.

A transition $\langle s, a, s' \rangle$ is *causally explained* according to D if its resulting state s' is the only interpretation of σ^{fl} that satisfies all formulas caused in this transition.

The *transition diagram* represented by an action description D is the directed graph which has the states of D as nodes and includes an edge from s to s' labeled a for every transition $\langle s, a, s' \rangle$ that is causally explained according to D.

Table 3. Abbreviations for Causal Laws

Abbreviation	Expanded Form	Informal Meaning
nonexecutable H if F.	caused $\bot$ after $H \wedge F$.	F is a precondition of H
H causes F if G.	caused F if $\top$ after $G \wedge H$.	F is true after H is executed in a state in which G is true
H may cause F if G.	caused F if F after $H \wedge G$.	F is true by default after H is executed in a state in which G is true
default F.	caused F if F.	F is true by default
constraint F.	caused $\bot$ if $\neg F$.	F must be true

Intuitively, if $\langle s, a, s' \rangle$ is a transition of the diagram, the concurrent execution of the atomic actions satisfied by a causes a transition from the state s to the state s'. Despite the fact that $\mathcal{C}$ consists of only two kinds of propositions, several others can be defined as abbreviations of either (1) or (2), modeling, e.g. actions' preconditions, actions' nondeterministic effects, fluents with default values, and inertial and exogenous fluents. The abbreviations used in this paper are given in Table 3, where F and G are fluent formulas, and H is an action formula.

4   Formal Modeling of Business Processes with $\mathcal{C}$

We now show how business processes under authorization constraints can be formally specified in the action language $\mathcal{C}$. This is done by using the LOP as a case study. The set of fluents involved comprises all the fluents listed in Table 4 suitably instantiated for all tasks and roles in Table 1 and the set of available agents. The fluents lowRisk and $\mathtt{pa}(r, t)$ are statically determined, that is their value is determined by means of static laws. The fluents $\mathtt{activated}(a, r)$ and $\mathtt{accessed}(a)$ are exogenous, i.e. they can arbitrarily change value in the transition from one state to the other (unless there is some other rule constraining their value). In addition, $\mathtt{activated}(a, r)$ is subject to

$$\mathbf{caused}\ \neg\,\mathtt{activated}(a, r)\ \mathbf{if}\ \neg\,\mathtt{ua}(a, r). \qquad (3)$$

to state that an agent cannot be active in a role she is not assigned to, and $\mathtt{accessed}(a)$ is subject to

$$\mathbf{caused}\ \mathtt{accessed}(a)\ \mathbf{after}\ \mathtt{accessed}(a). \qquad (4)$$

Table 4. Fluents and their informal meaning

Fluent	Meaning
$\mathtt{activated}(a, r)$	agent a is playing role r
$\mathtt{accessed}(a)$	agent a has accessed the information sent by the CB
$\mathtt{ua}(a, r)$	agent a is assigned to role r
$\mathtt{delegated}(a, r, t)$	agent a is delegated by an agent in role r to perform task t
$\mathtt{pa}(r, t)$	role r has the permission to perform task t
$\mathtt{granted}(a, r, t)$	agent a obtained by means of role r the permission to perform task t
$\mathtt{executed}(a, r, t)$	agent a has executed task t obtaining the authorization from role r
$\mathtt{invoked}(a, r, e)$	agent a has invoked entity e obtaining the authorization from role r
$\mathtt{senior}(r_1, r_2)$	role r_1 is more senior than or is as senior as r_2
$\mathtt{lowRisk}$	the risk associated with the loan is low
$\mathtt{highValue}$	the loan amount is high w.r.t. the financial status of the customer
$\mathtt{isIndustrial}$	the customer is industrial
$\mathtt{intRatingOK}$	the customer's internal rating is positive
$\mathtt{productOK}$	both the customer and the bank agree on the contract
$\mathtt{interrupted}$	the execution of the process is interrupted
$\mathtt{p_1}, \ldots, \mathtt{p_{11}}$	the places of the extended Petri net (cf. Figure 1)

to state that the access to the information exchanged in the process by an agent is not reversible. All the other fluents in Table 4 are inertial, i.e. they keep their value by default in the transition from one state to the other (unless there is some other rule constraining their value).

Each transition of the extended Petri net in Figure 1 (tasks execution, invocation of entities and empty activities) are actions. The preconditions of these actions have a common pattern, i.e. they always include the input places of the corresponding transition and the conditions associated with the arcs from the input places, if any. For example, the task approve is expressed by

$$\texttt{exec}(a, r, \texttt{approve}) \textbf{ causes } \quad \texttt{p}_{10} \wedge \neg \texttt{p}_9 \wedge \texttt{executed}(a, r, \texttt{approve})$$
$$\textbf{if} \quad \texttt{granted}(a, r, \texttt{approve}) \wedge \texttt{p}_9 . \quad (5)$$

$$\texttt{exec}(a, r, \texttt{approve}) \textbf{ may cause } \quad \texttt{productOK}$$
$$\textbf{if} \quad \texttt{granted}(a, r, \texttt{approve}) \wedge \texttt{p}_9 . \quad (6)$$

where $\texttt{exec}(a, r, \texttt{approve})$ is the action symbol. Causal law (6) states that productOK is a nondeterministic effect of $\texttt{exec}(a, r, \texttt{approve})$. As it appears from (5), each transition corresponding to a task t requires $\texttt{granted}(a, r, t)$ as further precondition.

Some actions can also require to be executed as soon as their preconditions hold, e.g. invoke creditBureau. This is expressed by the following set of causal laws.

nonexecutable $\texttt{invoke}(a, r, \texttt{creditBureau})$
   if $\neg \texttt{granted}(a, r, \texttt{extRating}) \vee \neg \texttt{p}_6 \vee \texttt{lowRisk} .$

caused $\texttt{invoke}(a, r, \texttt{creditBureau})$
   if $\texttt{granted}(a, r, \texttt{extRating}) \wedge \texttt{p}_6 \wedge \neg \texttt{lowRisk} . \quad (7)$

$\texttt{invoke}(a, r, \texttt{creditBureau})$
   causes $\neg \texttt{p}_6 \wedge \texttt{invoked}(a, r, \texttt{creditBureau}) \wedge \texttt{p}_7 .$

The execution of the task extRating is then expressed by

$$\texttt{exec}(a, r, \texttt{extRating}) \textbf{ causes } \texttt{p}_8 \wedge \neg \texttt{p}_7 \wedge \texttt{executed}(a, r, \texttt{extRating})$$
$$\textbf{if} \quad \texttt{invoked}(a, r, \texttt{creditBureau}) \wedge \neg \texttt{interrupted} . \quad (8)$$

Unlike the other tasks, extRating does not have $\texttt{granted}(a, r, \texttt{extRating})$ in its preconditions as it is implicit in $\texttt{invoked}(a, r, \texttt{creditBureau})$. Notice that $\neg$ interrupted represents the condition associated with the arc between place $\texttt{p}_7$ and the current transition. The fluent interrupted is an inertial fluent subject to the following static laws for all $a_1 \neq a_2$ and $r \neq \texttt{director}$:

caused interrupted **if** $\texttt{p}_7 \wedge \texttt{invoked}(a_1, r, \texttt{creditBureau}) \wedge \texttt{accessed}(a_2) .$
caused $\neg$ interrupted **if** $\texttt{p}_7 \wedge \texttt{invoked}(a, \texttt{director}, \texttt{creditBureau}) .$

As described in Section 2, the access control policy is given by an RBAC model enhanced with delegation and SoD constraints. The permission assignment relation is expressed by the statically determined fluents $\mathtt{pa}(r, t)$ defined by static laws according to Table 1, e.g.:

> **caused** $\mathtt{pa}(\mathtt{supervisor}, \mathtt{extRating})$ **if** $\neg\,\mathtt{interrupted}$.
> **default** $\neg\,\mathtt{pa}(\mathtt{supervisor}, \mathtt{extRating})$.
> **caused** $\mathtt{pa}(\mathtt{director}, \mathtt{extRating})$ **if** $\mathtt{interrupted}$.
> **default** $\neg\,\mathtt{pa}(\mathtt{director}, \mathtt{extRating})$.

The RBAC policy enhanced with delegation is given by static laws, e.g.:

$$\textbf{caused}\ \ \mathtt{granted}(a, r, t)\ \textbf{if}\ (\mathtt{ua}(a, r) \wedge \mathtt{activated}(a, r)\wedge$$
$$\mathtt{pa}(r_1, t) \wedge \mathtt{senior}(r, r_1)) \vee \mathtt{delegated}(a, r, t). \quad (9)$$

Each delegation rule originates a dynamic law. For example, rule D1 is modelled, for all $a_1 \neq a_2$, by

$$\mathtt{d1}(a_1, a_2)\ \textbf{causes}\ \mathtt{delegated}(a_2, \mathtt{supervisor}, \mathtt{extRating})$$
$$\textbf{if}\ \ \mathtt{ua}(a_1, \mathtt{supervisor}) \wedge \mathtt{ua}(a_2, \mathtt{postprocessor})\wedge$$
$$\mathtt{pa}(\mathtt{supervisor}, \mathtt{extRating}) \wedge \neg\mathtt{highValue}. \quad (10)$$

Finally, the SoD constraints of Table 2 are given by static laws constraining each set of critical tasks to be executed by at least two different agents. For example, constraint C3 is expressed by

$$\textbf{constraint}\ \neg(\mathtt{executed}(a, r_1, \mathtt{prepareContract})\wedge$$
$$\mathtt{executed}(a, r_2, \mathtt{approve}) \wedge \mathtt{executed}(a, r_3, \mathtt{sign})). \quad (11)$$

5   Experiments

We have fed CCALC with the specification of the LOP given in Section 4 and used it to determine whether the process can be run to completion. When this is the case a resource allocation plan (i.e. an assignment of agents to tasks) is extracted from the execution trace returned by the tool. Notice that if the assignment of agents to roles is not given (as it is the case in our case study) a possible agent-role assignment can also be obtained from the execution trace.

The process can take place in different scenarios characterized not only by different initial states (according to the initial value of $\mathtt{isIndustrial}$ and $\mathtt{highValue}$), but also by the different nondeterministic effects determined by some actions and effects of exogenous fluents. As a result, in order to verify the executability of the process for all the possible scenarios, we run CCALC against all possible initial states and all possible successful process completions. The initial states are those in which the fluent $\mathtt{p_1}$ and the fluents concerning the role hierarchy hold. The process ends successfully if it reaches a state in which both

p_{11} and `productOK` hold. We looked for a resource allocation plan for each of these scenarios. As further requirement, we looked for resource allocation plans involving the minimal number of agents. Thus we started by considering a single agent and then we incremented the number of available agents until an execution trace was found by CCALC. CCALC could not find any way to complete the process when a single agent was considered. This is not surprising as the SoD constraints require at least two agents to perform the critical tasks. When we considered two agents, say a_1 and a_2, CCALC found an execution trace that suggests a resource allocation plan where a_1 evaluates the internal rating and prepares the contract, while a_2 inputs the customer's data, and approves and signs the contract. The execution trace also suggests an agent-role assignment, i.e. a_1 is both `preprocessor` and `supervisor` while a_2 is both `preprocessor` and `manager`. This resource allocation plan leads to successful completion of the process in a scenario where the customer is not industrial, the loan is not `highValue` and the internal rating is ok. However CCALC could not find an execution trace for all the scenarios by involving only two agents. When we considered three agents, CCALC found an execution trace for all the scenarios but the ones where the internal rating is not ok and the process is interrupted. This brought to a further inspection of the policy that highlighted that the process executability was not ensured when `intRatingOK` does not hold and `interrupted` does. In fact, in these scenarios a director is required to execute tasks `extRating` and `approve` while the SoD constraint C3 prevents the same agent from performing both tasks. As a consequence we modified the policy disabling the constraint C3 when the internal rating is not ok and the process is interrupted. Considering the new access control policy CCALC verified the process executability by finding an execution trace and a corresponding resource allocation plan for each scenario by involving three agents.

6   Related Work

The use of the action language $\mathcal{C}$ for the specification of business processes has been faced in [7] where the research objective is to describe, simulate, compose, verify, and develop Web services. On the contrary, our approach takes into account access control policies and focuses on model checking of business processes subject to an access control policy with the objective of verifying properties.

The problem of specifying a workflow process in the action language $\mathcal{C}$ has been also faced in [8]. In particular this paper considers activities with duration and the cost of a workflow execution but, differently from our approach, it does not take into account complex access control policies, mandatory requirements, and the problem of finding resource allocation plans.

The use of model checking for the automatic analysis of business has been put forward and investigated in [1]. The paper uses NuSMV, a state-of-the-art model checker originally designed for hardware circuits, to carry out the analysis of the LOP w.r.t. a variety of SoD properties. Our approach, by using an action language, allows for a natural and concise modeling of the business process and the associated access control policy which is much closer to the process being modeled. This greatly simplifies the specification process considerably reducing the probability of introducing bugs in the specification.

A formal framework that uses the SAL model checker to analyze SoD properties as well as to synthesize a resource allocation plan for business process has been put forward in [2]. However, differently from our approach, this framework does not offer a natural modeling and RBAC is the only access control model supported (with tasks rigidly associated with specific roles). Finally, the paper assumes an interleaving semantics while our approach allows multiple actions to be executed simultaneously.

7 Conclusions

The design and verification of business processes under authorization constraints is a time consuming and error-prone activity. Moreover, due to the complexity that business processes subject to an access control policy may reach, it can be difficult to verify even basic properties such as the executability of the process w.r.t. the available resources by manual inspection only.

In this paper we have presented an action-based approach to the formal specification and automatic analysis of business processes under authorization constraints. Our approach improves upon the state-of-the-art by greatly simplifying the specification activity while retaining the ability to perform a fully automatic analysis of the specifications by means of the Causal Calculator CCALC. Our experiments indicate that model checking of $\mathcal{C}$ specifications can be profitably used to verify the process executability and to identify resource allocation plans complying with the security policy.

References

1. Schaad, A., Lotz, V., Sohr, K.: A model-checking approach to analysing organisational controls in a loan origination process. In: SACMAT 2006, pp. 139–149. ACM, New York (2006)
2. Cerone, A., Xiangpeng, Z., Krishnan, P.: Modelling and resource allocation planning of BPEL workflows under security constraints. Technical Report 336, UNU-IIST (2006), http://www.iist.unu.edu/
3. Giunchiglia, E., Lifschitz, V.: An action language based on causal explanation: Preliminary report. In: AAAI 1998, pp. 623–630. AAAI Press, Menlo Park (1998)
4. Texas Action Group at Austin: The causal calculator (2008), http://www.cs.utexas.edu/users/tag/cc/
5. Peterson, J.L.: Petri Net Theory and the Modeling of Systems. Prentice Hall PTR, Upper Saddle River (1981)
6. Sandhu, R.S., Coyne, E.J., Feinstein, H.L., Youman, C.E.: Role-based access control models. Computer 29(2), 38–47 (1996)
7. Chirichiello, A.: Two Formal Approaches for Web Services: Process Algebras & Action Languages. PhD thesis, "Sapienza" University of Roma (2008)
8. Koksal, P., Cicekli, N.K., Toroslu, I.H.: Specification of workflow processes using the action description language $\mathcal{C}$. In: AAAI Spring 2001 Symposium Series: Answer Set Programming, pp. 103–109 (2001)

A Formalization of HIPAA for a Medical Messaging System

Peifung E. Lam[1], John C. Mitchell[1], and Sharada Sundaram[1,2]

[1] Stanford University, Stanford, CA
[2] Tata Research Development and Design, Pune, India
{pflam,mitchell,shas}@cs.stanford.edu

Abstract. The complexity of regulations in healthcare, financial services, and other industries makes it difficult for enterprises to design and deploy effective compliance systems. We believe that in some applications, it may be practical to support compliance by using formalized portions of applicable laws to regulate business processes that use information systems. In order to explore this possibility, we use a stratified fragment of Prolog with limited use of negation to formalize a portion of the US Health Insurance Portability and Accountability Act (HIPAA). As part of our study, we also explore the deployment of our formalization in a prototype hospital Web portal messaging system.

1 Introduction

In regulated sectors such as healthcare, finance, and accounting, laws such as the U.S. Health Insurance Portability and Accountability Act (HIPAA), the Gramm-Leach-Bliley Act, the Sarbanes-Oxley Act, and related European laws have been enacted over the past decade to establish new or enhanced standards. The length of these laws, the opacity of the legal language, and the complexity of these acts make it very difficult for practitioners to determine whether they are in compliance [17]. This complexity becomes even more significant if computer programmers and information technology professionals wish to build and configure automated systems to help business professionals comply with applicable laws. The HIPAA regulation, in particular, appears complex for non-experts to follow for a number of reasons. To give one example, the law generally allows protected information to be shared between appropriate entities for the purpose of treatment. However, clause *164.508.a.2* [27] apparently contradicts this by stating that if the protected information is a *psychotherapy note* then a covered entity, i.e., a health plan, a health care provider or a clearinghouse, must obtain an *authorization* before disclosure. Thus simple reasoning based on actions allowed by one portion of the law, without accounting for prohibitions in other portions of the law, may give erroneous results.

Motivated by issues encountered in connection with the Myhealth@Vanderbilt system [28,15] developed by the Vanderbilt University Medical Center, we decided to see if we could produce a formalization of applicable parts of the HIPAA regulation in a form that could be used as part of the MyHealth system. Through

S. Fischer-Hübner et al. (Eds.): TrustBus 2009, LNCS 5695, pp. 73–85, 2009.

Web access to a centralized system, MyHealth allows patients and medical professionals to exchange messages and potentially request and view information such as prescriptions or lab test results. We also envision future use of such systems to respond to requests from other hospitals and clinics, law enforcement, insurers, and other organizations. Our intent is to construct a compliance module that can decide, as messages are composed or entered into the system, whether a message complies with HIPAA. Further, we expect that HIPAA could be augmented by additional constraints, in accordance with Vanderbilt University Medical Center policy decisions.

Starting with a view of privacy policy, business processes, and compliance developed in previous work [5,6], we chose to experiment with a stratified fragment of the logic programming language Prolog [18] with limited use of negation. In addition to representing HIPAA precisely enough to determine whether any particular action within the scope of the messaging system would comply with law, we also hope to produce a formalization that could be verifiable by lawyers, medical and computer professionals alike. For this reason, we have tried as much as possible to formalize the law so that the Prolog presentation can be read and understood section by section, with the meaning of the entire presentation determined in a systematic way from the meaning of its parts. In addition to supporting outside review and audit, this approach also helps make it possible to combine the HIPAA formalization with additional policies adopted by regulated enterprises. While there have been previous general studies on formulating laws in logical formalisms, e.g. [23,9], our effort is distinguished by our focus on a specific privacy law, identification of a specific fragment of stratified Datalog that appears appropriate to the task, and our reliance on a general theory of privacy previously articulated for a more expressive but less commonly implemented logical framework [5,6].

The main contribution of this paper is threefold: First we have identified a specific fragment of stratified Datalog with one alternation of negation, which we refer to for simplicity as pLogic, which suits our approach and supports a certain degree of policy compositionality. Secondly we use this framework to formalize the part of the HIPAA law that regulates information sharing in a healthcare provider environment. The structure of logic programming with predicates, query, and facts correspond to the legal clauses, actions being performed, and relations like roles defined in the law. Being a subset of logic programming, pLogic makes it easy to add cross references as present in the law. Finally we have implemented a prototype compliance checker and message system that is based on the Vanderbilt Medical Center MyHealth web portal [24]. This prototype is used to decide if a message that a practitioner is about to send is in compliance with the HIPAA regulation. We have also used our formalization to examine conflicts in the HIPAA regulation. While this paper focuses on the formalization of HIPAA, our approach appears to apply generally to a broad class of privacy regulations, such as those consistent with Nissenbaum's theory of Contextual Integrity [19] as formalized in [5].

The remainder of the paper is organized as follows. Section 2 introduces the key features and structure of the HIPAA policy and our information sharing model. Section 3 depicts the language pLogic that we use to model the HIPAA policy and our rule composition approach. Section 4 reviews related work. Finally Section 5 concludes.

2   Modeling HIPAA

2.1   HIPAA Overview

The U.S. Health Insurance Portability and Accountability Act (HIPAA) title II was enacted in 1996. As stated on an explanatory U.S. Government web site [26], HIPAA both explicitly permits certain transfers of personal health information, and prohibits some disclosures: "The Privacy Rule provides federal protections for personal health information held by covered entities and gives patients an array of rights with respect to that information." HIPAA Administrative Simplification, Regulation Text: 45 CFR Parts 160, 162, and 164 [27] regulate the use and disclosure of personal health information.

In HIPAA terminology, a *covered entity* is a health plan, a health care clearinghouse, or a health care provider who transmits health information in electronic form and *protected health information* is individually identifiable health information that is transmitted or maintained in electronic or other media.

The main focus of this paper is *section 164 of HIPAA,* which regulates the security and privacy issues in the health care industry. It covers general provisions, security standards for the protection of electronic health information, and privacy of individually identifiable health information. We are especially concerned with subpart 164.502, which covers the general rules for uses and disclosures of protected health information. Of the many subparts it refers to we consider subpart 164.506, which covers uses and disclosures to carry out treatment, payment, or health care operations, and subpart 164.508, which covers uses and disclosures requiring an authorization.

2.2   Actions

In our motivating application, patients or professionals enter a message into a centralized message system that can "deliver" the message by making it visible to other users. Messages may be simple questions from a patient, or may contain lab test results or other forms of protected medical information. Given information about the message, and other information such as the roles of the sender and receiver in the hospital, the HIPAA compliance module must decide whether delivery of the message complies with HIPAA. While portions of HIPAA regulate how data may be used after it is disclosed, or specify notifications that must be given after the disclosure, we currently focus only on whether to allow a message from a sender to a recipient.

Based on our understanding of HIPAA and the information available to the MyHealth system, our compliance engine is designed to make compliance decisions based on eight message characteristics: *To, From, About, Type, Purpose, In Reply To, Consented By* and *Belief.* The *To* and *From* fields indicate the recipient and sender of the message. The *About* field identifies whose personal health information is contained in the message. The *Type* field defines what kind of information would be passed, such as name or location. The *Purpose* field indicates a reason the message is being sent, such as for medical treatment. When the purpose is needed to determine compliance, we assume that some professional has asserted a purpose, or an asserted purpose is in some way inferred and made available as input to the compliance module. (Our prototype messaging system can infer when a purpose is needed, and supply the sender with a pulldown menu indicating purposes that would allow the message to be sent.) The *In Reply To* field was added to describe a disclosure where the message is sent as a response to some earlier message. The *Consented By* field indicates which people have consented to the message disclosure. The *belief* field contains a collection of assertions about the current situation, such as whether this is a medical emergency, or whether disclosure is (in the opinion of the sender) in the best interest of the health of the patient. Some beliefs may not be indisputable facts in the sense that another person may think differently. However, a sender may assert a belief (e.g., from a pulldown menu) or the sender's belief may be established by some other means. Once a message is allowed based on a belief, this reason may be recorded and later subject to audit. (We considered ways of processing audit logs based on policy in [6].)

Action (Definition 1). For the purpose of determining compliance, a message *action* is represented as an eight-tuple $a = \langle u_{src}, u_{dst}, u_{abt}, m_{typ}, m_{pur}, a_{reply}, c, b \rangle$, where (using underlining to indicate a set)

$u_{src}, u_{dst}, u_{abt}$	$\in U$	(the set of users or agents),
m_{typ}	$\in T$	(the set of types of messages),
m_{pur}	$\in P$	(the set of purposes),
a_{reply}	$\in A$	(the set of actions),
$c = \langle \underline{u_{by}}, \underline{ct_{typ}} \rangle$	$\in C$	(the tuple of consents) *with*
$\underline{u_{by}}$	$\in U$	*(the set of users) and*
$\underline{ct_{typ}}$	$\in CT$	*(the set of consent types),*
$b = \langle \underline{u_{by}}, \underline{u_{abt}}, \underline{bf} \rangle$	$\in B$	(the tuple of beliefs) *with*
$\underline{u_{by}}, \underline{u_{abt}}$	$\in U$	*(the set of users) and*
$\underline{bf}$	$\in BF$	*(the set of beliefs).*

HIPAA Policy (Definition 2). A HIPAA policy is a function from actions to Booleans (true or false), indicating permission or prohibition.

$$U \times U \times U \times T \times P \times A \times C \times B \to \{T, F\}$$

Categories. A category is a set of field values definining the conditions when a legal clause is applicable to a particular action. For example, one common category of actions are those with type indicating protected health information and purpose indicating medical treatment.

Subcategories. Naturally, some field values may indicate that the action belongs to a subcategory of another category of actions. For example *psychotherapy note* is a subtype of *health records*, which implies that policy about *health records* could also affect decisions about *psychotherapy note*, but not vise versa. More generally, the possible values associated with any field may be partially ordered.

Roles. While it is possible to express policy about specific individuals, HIPAA policies are written using roles. For example, an individual could be a nurse or a doctor. When an action is considered, our system receives the names of the sender and recipient, for example, and then uses information about the hospital to determine the respective role(s). For patients, similar processing (formalized in Prolog) is used to determine whether the patient is an adult or a minor.

3 Formalization of HIPAA

3.1 Overview

We introduce further concepts for the formalization of HIPAA, using *164.508.a.2* of HIPAA as a running example. As stated in the previous section, 164.508 as a whole governs uses and disclosures of protected health information that require an authorization. Specifically, *164.508.a.2* states, among other things, that a *covered entity* must obtain an authorization for any use or disclosure of *psychotherapy note*, except if it is to be used by the originator of the *psychotherapy note* for treatment.

Requirement. An action that falls into the category of a legal clause is allowed only if the *requirement* in the clause is satisfied. For example, *164.508.a.2* states that the specified action is allowed only if an authorization is obtained.

Exception. An exception in a legal clause qualifies its category. For example, *164.508.a.2* states that if the purpose of the action is for use by the originator of the *psychotherapy note* for treatment, then the requirement does not apply.

Clause vs. Rule. For ease of exposition, we call a labeled paragraph in the HIPAA law a clause, and its translation into logic rules.

To illustrate our terminology, a clause with *category* given by predicate a, *requirement* predicate c and *exceptions* e can be expressed as the following rules:

$$permitted\_by_R \Leftarrow (a \wedge \neg e) \wedge c$$
$$forbidden\_by_R \Leftarrow (a \wedge \neg e) \wedge \neg c$$
$$R\_not\_applicable \Leftarrow \neg a \vee e$$

Combination. A central concept in our approach is the way that a policy composed of several legal clauses is expressed by a combination of the associated *permitted_by* and *forbidden_by* rules. Given rules $R_1 \ldots R_m$, any action is consistent with the policy of these rules if it is permitted by some of the rules and *not forbidden* by any of them.

$$compliant\_with_{R_1 \ldots R_m} \Leftarrow (permitted\_by_{R_1} \vee \ldots permitted\_by_{R_m}) \wedge$$
$$\neg(forbidden\_by_{R_1} \vee \ldots forbidden\_by_{R_m})$$

This approach allows each clause to be translated into rules that are then combined in a systematic way to express the requirements of the law.

Cross-Reference. Frequently a *requirement* of a clause involves a reference to other clauses of the law. In our formal definition below, we will require an acyclicity condition so that the cross-reference relation among HIPAA clauses forms a directed acyclic graph.

3.2 Expressing Policy in pLogic

We have identified a fragment of stratified Datalog with one alternation of negation, which we refer to for simplicity as pLogic, which suits our formalization approach and supports a certain degree of policy compositionality. It is designed so that given an action we can verify whether the action is compliant with the written policy.

Our method for translating HIPAA into stratified Datalog with one alternation of negation is structured according to the form of *pLogic* rules and *pLogic* policies given below. As is standard in logic programming [18], a predicate is a symbol with an associated arity. Since we are using only Datalog, a term is a variable (starting with an upper-case letter) or an object constant (starting with a lower-case letter). An atom is an n-ary predicate applied to n terms. A literal is an atom. An expression is ground if it contains no variables.

Intuitively, a *pLogic* rule is a translation of a HIPAA clause into permitted and forbidden conditions. Each rule R therefore gives conditions on predicates *permitted_by$_R$* or *forbidden_by$_R$*, taking actions as arguments, indicating whether the action should be allowed or denied. *pLogic* facts may be used to define subsidiary predicates or other inputs to the compliance process.

pLogic Facts (Definition 3). A *pLogic* fact is an atom $g_i(a_1, \ldots, a_n)$ written using any relation g_i of arity n.

pLogic Rule (Definition 4). The *pLogic* rules associated with a HIPAA clause R_i possibly cross-referencing clauses $R_j, \ldots, R_k$ have the form:

$$permitted\_by_{R_i}(A) \Leftarrow category\_R_i(A) \wedge \neg exception\_R_i(A) \wedge requirement\_R_i(A)$$
$$\wedge(permitted\_by_{R_j}(A) \; op_{i,j+1} \; \ldots \; op_{i,k} \; permitted\_by_{R_k}(A))$$
$$forbidden\_by_{R_i}(A) \Leftarrow category\_R_i(A) \wedge \neg exception\_R_i(A) \wedge (\neg requirement\_R_i(A)$$
$$\vee forbidden\_by_{R_j}(A) \vee \ldots \vee forbidden\_by_{R_k}(A))$$

where

- $permitted\_by_{R_i}$, $forbidden\_by_{R_i}$, $category\_R_i$, $exception\_R_i$ and $requirement\_R_i$ are predicates on actions,
- each $op_{i,x}$ is either the $\wedge$ (AND) or the $\vee$ (OR) operator, as specified in the corresponding legal clause in HIPAA,
- $category\_R_i$, $exception\_R_i$ and $requirement\_R_i$ may appear as the head of additional Datalog rules we consider part of the rule expressing the clause,
- Every variable in the body must appear in the head,
- As indicated, $permitted\_by_{R_i}$ may depend on $permitted\_by_{R_j}$ for another clause R_j, but not $forbidden\_by_{R_j}$, and similarly $forbidden\_by_{R_i}$ may depend on another $forbidden\_by_{R_j}$ but not $permitted\_by_{R_j}$.

In the definition given above, the requirements are considered to be both *may* and *must*. However, the definition could easily be generalized to put one requirement in the permit rule and another in the forbid rule.

***pLogic* Policy** (Definition 5). An *pLogic* policy is a set Δ of *pLogic* rules and *pLogic* facts whose dependency graph (defined below) is acyclic.

The dependency graph $\langle V, E \rangle$ of Δ is defined as follows. The vertices V are predicates occurring in Δ and E contains a directed edge from u to v exactly when there is a rule in Δ where the predicate in the head is u and the predicate v appears in the body. The acyclicity condition ensures a nonrecursive stratified Datalog program.

Entailment for *pLogic* is based on the usual stratified semantics from deductive databases and logic programming.

pLogic policy is decidable. *pLogic* policy is a nonrecursive logic program with negation and without function constants. Restricting the arity of the predicates to a constant reduces the complexity to polynomial time [18].

3.3   Rule Combination and Conflicts

pLogic is designed so that prohibition takes precedence over permission. However, we have found that some care must be taken in translating HIPAA into *pLogic* when it comes to overlapping clauses. We say that two rules *overlap* if the category and exceptions of the two rules allow them to apply to the same action, and one is a *subcase* of the other if its category and exception make it apply to every action satisfying the category and exceptions of the other. Two overlapping rules *conflict* if one permits an action while another forbids it; two rules are disjoint if there exists no action to which both apply.

Some example relationships between rules are illustrated in *Table 1*. All three rules presented in the table are pairwise overlapping. However, only rule $R_{502a1ii}$ has a category that is a subcategory of another, specifically rule $502a1v$.

Based on our experience with HIPAA, we believe that when two rules are disjoint or overlapping, but neither is a subcase of the other, the general approach described in sections 3.1 and 3.2 gives the correct results: an action is permitted if it is permitted by at least one rule and not forbidden by any. However, when

Table 1. This table shows some examples of overlapping rules in HIPAA

		Category				Requirement
		A_{from}	A_{type}	$A_{purpose}$	$A_{consent}$	
$R_{502a1ii}$	+	covered entity	health records	treatment	*	$permitted\_by_{R_{506}}(A)$
	-	covered entity	health records	treatment	*	$forbidden\_by_{R_{506}}(A)$
R_{502a1v}	+	covered entity	health records	*	*	$permitted\_by_{R_{510}}(A)$
	-	covered entity	health records	*	*	$forbidden\_by_{R_{510}}(A)$
R_{508}	+	*	psy-therapy note	*	⟨ x, authz ⟩	
	-	*	psy-therapy note	*	¬⟨ x, authz ⟩	

one clause addresses a subcase of another, it often appears to be the expressed intent of the law to have the more specific clause take precedence over the other clause. In other words, it appears correct to disregard both the permitted and forbidden conditions of the less specific clause, and use only the more specific clause. Fortunately, we can handle this correctly within pLogic, by using exceptions to narrow the scope of the less specific rule so that it is not applied in the conflicting subcase.

Generally, disregarding the added complexity of cross-references and exceptions, conflicts happen when the *category* of an action matches two or more rules, the *requirement* for one rule is satisfied and the requirement for the other is violated. In the above example, an action like ⟨ *from: covered entity, type: health records, for: treatment, requirement*:- as satisfying R_{506}⟩ is permitted by $R_{502a1ii}$ but forbidden by R_{502a1v}. Because pLogic is designed to give precedence to parts of the law that forbid an action, an action that is permitted by one of two overlapping rules and forbidden by the other will be considered forbidden.

In cases where one rule specifies a category that is a proper subset of the category of another rule, giving precedence to denial may be incorrect because the more specific clause of the law was intended to have higher priority. A simple way to modify the translation of the law into rules is to add exceptions to the more generic rule to make the two rules disjoint. In the example illustrated above (in the table), we add an exception to rule $R_{502a1ii}$ specifying *for:* ¬ *treatment*. This causes rule $R_{502a1ii}$ not to be applied when the purpose is treatment, eliminating the problematic conflict. Another solution suggested in [12] is to assign priorities and split all the overlapping rules to make them disjoint. If applied throughout, the alternative approach could produce a more efficient compliance checker, but we believe that it require substantial effort to properly split all rules, as many HIPAA rules are overlapping. Additionally, our approach has the advantage that it better preserves the correspondence between the logic rules and the corresponding legal clauses. To elucidate the structure of HIPAA and its translation in logic we have included an example in the appendix.

3.4   Extensions to the Model

Three extensions to the work described in this paper involve audit, implicit information, and obligations (as considered in [5,6], for example).

As mentioned earlier in connection with beliefs asserted by the sender of a message, compliance decisions depend on the accuracy of the information provided by the users. It seems natural to generally assume that the users of a hospital medical system are professional practitioners who will provide correct information. However, there may be some instances in which faulty or questionable information is entered. To provide accountability, auditing systems can be added to provide trace logs of how decisions are made and when beliefs or other potentially questionable input is used. Some related discussion involving non-compliant actions and audit appears in [6].

Another enhancement could infer relevant information, to reduce the amount of information the user has to provide to send a message. This could be achieved by extracting information from the message itself or by reasoning about the context of an action, information in previous messages, and so on.

Since obligations to perform future actions arise in many privacy contexts [5,6], it may be useful to extend our *pLogic* approach to support such obligations. However, Prolog and Datalog do not inherently have any concept of past or future. While we represent the past explicitly through the in-reply-to field of messages, which produces linked structures of relevant past actions, future obligations requires an additional approach. One method may be to periodically run a scheduled process which looks through the log and checks whether, for any particular action, any further action is required and notify the concerned person. In fact, this corresponds to the current manual process at Vanderbilt, where a staff person checks every Friday afternoon to make sure that messages requiring a response are addressed.

4   Related Work

Access control mechanisms have been widely studied and deployed. Discretionary access control [10,14], for example, allows the owner of a resource to specify access conditions, while mandatory access control [8] enforces policy of an organization. Role based access control [21] provides simplified policy entry and maintenance.

Regulations have been formalized using a variety of policy languages [3,4,2]. Privacy APIs [16], based on HRU access control, have been used to express some privacy legislation but are not tailored to compliance analysis or conflicts in policy. One approach to eliminating conflicts is shown in [12].

One widely available system for expressing and checking privacy policy is P3P [11]. In [1], the authors examine ways to use P3P to enforce policies in database systems where the type of information is known explicitly. P3P has limited expressiveness [25].

The EPAL language [22] privacy policy designed by IBM has been used to enforce privacy enterprise policies but it is not currently supported. XACML [20] is a prominent authorization algorithm, with some advantages and limiations [7].

The Logic of Privacy and Utility is based on the privacy language CI [5], a formalization of contextual integrity's transmission norms which has received some recent media attention [13]. The idea of contextual integrity was first proposed by Helen Nissenbaum [19].

5   Conclusions and Future Work

In this paper, we identified a fragment of stratified Datalog with limited use of negation, and developed a specific format for compostionally representing clauses of a law as Datalog rules, which we refer to for simplicity as pLogic. We used this framework to formalize the part of the US Health Insurance Portability and Accountability Act (HIPAA) that regulates information sharing in a healthcare provider environment. We tested this executable formalization of legal regulation by implementing a prototype web-based message system and compliance checker based on the Vanderbilt Medical Center MyHealth web portal [28]. This prototype is publicly accessible, allowing anyone to try the system and view sample Prolog HIPAA source [24].

We have also used our formalization to examine conflicts in the HIPAA regulation. By querying the logic program to return all the possible agents who could gain access to patient information, we found some anomalies regarding lack of regulation of government employees who are granted access to medical data, for example. While this paper focuses on the formalization of HIPAA, our approach appears to apply generally to a broad class of privacy regulations, such as those consistent with Nissenbaum's theory of Contextual Integrity [19] as formalized in [5].

A number of possible future directions seem promising. While we have not formalized all parts of HIPAA, it is possible to continue the effort to other portions of the law, if desired. We also look forward to collaborating with others, in hopes that there could be an open-source HIPPA formalization process. By sharing a formal presentation of HIPAA among many researchers and healthcare organizations, it may be possible to develop confidence in the formal presentation and use it widely across many enterprises. Another promising direction involves generating meaningful annotated audit logs, as by logging messages with semantic information about each action and compliance issues associated with it. In addition to automating compliance tasks, we also believe that a formal presentation of HIPAA (or other regulations) could also be useful in training medical personnel about the consequences and non-consequencs of the law.

References

1. Agrawal, R., Kiernan, J., Srikant, R., Xu, Y.: An XPath-based preference language for P3P. In: Proceedings of the Twelfth International Conference on World Wide Web, pp. 629–639. ACM Press, New York (2003)
2. Antón, A.I., Earp, J.B., Reese, A.: Analyzing website privacy requirements using a privacy goal taxonomy. In: Requirements Engineering 2002, pp. 23–31 (2002)
3. Anton, A.I., Eart, J.B., Vail, M.W., Jain, N., Gheen, C.M., Frink, J.M.: Hipaa's effect on web site privacy policies. IEEE Security and Privacy 5(1), 45–52 (2007)
4. Antón, A.I., He, Q., Baumer, D.L.: Inside JetBlue's privacy policy violations. IEEE Security and Privacy 2(6), 12–18 (2004)
5. Barth, A., Datta, A., Mitchell, J.C., Nissenbaum, H.: Privacy and contextual integrity: Framework and applications. In: IEEE Symposium on Security and Privacy, pp. 184–198. IEEE Computer Society, Los Alamitos (2006)

6. Barth, A., Mitchell, J., Datta, A., Sundaram, S.: Privacy and utility in business processes. Computer Security Foundations Symposium, IEEE, 279–294 (2007)

7. Barth, A., Mitchell, J.C.: Enterprise privacy promises and enforcement. In: Workshop on Issues in the Theory of Security, pp. 58–66. ACM Press, New York (2005)

8. Bell, D.E., La Padula, L.J.: Secure computer systems: Mathematical foundations. Technical Report 2547, MITRE Corporation (1973)

9. Borrelli, M.A.: Prolog and the law: using expert systems to perform legal analysis in the United Kingdom. Softw. Law J. 3(4), 687–715 (1990)

10. Crampton, J.: On permissions, inheritance and role hierarchies. In: Proceedings of the 10th ACM Conference on Computer and Communication Security, pp. 85–92. ACM Press, New York (2003)

11. Cranor, L.F., Langheinrich, M., Marchiori, M., Presler-Marshall, M., Reagle, J.: The platform for privacy preferences 1.0 (P3P1.0) specification (2002), http://www.w3.org/TR/P3P/

12. Cuppens-Boulahia, N., Cuppens, F., Haidar, D.A., Debar, H.: Negotiation of prohibition: An approach based on policy rewriting. In: IFIP International Federation for Information Processing, vol. 278, pp. 173–187. Springer, Boston (2008)

13. Evans-Pughe, C.: The logic of privacy. The Economist 382(8510), 65–66 (2007)

14. Jajodia, S., Samarati, P., Sapino, M.L., Subrahmanian, V.S.: Flexible support for multiple access control policies. ACM Trans. Database Syst. 26(2), 214–260 (2001)

15. Masys, D.: Electronic medical records and secure patient portals as an application domain for team research in ubiquitous secure technologies (2005), http://dbmi.mc.vanderbilt.edu/trust/TRUST_for_patient_portals.pdf

16. May, M.J., Gunter, C.A., Lee, I.: Privacy APIs: Access control techniques to analyze and verify legal privacy policies. In: IEEE Workshop on Computer Security Foundations, pp. 85–97. IEEE Computer Society Press, Los Alamitos (2006)

17. Ness, R.B.: A year is a terrible thing to waste: early experience with HIPAA. Annals of Epidemiology 15(2), 85–86 (2005)

18. Nilsson, U., Maluszynski, J.: Logic, Programming and Prolog, 2nd edn. Wiley, Chichester (1995)

19. Nissenbaum, H.: Privacy as contextual integrity. Washington Law Review 79(1), 119–158 (2004)

20. OASIS. eXtensible Access Control Markup Language (XACML) 2.0, http://docs.oasis-open.org/xacml/2.0/access_control-xacml-2.0-core-spec-os.pdf

21. Sandhu, R.S., Coyne, E.J., Feinstein, H.L., Youman, C.E.: Role-based access control models. IEEE Computer 29(2), 38–47 (1996)

22. Schunter, M., Ashley, P., Hada, S., Karjoth, G., Powers, C., Schunter, M.: Enterprise privacy authorization language, EPAL 1.1 (2003), http://www.zurich.ibm.com/security/enterprise-privacy/epal/Specification/

23. Sherman, D.M.: A prolog model of the income tax act of Canada. In: ICAIL 1987: Proceedings of the 1st international conference on Artificial intelligence and law, pp. 127–136 (1987)

24. Stanford Privacy Group. HIPAA Compliance Checker, http://crypto.stanford.edu/privacy/HIPAA

25. Stufflebeam, W.H., Antón, A.I., He, Q., Jain, N.: Specifying privacy policies with P3P and EPAL: lessons learned. In: WPES 2004: Proceedings of the 2004 ACM workshop on Privacy in the electronic society, pp. 35–35. ACM, New York (2004)

26. U.S. Department of Health and Human Services. Understanding HIPAA privacy, http://www.hhs.gov/ocr/privacy/hipaa/understanding/index.html

27. U.S. Department of Health and Human Services. HIPAA administrative simplification (2006), http://www.hhs.gov/ocr/privacy/hipaa/administrative/privacyrule/adminsimpregtext.pdf
28. Vanderbilt Medical Center. MyHealthAtVanderbilt, https://www.myhealthatvanderbilt.com/

A An Example of the Encoding of the Law

We consider the part of clause $R_{164.502}$ which states that a *covered entity* can give out *health records* if it adheres to R_{502b} or R_{506a2} and satisfies additional conditions. We begin with 164.502.b.

```
164.502.b      Standard: Minimum necessary
  164.502.b.1Minimum necessary applies.
    When using or disclosing protected health information or when
    requesting protected health information from another covered
    entity, a covered entity must make reasonable efforts to limit
    protected health information to the minimum necessary to accomplish
    the intended purpose of the use, disclosure, or request.
  164.502.b.2 Minimum necessary does not apply.
    This requirement does not apply to:
    (i) Disclosures to or requests by a health care provider for treatment;
```

In short R_{502b} implies that when the *covered entity* is giving out the information to another *covered entity*, it should ensure that it is *minimal* information except for the purposes of treatment. Thus the *category* for this clause is *from: covered entity* and *to: covered entity* and *type: health records*. The requirement is *belief: minimal*. The exception is *for: treatment*.

```
164.502 Uses and disclosure of protected health information
  164.502.a Standard: A covered entity may not use or disclose protected
    health information, except as permitted or required by this
    subpart or by subpart C of part 160 of this subchapter.
    164.502.a.1 Permitted uses and disclosures. A covered entity
      is permitted to use or disclose protected health
      information as follows:
      (ii) For treatment, payment, or health care operations,
        as permitted by and in compliance with 164.506;
```

The clause R_{502aii} implies that when a *covered entity* is sending *health records* for the purposes of *treatment* then it should also comply with R_{506}. Here the *category* is *from: covered entity* and *type: health records* and *purpose: treatment*. The *requirement* is to comply with R_{506}.

Thus the logic translation of the two clauses would look like:

Rules:-

$permitted\_by_{R_{502b}}(A) \Leftarrow$

$\quad (A_{from} = covered\ entity) \wedge (A_{type} = health\ records) \wedge (A_{to} = covered\ entity) \wedge$

$\quad \neg(A_{purpose} = treatment) \wedge (A_{belief} = minimal)$

$forbidden\_by_{R_{502b}}(A) \Leftarrow$

$\quad (A_{from} = covered\ entity) \wedge (A_{type} = health\ records) \wedge (A_{to} = covered\ entity) \wedge$

$\neg(A_{purpose} = treatment) \land \neg(A_{belief} = minimal)$

$permitted\_by_{R_{502aii}}(A) \Leftarrow$

$\quad (A_{from} = covered\ entity) \land (A_{type} = health\ records) \land (A_{purpose} = treatment) \land$

$\quad permitted\_by_{R_{506}}(A)$

$forbidden\_by_{R_{502aii}}(A) \Leftarrow$

$\quad (A_{from} = covered\ entity) \land (A_{type} = health\ records) \land (A_{purpose} = treatment) \land$

$\quad forbidden\_by_{R_{506}}(A)$

Policy:-

$compliant\_with_{HIPAA} \Leftarrow$

$\quad permitted\_by_{R_{502b}} \lor permitted\_by_{R_{502aii}} \land \neg(forbidden\_by_{R_{502b}} \lor forbidden\_by_{R_{502aii}})$

Attributes:-

We can define attributes and relations. Consider a relation called *inRole* that identify a particular individual and their role. It is simple to consider an example from the sitcom *Scrubs* where *dr_cox*, a doctor and *carla*, a nurse work for the *Sacred Heart Hospital.*

$inRole(carla, nurse)$

$inRole(dr\_cox, doctor)$

$inRole(doctor, covered\ entity)$

$inRole(nurse, covered\ entity)$

$inRole(sacredHeart, covered\ entity)$

$employeeOf(sacredHeart, dr\_cox)$

$employeeOf(sacredHeart, carla)$

We can also have a transitive closure of these rules which would imply that *carla* and *dr_cox* are *covered entity.*

Given this policy and the list of attributes, assuming *dr_cox* and *carla* work for the same hospital and R_{506} is satisfied, an action that would be allowed with this particular rule system is:

$$(from : carla, to : dr\_cox, type : health\ records, for : treatment)$$

The policy would permit this action because of the rule R_{502aii}
An action like

$$(from : carla, to : xyz, type : health\ records, for : treatment)$$

would not be allowed as there is no relation stating that *xyz* is some kind of *covered entity* and there is no other rule in the policy permitting this action.

Adaptive Dispatching of Incidences Based on Reputation for SCADA Systems

Cristina Alcaraz, Isaac Agudo, Carmen Fernandez-Gago,
Rodrigo Roman, Gerardo Fernandez, and Javier Lopez

Computer Science Department - University of Malaga,
29071 - Malaga, Spain
{alcaraz,isaac,mcgago,roman,gerardo,jlm}@lcc.uma.es

Abstract. SCADA systems represent a challenging scenario where the management of critical alarms is crucial. Their response to these alarms should be efficient and fast in order to mitigate or contain undesired effects. This work presents a mechanism, the Adaptive Assignment Manager (AAM) that will aid to react to incidences in a more efficient way by dynamically assigning alarms to the most suitable human operator. The mechanism uses various inputs for identifying the operators such as their availability, workload and reputation. In fact, we also define a reputation component that stores the reputation of the human operators and uses feedback from past experiences.

Keywords: SCADA systems, Critical Control Systems, Reputation.

1 Introduction

Part of our society comprises a set of critical infrastructures most of them belonging to the industrial sector. These critical infrastructures are controlled by specialized and complex control systems known as Supervisory Control and Data Acquisition Systems (SCADA). Through them, the operators could know the state of the infrastructure in real-time, by simply observing those data come from RTUs (*Remote Terminal Units*) and sensors deployed in all the development area. Even though the main requirement of a SCADA system is to ensure the performance and availability of the controlled system, security issues should be taken into consideration since a failure in the controlling process or a threat could mean a harmful cascade effect in the whole system [4]. Hence, SCADA systems are considered critical infrastructures by themselves as well.

During the controlling process, a set of incidences generated and categorized by the type of criticality of their associated alarms can appear. These incidences have to be managed by authorized operators. However, nowadays, most of them are not always suitable for attending them. The reasons may be several: lack of knowledge/skill, disinterest to take it up, or malicious goals. This paper presents a mechanism based on reputation that allows a SCADA system to identify the best staff to attend an incidence, maximizing reaction time and minimizing future risks.

S. Fischer-Hübner et al. (Eds.): TrustBus 2009, LNCS 5695, pp. 86–94, 2009.

The paper is organized as follows. In Section 2 we explain the procedures for action control in SCADA systems and highlight our contribution. Section 3 justifies the importance of reputation in SCADA systems and introduces a reputation component that stores human operators' information. In section 4 we detail the mechanism that assigns a certain incidence to an operator and discuss the practicability of using such a mechanism. Section 5 concludes the paper and outlines the future work.

2   Procedures for Action Control in SCADA Systems

SCADA systems are composed of two types of foundation networks: the *control network* and the *corporative network* (see Figure 1). The control network is in charge of receiving measurements or alarms from substations and managing control tasks (e.g open/close a pump). The operations performed by the corporative network are more related to the general supervision of the system. Both networks can make use of different communication infrastructures and specific SCADA communication protocols [8,9,16,17]. Furthermore, Some SCADA systems could offer web and mobile services as well as control operations between critical control systems.

From a security point of view, both networks and all their components can be threatened either by insiders (negligence or malicious acts of the staff) or outsiders (vulnerabilities of the protocols and software components [3]). In fact, Byres et.al. [5] used public databases[14,15] to infer that the number of external threats are increasing since the SCADA systems are connected to other external networks. Due to all these security problems, experts from different fields [6,7] are joining their efforts in order to improve the overall security of these critical

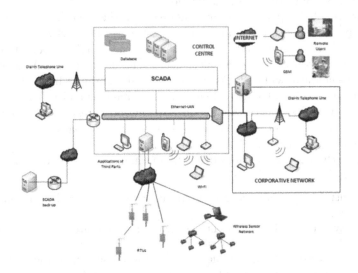

Fig. 1. A SCADA network architecture

infrastructures. Special attention should be also paid to the management of human operators since their responsibilities and their influence in the system are very high. Basically, this is currently done by using formal procedures such as security policies, access control policies and auditing mechanisms.

Security policies have to define the steps and responsibilities that can be performed by the different elements of the system. For that reason, their foundations should be based on generic security control standards [10,11,12] being extended to specific requirements of SCADA systems [12,13]. In contrast, access control policies must be able to manage and control every user identification and authorization process in all the components of the system.

Finally, auditing mechanisms provide a general overview of the state of the system by inspecting the actual functionality and the responsibilities of all the components and members of an organization. Such inspections must be regulated by formal procedures and standards, e.g. NIST SP 800-53 revision 2 [12].

2.1   Our Contribution

While the policies and mechanisms presented in Section 2 are necessary for securing a SCADA system, it would be also interesting to provide security mechanisms for controlling activities of the human operators. These mechanisms could work in parallel with all the policies and mechanisms mentioned above and can provide a more accurate control. Note that any mechanism of this sort should not interfere with the normal functionality of a SCADA system due to the criticality of its operations.

From a research point of view, this field is still unexplored in SCADA systems. A related work was proposed by Bigham et. al. in 2004. They presented an architecture based on an agent-based system to monitor the system and derive automated trust and privileges re-allocation.

The purpose of this paper is to investigate one of these mechanisms: an automated adaptive response mechanism able to estimate the most suitable human operator to effectively respond to incidents and alarms in a SCADA system. This will reduce the possibility that an alert could remain untreated. As a primary input, this mechanism will make use of a *Reputation* module where all operators are assigned a certain value according to their behaviour and to their reaction when dealing with incidences. Again, since the adaptive response mechanism is decoupled from the reputation module (i.e. they work in parallel), the impact on the availability of the SCADA system is minimal.

Therefore, the expected results from the mechanism presented in this paper are as follows:

1. Task control and monitoring without reducing the overall performance of the system.
2. Reliability. The mechanism identifies the human operator that is more suitable for performing a certain task.
3. Security. The reputation module manages the behaviour of the elements of the system and it can be used for detecting some malicious activities coming from internal attackers.

4. Availability of the resources of the system. The mechanism works in parallel with the other elements of the system.

3 Reputation Module for a SCADA System

The concept of reputation is defined by the Concise Oxford Dictionary as 'what is generally said or believed about a person's or thing's character or standing'. Reputation can be measured in several ways [1]. According to Resnick [2], a working reputation system must have at least the following three properties:

1. Entities must be long lived, so that with every interaction there is always an expectation of future interactions.
2. Feedback about current interactions is captured and distributed. Such information must be visible in the future.
3. Past feedback guides buyer decisions. People must pay attention to reputations.

Entities in SCADA systems are long lived and there are always expectations for future interactions as in these type of systems there are always incidences or alarms to attend. Also, the information about interactions is something we intend to capture and store. Besides, we believe that a reputation system is more effective when there are some incentives for maintaining a good reputation level and when it is difficult to get rid of bad ratings. We classify the aims of a user for improving his reputation into the following categories: *Profit, Reward, Ego* and *Fear*. The reputation system that we propose for SCADA systems fall into the Reward or Fear categories. Operators with a higher reputation could be rewarded with some benefits such as a pay raise or a promotion. On the other hand, if they continuously fail in performing their tasks or they are not performed as well as the system requires they could be given a worse position in the organization or even be fired.

In order to provide a mechanism based on reputation for a critical and complex control system we will design a reputation module for such a systems. This reputation system will monitor all the feedbacks and will compute reputation values for each operator. This information will be gathered later by a specialized component of incidences. Some minimal requirements are though needed. First of all, users (operators in this case) are assigned initial values of reputation. This initial reputation could be the same for all of them assigned accordingly to their experience or knowledge. The values of reputation are increased or decreased depending on how the human operator manages system incidences. The increase or decrease will vary based on how critical the alarm is and what the feedback from an operator with a higher reputation level who takes the role of the 'supervisor' is.

When we require a feedback for a given incidence the system must allocate two available operators. One of them will manage the incidence and the other one will send a feedback to the system informing how satisfactory was the measure taken by the first operator. The feedback system allows supervisors to include some textual description and forces them to rate the incidence management with one of the following values: Bad (1), Neutral (2) and Good (3).

As mentioned above the level of criticality is an input parameter for the management of reputation. This level will be measured ranging from 1 to 5, for example. In order to combine the feedback with this other factor, we can multiply them and obtain a modified feedback: "$Criticality \times Feedback$". We also consider the reputation of the supervisor as a parameter for modifying the feedback. This way, the higher the reputation of the supervisor is, the more relevant the feedback will be. The new feedback value can be computed as "$Criticality \times SupervisorReputation \times Feedback$". Note that other combinations are possible but we have chosen this as an initial approach.

4   Adaptive Assignment of Human Operators for a SCADA System

The reputation module is useful for storing the overall behaviour of the human operators, but it does not hold any decision-making capabilities. Therefore, for developing our automated adaptive response mechanism, we need an "Incidence Manager" component: the *Adaptive Assignment Manager* (AAM) (see Figure 2). This component takes an alarm as an input, and it determines which operator and supervisor are the most appropriate to take it up. The AAM is also in charge of updating the reputation of the operators in the reputation module by using the feedback of the supervisors.

The AAM component does not pretend to completely replace the response and alert management capabilities of human operators and supervisors. Instead, it facilitates their work by selecting, in the first instance, the most skilled staff that could provide an early and effective response to the incidence, offering all the relevant information to supervisors in a way that they can do their job in an assisted manner. In order to determine which operator or supervisor are the most suitable for taking care of an incidence, the AAM considers the following set of parameters:

- **Criticality of the alarm.** The alarms are categorized by the type of criticality of an event occurred in the system. Such alarms are received by a SCADA server, which generates the associated incidences.
- **Reputation** of the operator and supervisor, obtained from the reputation module.
- **Availability** of the operator and supervisor according to their contracts. They should be authorized in the system and being available in their work place.
- **Load of work** of the operator and supervisor. This parameter is related to the overload of critical incidences that an operator might be dealing with at a certain time. If an operator is attending a number of non very critical incidences he could be still available for taking up a more critical one.

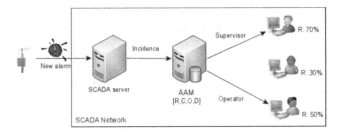

Fig. 2. Functionality of an Adaptative Assignement Manager (AAM)

However, if the operator is dealing with other critical incidences (even if it is only one) the system should identify another operator who could deal with it. The process is analogous for the supervisor.

Another task of the AAM is to serve as an interface to the values stored inside the reputation module. This way, the managers can determine the knowledge of the operators and even the level or mistakes made by them during the life time of a system. For example, an operator can i) reach the minimal reputation value, or ii) reach the maximal reputation value. In the first case the system should notify it to the responsible managers of the organization owning the SCADA system, thus that they are aware of the situation. However, in the second case the organization should reward these employees in order to maintain this high threshold of reputation.

4.1   Discussions

The implications of using the Adaptive Assignment Manager (AAM) presented previously in a real environment need to be carefully analyzed. First, it is necessary to consider in which order we should process the four parameters (C, R, A, L). Next, we should check the different situations that can be found in the management of an incidence by an operator assigned by the AAM system.

At first, the order of processing the four parameters employed by the AAM system could be crucial for quickly reducing the set of candidates to be chosen as operators and supervisors. This is a key point when critical alarms need to be dispatched as soon as possible. Availability (A) seems to be the first parameter to be processed from the set of the four parameters presented in Section 4. It can reduce the group of operators to be evaluated in a speedy way as it puts aside those employees that are not actually at work. The rest of variables can be sorted in different ways depending on each scenario but a logical sequence that can be used is to take into account criticality (C) of alarms. This can be used in a third step to select those personnel that are less busy (L), and from them the one with a higher reputation (R).

As for incidence management, after selecting a human operator to manage an incidence received by the AAM system, a supervisor is chosen for monitoring the

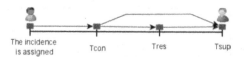

Fig. 3. Counter to be used in this schema

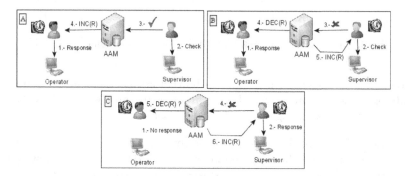

Fig. 4. Three main situations in the management of an incidence in a SCADA system

way it is going to be resolved by him/her. The operator must confirm the acceptance of the assignment before a defined time (*Tcon*). At that moment the resolution of the incidence starts. The supervisor is informed of the assignment done by the AAM system and a time counter (*Tres*) for determining how long it has been spent for resolving the incidence is started. This counter will warn the supervisor when an incidence remains unresolved for longer than it should. Thus, this counter could also help to calculate the efficiency of the operator in the resolution of incidences. Finally, a third counter must be used (*Tsup*) to check that the maximum time spent by a supervisor for managing an incidence not resolved by an operator is reached. These three counters are shown in Figure 3.

At this point, three situations can happen (see Figure 4).

- The incidence is successfully resolved by the operator assigned before *Tres* is reached. Nonetheless, the supervisor checks his/her resulting action after this counter is reached. The operator's reputation must be increased. (Figure 4-A).
- The incidence is not successfully resolved by the operator and *Tres* is reached. The supervisor checks the operator's action to be in charge of resolving it again. Finally, the operator and supervisor's reputation are changed (Figure 4-B).
- The operator could not confirm the acceptance of the assignment done by the AAM system. This situation is detected because *Tcon* is reached. The supervisor will be in charge of the incidence if this counter is overtaken increasing his final reputation. (Figure 4-C).

When a supervisor is in charge of managing the incidence, the AAM system must offer him all the information generated for the assignment. Thus, the supervisor can use this report in order to evaluate the reason why the incidence was not successfully resolved in such a way that he can deal with it in a more accurate way. Besides this, the supervisor must make a decision about how to proceed with the resolution of the incidence before $Tsup$ is reached, otherwise his reputation must be modified by the AAM system conveniently.

Finally, an AAM system could not find any operator with enough reputation and the load of work needed to be selected for the assignment of an incidence. Also, supervisors could have a parameter showing their load of work that could drive to a similar situation. These states must be evaluated for each scenario as in some cases it could be solved by re-sorting actual incidences and the staff assigned to them. Some other times these incidences can be queued waiting for an operator and a supervisor to deal with them.

5 Conclusions and Future Work

This paper presents an approach based on reputation that intends to improve the incidence management in a SCADA system. Basically, reputation will allow the system to identify which human operator is more suitable to attend it and those supervisors to check the resulting action. Such identification is made by an incidence manager (AAM) which will identify not only the best candidates but also will manage their final reputation level. To this end, a reputation module and a set of input parameters has been defined as well as some important situations (discussed in Section 4.1).

Any data associated to the reputation and the human operator's operations must be registered for future analysis processes. Basically, these will allow managers or staff in charge of a critical and complex system to be able to determine the operators' knowledge level in real time and/or even the presence of suspicious actions. Moreover, these registers will improve the response processes, the control procedures and the development of new and interesting tools such as auditing and maintenance of the system.

In order to show the validity of this approach this work is being currently formalized through a mathematical model. Besides, we are working on extending it and thus to take into account web and mobile services as well as remote control from other control systems.

Acknowledgments

This work has been funded by MEC I+D and MICT of Spain under the research projects: CRISIS (TIN2006-09242), ARES (CSP2007-00004) and PROTECT-IC (TSI-020302-2008-46).

References

1. Jøsang, A., Ismail, R., Boyd, C.: A Survey of Trust and Reputation Systems for Online Service Provision. Decision Support Systems 43(2), 618–644 (2007)
2. Resnick, P., Zeckhauser, R., Friedman, E., Kuwabara, K.: Reputation Systems. Communications of ACM 43(12), 45–48 (2000)
3. Cardenas, A., Amin, S., Sastry, S.: Research Challenges for the Security of Control Systems. In: HotSec 2008 (2008)
4. Peerenboom, J.P., Fisher, R.E.: Analyzing Cross-Sector Interdependencies. In: IEEE Computer Society, HICSS 2007, pp. 112–119. IEEE Computer Society, Los Alamitos (2007)
5. Byres, E., Lowe, J.: The myths and facts behind cyber security risks for industrial control systems. In: 'VDE Congress, VDE Association For Electrical, Electronic Information Technologies, British Columbia Institute of Technology and PA Consulting Group (2004)
6. Department of Energy Office of Energy Assurance. In: Steps to Improve Cyber Security of SCADA Networks, white paper (2002)
7. NISCC, National Infrastructure Security Co-ordination Centre, NISCC Good Practice Guide on Firewall Deployment for SCADA and Process Control Networks, BCIT (2005)
8. IEC 60870-5-104, International Electrotechnical Commission (2006)
9. IEC 60870-6, ICCP/TASE2, International Electrotechnical Commission (2008)
10. ISACA, Control Objectives for Information and related Technology, rev. 4.1 (2007)
11. ISO/IEC 17799:2005, Code of Practice for Information Security Management (2005)
12. NIST Special Publication 800-53 revision 2, Recommended Security Controls for Federal Information Systems (2007)
13. NIST Special Publication 800-82, DRAFT - Guide to Industrial Control Systems (ICS) Security (2007)
14. BCIT, British Columbia Institute of Technology (2008), http://www.bcit.ca/
15. CERT, Carnegie Mellon Software Engineering Institute, CERT/CC Statistics (1988-2008), http://www.cert.org/stats/vulnerability_remediation.html
16. DNP3, DNP Users Group (2008), http://www.dnp.org
17. Modbus-IDA, The Architecture for Distributed Automation (2005), http://www.modbus.org/

Steering Security through Measurement

Jose M. Torres, Jose M. Sarriegi, Josune Hernantes, and Ana Lauge

Tecnun, University of Navarra, Spain
{jmtorres,jmsarriegi,jhernantes,alauge}@tecnun.es

Abstract. This paper presents the results of a security management survey of IT administrators from small and medium sized enterprises (SMEs) who ranked predefined Critical Success Factors (CSFs) and Indicators. The outcome of this study relies on the development of a set of security management guidelines that allows IT administrators to adopt assessment and managerial security routines. The secondary contribution relies on allowing IT administrators to establish a culture of implementing and tracking the effectiveness of technical and non-technical security controls. The survey results describe how IT administrators would like the most critical aspects of security to evolve.

Keywords: Industrial Research, Management Model, Security Management, Critical Success Factors, Indicators.

1 Introduction

Information security has become the process of achieving a well-informed sense of assurance that information risks and technical, formal and informal controls are in dynamic balance [1]. Nevertheless, it is very hard to find a SME that manages the effectiveness of its implemented security controls.

The staff in charge of information security in SMEs, usually the IT-administrator, perceives current management and measuring methods as unavailable, complex and time consuming. Further complicating the situation, organizations that do implement security metrics use them as isolated reference points and do not see them as part of a continuous improvement process [2].

The complexity, unavailability and prohibitive size of current security management models such as the ISO 27000 series cause continuous measuring and management of technological, organizational and human aspects of security to continue to be under-developed. Building a security management and measuring culture in SMEs is crucial to limit damages from and prevent future incidents.

In this paper we present results from a survey of IT administrators from SMEs. The study is a continuation of previous research [3] where personal interviews and litera-ture reviews led to the identification of critical success factors (CSFs) and a set of security indicators. To elicit industry opinion, we built a survey where IT Administra-tors were asked to: a) rank 11 identified security management critical success factors; and b) rank indicators of each factor depending on their effectiveness and handiness. The outcome of this work aims to provide SMEs with guidelines that allow IT admin-istrators to track the evolution of their information security and systematically apply

S. Fischer-Hübner et al. (Eds.): TrustBus 2009, LNCS 5695, pp. 95–104, 2009.

measures to improve it. Owing to resource constraints, practitioners in SMEs need tools that provide less complicated, scaled down security management practices that can be implemented in a reasonable time frame with available resources.

2 Survey Methodology

We chose an online exploratory questionnaire to rank our previously designed CSFs and indicators by means of practitioners. The questionnaire was accessible through a website and the link was sent by e-mail to 170 IT Administrators from organizations with less than 250 employees (SMEs) located in Spain with a security budget of about 10% of IT budget. The questionnaire was answered anonymously and the main objective was to classify, by importance, 11 CSFs and 62 indicators so IT administrators could build a personal security scorecard choosing the CSFs and indicators that fit best. It was also possible to suggest additional CSFs and indicators during the survey execution.

The survey had two sections. Part one, with an average response time of 10 minutes, provided the 11 CSF definitions and asked IT administrators to rank from 1 to 11 all CSFs (1 being the most important and 11 being the least important). Part 2, with an average response time of 30 minutes, provided predefined indicators for each CSF and asked IT administrators to set the following two values for each indicator:

- Effectiveness: How well the indicator measures the CSF
- Handiness: How easy it is to implement and track this indicator

It must be noticed that obtaining real data about security incidents and their causes and effects is extremely difficult since the companies are usually reluctant to share this information due to confidentiality and reputation issues.

At this moment, a considerable large number of SMEs are approaching information security as a merely technological issue. Therefore, it is widely recognized the need of empirical studies, regardless of size, in order to help SMEs to achieve a successful implementation of security management. Despite the difficulty in gathering this type of information, we managed to obtain 40 responses (23.52% response rate) with the geographical and sector distribution showed in Figure 1.

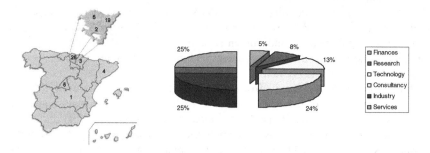

Fig. 1. Geographic/sector distribution of companies involved in the study

From a statitistal point of view, the above sample allows us to provide an exploratory analysis about the priorities of IT administrators and how they perceived and understand information security duties rather than a confirmatory analysis.

3 Survey Results

IT-administrators were asked to rank the 11 factors presented above. The question was phrased as follows: Please rank the 11 CSFs (1 being the most influential factor and 11 being the less influential) that in your opinion affect information security the most. The obtained results are shown in Figure 2. For instance, Top Management Commitment resulted to be the most important CSF resulting in 3.38 to IT-administrators (169 total points divided by 40 responses). Security Strategy came in second with 4.92 (246 points divided by 40 responses) and so on.

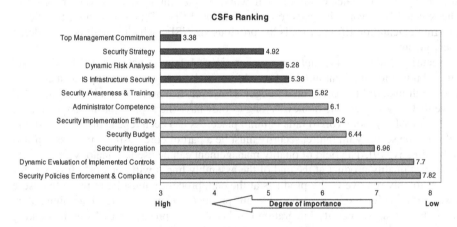

Fig. 2. CSFs Ranking Results

That Top Management Commitment (3.38) was ranked first is hardly surprising. Without it, resources will not be allocated and ear-marked for security. In our experience most SMEs do not have a budget dedicated to security, but money must be taken from the IT-budget to cover those expenses. When there is competition for resources, funds will be allocated to that which management prioritizes.

The second priority set by practitioners after top management commitment, is Security Strategy (4.92). Literature also points out how "defining the security strategy" represents an early key factor to carry out since the strategy usually shapes security implementations and managerial activities [4], [5]. An important distinction to be made is not whether an SME has a security strategy but how proactive, formal, reviewed and accepted it is.

Dynamic Risk Analysis (5.28) is considered by IT-administrators to be the third most important issue. Without some form of risk assessment one can not know what the threats are and what needs to be secured.

IS Infrastructure Security (5.38), ranked fourth, reflects the technical orientation of most IT-administrators. Their educational background and daily work emphasizes technical solutions to problems.

We consider it heartening that Security Awareness and Training (5.82) ranks in at number five. As many authors have pointed out, security is no longer and has indeed never been purely a technological issue [6], [7], [8]. It is therefore worth mentioning that IT-administrators, who have a highly technical background, have started to recognize this issue.

In sixth place is Administrator Competence (6.1). Since IT-administrators are usually primary in charge of security in SMEs we had expected Administrator Competence to rank much higher. However, it seems that respondents of this survey recognize that there is only so much one individual can do without the support of management and constructive processes in place to support them.

Next on the list we find Security Implementation Efficacy (6.2). Implementing something without later checking if it works is meaningless. However, in order to check whether it works it needs to be implemented first. Thus it is natural that Security Implementation Efficacy trails the previous six CSFs, which can all be considered prerequisites.

Security Budget (6.44) ranks as number eight. A fair expectation would be for security budget to rank in at number four. After a risk analysis has been performed there is enough material to decide on a budget. However, it may be that administrators believe that they will get the money as long as they have the support of management.

Security Integration (6.96) falls in ninth place. As has been repeatedly pointed out in information security literature, security must be a part of core business processes if it is to be effective [9]. The field of quality management can be used as analogy. If one tries to inspect quality product at the end of the assembly line it will not work. It is not sufficient to only remove faulty products at the end, processes must be in place to ensure that as few faulty products as possible are produced. However, the IT-administrators might have ranked Security Integration low because the preceding CSFs in the ranking for a large part are prerequisites. For example, to successfully integrate security into a business process the staff needs to have some security knowledge.

Dynamic Evaluation of Implemented Controls (7.7) is second to last at tenth position. To steer the security ship it is needed not only to know where the "security north" is, but also where the ship is relative to the north. Knowing where you are is a prerequisite to deciding on where to go next. Nothing is worse than wasting resources on controls that are not working. Why then, is Dynamic Evaluation of Implemented Controls is so low on the list? A reason may be that internal audits of implemented security controls are not executed on a regular basis because IT administrators do not see themselves as potential targets for attackers. Another possibility is that they might see this as too time consuming, and hence, unfeasible to do.

Security Policies Enforcement and Compliance (7.82) rounds out the list. Enforcing implemented security policies, meeting security law requirements and monitoring user compliance is considered fairly important to practitioners but difficult to follow for the immediate future.

It is likely that some of the CSFs would trade places on the list given a different sample. However, we are not aiming at creating a universal law. Our purpose is to create a practical security management roadmap for SMEs and the ranking of the CSFs provide a useful guideline.

4 Security Indicators Rank

Each IT administrator was asked to grade (high, medium, low) the Effectiveness and Handiness of each CSF; being the meaning of Effectiveness how well the indicator measures the CSF (high, medium, low) and Handiness being how easy it is to implement and track the indicator (high, medium, low) (see figure below). We replaced the high, medium, low ratings with 3, 2, 1 respectively and calculated the average of responses. We used the square root of the product between effectiveness & handiness (the geometric mean) to rank the 62 indicators.

#	CRITICAL SUCCESS FACTOR	Effective	Handy	Rank
	INDICATOR	e	h	(√e*h)
	FORMULA [UNITS]			

Most of the indicators for Top Management Commitment got similar scores, with the exception of number 6, which is significantly below the others. Looking at the nature of the indicators it seems that the respondents preferred tangible indicators which are easy to count and which do not require a lot of effort to collect. Perhaps the IT-administrators feel that it is too difficult to keep track of what management is doing in relation to security promotion. Management may for example not only promote security in meetings or informal settings where the IT-administrator also attends. To continuously ask management what they have been doing is time consuming. In addition, a manager may not remember exactly how or when he promoted security.

For Security Strategy, indicators 7 and 8 attain significantly higher scores than the others. The respondents view actual fulfillment of objectives as the best indicator. This correlates with interviews we have done with IT administrators. A typical comment is that everybody is very enthusiastic when a security program is launched, but everyone has forgotten about it three weeks later. The IT-administrators also care about how many others in the organization that are qualified in security. The IT-administrator can not secure a whole enterprise without help from its staff. The security community highlights a company encompassing security culture as crucial in security management work [10]. However, it is a bit strange that indicator 11 which is highly related to security qualification obtained such a low score. The reason for it might be that in many SMEs the IT administrator is the only one working on security.

Outsourcing of security tasks is relatively uncommon in SMEs, and that may explain why indicators 9 and 12 got low scores. In addition, a high percentage of outsourced tasks do not necessarily mean that security is bad and vice versa. It depends on the way in which security is managed, not who manages it.

Indicator 10 requires a significant amount of effort to keep track of, and a busy IT-administrator who has many other tasks may find the extra time it takes an unnecessary burden.

Top Management Commitment	Effective	Handy	Rank
1. Downstream security communication	2.214	2.238	**2.226**
(Σ of meeting between security leaders & top management per year) [meetings/year]			
2. % of security budget spent on training	2.19	2.214	**2.202**
(Budget spent on training*100)/(Security budget) [%]			
3. % of security policies approved	2.143	2.071	**2.107**
(Σ of policies approved*100)/(Σ of policies suggested per year) [%]			
4. Average training hours received per year	2.143	1.976	**2.058**
(Hours dedicated to training)/(Average staff during 1 year) [hours/user-year]			
5. % of security related reports asked	1.905	2.19	**2.043**
(Σ of security reports asked per year) [reports/year]			
6. % of security training activities promoted by management	1.619	1.571	**1.595**
(Σ of activities promoted by management*100)/(Σ of training activities executed per year) [%]			

Security Strategy	Effective	Handy	Rank
7. % of strategy maturity	2.514	2.343	**2.427**
(Σ of security objectives achieved*100)/(Σ of objectives initially set or advised by a guide) [%]			
8. % of security qualified staff	2.229	2.4	**2.312**
(Qualified security staff*100)/(Average IS staff during 1 year) [%]			
9. Σ of audits to the security outsourced firm(s)	1.914	1.857	**1.885**
Σ of audits per year [audits/year]			
10. Delays in security tasks	1.943	1.8	**1.870**
(Σ (Days estimated to complete task "n"-Days to complete task "n")/ Total tasks per year) [days behind]			
11. Security responsibility sharing	1.912	1.706	**1.806**
(Σ of responsibilities assigned to a single staff member*100)/(Σ of all security responsibilities) [%]			
12. % of outsourced security processes	1.486	2.057	**1.748**
(Σ of security processes outsourced*100)/(Σ of business security processes) [%]			

Indicators 13 and 14 have high scores in both effectiveness and handiness. Indicators 15-18 generally score high in effectiveness, but low in handiness. For example, indicator 17 is actually ranked higher than 13 and 14 in effectiveness, but it requires a significantly higher effort to keep up to date. Owing to scarce resources, IT-administrators can not dedicate all of their time to a single task. Thus, even though some indicators may be considered quite effective, they are unlikely to be implemented because they are very time consuming.

Dynamic Risk Analysis	Effective	Handy	Rank
13. Average risk assessment review time	2.405	2.432	**2.419**
(Time between consecutive reviews) [months]			
14. % of countermeasures implemented	2.5	2.214	**2.353**
(Σ of implemented countermeasures*100)/(Σ of identified countermeasures in the D.R.A) [%]			
15. Potential loss of critical assets	2.649	1.892	**2.239**
(Current value for each critical asset) [€]			
16. Σ of high-impact incidents on processes not contemplated in previous D.R.A.	2.108	1.865	**1.983**
Σ of incidents not contemplated [incidents not contemplated]			
17. Current level of risk by critical area	2.514	1.514	**1.950**
(((Threats*vulnerability)/countermeasures)*value for each area) [potential impact (-€)]			
18. Σ of identified potential threats	2.027	1.622	**1.813**
Σ of potential threats identified per year [threats/year]			

One of the most likely threats to a SME is theft, which explains why physical protection occupies two of the three top slots. The fact that indicator 20 is in second place reflects another major concern: viruses, worms and other intrusions in the company network. It also seems that the respondents are concerned with insider activity, reflected by indicator 22 occupying fourth place on the list.

IS Infrastructure Security	Effective	Handy	Rank
19 % of critical equipment with adequate physical protection	2.615	2.538	2.577
(Average physically protected equipment per year*100)/(Critical business equipment) [%]			
20 % of secured configurations	2.684	2.316	2.493
(Σ of configurations secured according to the security strategy*100)/(total configurations) [%]			
21 % of secured areas	2.564	2.41	2.486
(Σ of secured areas*100)/(Total areas identified as critical) [%]			
22 Access privileges update	2.447	2.211	2.326
(Privileges to access the system update date - date of revoking privileges) [days]			
23 Σ of internal & external technical audits	2.205	2.282	2.243
Σ of internal & external technical audits per year [audits/year]			
24 N^0 of severe incidents with productivity loss	2.282	1.846	2.053
(Σ of severe incidents per year) [incidents/year]			
25 Σ of users with administrator passwords per workstation	2.000	2.079	2.039
Σ of users with access or administrator privileges per critical workstation [users/critical station]			
26 N^0 high risk technical vulnerabilities	2.263	1.816	2.027
(Σ of high risk vulnerabilities identified per year) [vulnerabilities/year]			
27 % of software and hardware classified	2.184	1.842	2.006
(Σ of software & hardware classified*100)/(Σ of total software & hardware) [%]			
28 Σ of contracts with third parties service suppliers	1.605	1.868	1.732
(Σ of formalized contracts*100)/(Total externalized services) [%]			

In our experience backups are one of the main security activities in SMEs. This partly explains why indicator 29 occupies the top of the Security Awareness and Training list. Another reason is that this is something the IT-administrators can do largely on their own, thus they do not need to involve a lot of other people.

Overall, there is not much difference in effectiveness or handiness for indicators 30, 31 and 32. However, it seems that respondents do not believe that the presence of written security communication indicates security awareness, as indicator 33 comes second to last on the list. They, like others, may be all too familiar with the document overload all too common in enterprises.

Indicator 34 is difficult to keep track of and would require quite a lot of effort, which explains the low score it obtained in handiness.

Security Awareness & Training	Effective	Handy	Rank
29 Average critical data recording time	2.382	2.529	2.455
(Time between two consecutive recordings) [hours]			
30 Incidents reported per employee	2.471	2.294	2.381
(Σ of incidents reported)/(Average employees during 1 year) [incidents/user per year]			
31 % of incidents investigated	2.515	2.152	2.326
(Σ of incidents investigated*100)/(Σ of detected incidents per year) [%]			
32 Business critical data recovery time	2.353	2.029	2.185
(Σ of hours needed to recover lost critical data or system functioning)/(DoS) [hours/DoSs]			
33 Security-related reports, newsletters, memorandums sent	1.941	2.176	2.055
(Σ of memorandums sent per year) [memorandums/year]			
34 Degree of implication by type of user (management, IT staff, end users, etc)	1.912	1.5	1.693
(Σ of voluntary activities per year to ensure or improve IS Security) [activities/year]			

Respondents value staff education. However, they seem to be less concerned with whether it is accomplished or not. The lower score of indicator 37 may be caused by the extra effort involved in following up whether staff has actually undertaken training. Still, the difference in score is not significant enough to say that they consider it unimportant.

Administrator Competence	Effective	Handy	Rank
35	Staff education	2.353	2.353	2.353
	(Hours dedicated to security training)/(Average IS staff during 1 year) [hours/staff member per year]			
36	Upstream security communication	2.235	2.382	2.308
	(Σ of meetings with executive management or reports sent per year) [meetings/year]			
37	% of training activity accomplishment	2.029	2.029	2.029
	(Σ of successfully finalized training activities*100)/(Σ of training activities scheduled per year) [%]			

The difference in scores for the Security Implementation Efficacy is relatively small. Respondents seem to value actual tangible results in the form of implemented controls rather than planning activities. Indicators 42 and 43 do not really reflect the actual security level, rather they reflect the planned future security level. This may explain why they have the lowest score of all indicators.

Security Implementation Efficacy	Effective	Handy	Rank
38	Hours dedicated towards upgrading activities	2.143	2.143	2.143
	(Hours dedicated to review and upgrade)/(Average qualified staff during 1 year) [hours/team member per year]			
39	% of controls documented and approved	2.143	2.143	2.143
	(Σ of controls documented & approved*100)/(Σ of total controls identified in the D.R.A.) [%]			
40	Hours dedicated to implement controls	1.943	2.143	2.040
	(Hours dedicated to implement)/(Average qualified staff during 1 year) [hours/team member per year]			
41	Maturity level of implemented controls	2.286	1.8	2.028
	(Σ of stops or productivity losses per year) [stops or €]			
42	% of controls (policies & procedures) into the design phase (not approved)	1.769	1.885	1.826
	(Σ of controls into design*100)/(Σ of total controls identified in the D.R.A.) [%]			
43	Hours dedicated to design controls	1.714	1.857	1.784
	(Hours dedicated to design)/(Average qualified staff during 1 year) [hours/team member per year]			

Complicated tasks, such as cost-benefit analysis, are not always welcome for practitioners, not because they are not helpful but owing to lack of time. Keeping track of the difference between this and last years security budget is much feasible.

Security Budget	Effective	Handy	Rank
44	Security budget evolution	2.275	2.366	2.320
	(Budget spent on IS security*100)/(Total IT budget spent every year) [%]			
45	Security budget segregation	1.902	1.829	1.865
	(Budget spent on the analyzed area*100)/(Security budget) [%]			
46	Σ of cost-benefit analysis (NPV, IRR, ROSI, ALE, GLEIS)	2.024	1.61	1.805
	(Σ of cost-benefit analysis executed per year) [analysis/year]			

Respondents value system availability and files' protection. Practitioners in SMEs want their systems up and running with appropriate critical files protection and short response time to vulnerabilities and incidents 47, 48, 49. As said at the introduction, certification is not achievable for SMEs. As a result, they seem to be less concerned with whether it is accomplished or not. Certification of security is something that seems to be far from where they stand at the moment and it explains the low score of indicators 50. Indicator 51 BSP incentives, best security practice, is the lowest because practitioners are not fully convinced about the value of best security practice incentives in SMEs.

Data recovery testing ranks highest both in effectiveness and handiness. This correlates well with the top Security Awareness and Training Indicator, timely backups. As mentioned earlier, executing backups is one of the main security activities of SMEs.

	Security Integration	Effective	Handy	Rank
47	% of systems availability	2.706	2.235	2.459
	(Σ of hours available*100)/(Σ of hours expected to be available) [%]			
48	Σ of protected files	2.441	2.441	2.441
	(Σ of files in the backup folder*100)/(Σ of files identified as critical) [%]			
49	Vulnerabilities fixing time	2.316	1.947	2.124
	(Σ of (detection date-fixing date)/(Σ of total identified vulnerabilities) [time/vulnerability fixed]			
50	Certification status	1.806	1.639	1.720
	(Σ of man-hours per week needed to achieve a security certification) [man hours/week]			
51	Σ of BSP incentives	1.647	1.765	1.705
	(Σ of best security practice incentives given/month) [incentives/month]			

All the indicators have good scores, but in general effectiveness is higher than handiness for each indicator. For example, process monitoring (indicator 54) is potentially very effective, but requires a lot of time.

	Dynamic Evaluation of Implemented Controls	Effective	Handy	Rank
52	Data recovery testing activities	2.667	2.406	2.533
	(Σ of data recovery testing activities/year) [data recoveries/year]			
53	% of maintenance processes executed	2.394	2.333	2.363
	(Σ of maintenance process executed*100)/(Σ of total maintenance processes scheduled) [%]			
54	% of monitorized processes	2.545	2.121	2.324
	(Σ of processes monitorized daily*100)/(Σ of critical business processes) [%]			
55	Average wireless and no wireless devices upgrade time	2.375	2.031	2.196
	Σ (current upgrade date (s)-date of last review (s))/(Σ of all critical devices) [days/device]			
56	% of system improvement	2.303	2.091	2.194
	(Σ of nonconformity aspects fixed*100)/(Σ of all nonconformity aspects detected during audit) [%]			
57	Average time to respond to severe incidents	2.469	1.938	2.187
	Σ (detection time (s)- response time (s)) in days)/(Σ of incidents with productivity loss [time/detected incident]			
58	% of successful vulnerability penetrations per audit	2.281	1.938	2.102
	(Σ of successful penetrations*100)/(Σ of penetrations executed) [%]			
59	System assessment	2.061	1.97	2.015
	(Σ of hours dedicated to evaluation & assessment activities by qualified staff monthly) [hours/month]			

If we compare best-in-class in each section then, indicators 60 and 61 have low scores. Practitioners still do not have a precise idea about the advantage of complying with external security regulations. Although internal policies monitoring appears to be helpful it demands a high number of resources. In regards to imposing penalties to users, they do not seem to be of the same opinion to execute such actions.

	Security Policies Enforcement & Compliance	Effective	Handy	Rank
60	% of monitorized policies	2.412	2.000	2.196
	(Σ of monitorized policies*100)/(Σ of implemented policies) [%]			
61	% of fulfilled regulations	2.206	2.000	2.100
	(Σ of regulations fulfilled*100)/(Σ of regulations recommended by authorities) [%]			
62	% of penalties imposed to users	1.882	1.412	1.630
	(Σ of penalties imposed*100)/(Σ of security bad practices detected) [%]			

5   Conclusions

The presented management guidelines allow IT administrators to build their personal security scorecard choosing the CSFs and indicators that fit best. This empirical study provides fast and straightforward security management procedures that not only allows SMEs to track the evolution of information security but also makes them evolve in technical, managerial and human aspects of information security.

Certainly, there could be more complex and accurate ways to manage and measure information security. However, the limited resources available to practitioners make it necessary to have an accessible, handy and user-friendly method to estimate previously often unknown security levels.

The proposed work benefits from ongoing research that focuses on the definition of security management maturity levels that will ease the transition from merely technical approaches to managerial oriented.

References

1. Torres, J.M.: ISSMF. An Information System Security Management Framework for SMEs. In: TECNUN. University of Navarra, Donostia (2007)
2. Sademies, A.: Process Approach to Information Security Metrics in Finnish Industry and State Institutions. Espoo (2004)
3. Santos, J., Sarriegi, J.M., Torres, J.M., Serrano, N.: Empirical study of the Information Systems Security Management in Basque Country SMEs. In: Proceedings of the 8th International Conference of the DS - IESE, pp. 884–893 (2005)
4. Berinato, S., Cosgrove, L.: Six Secrets of Highly Secure Organizations. CIO magazine (2004)
5. Theoharidou, M., Kokolakis, S., Karyda, M., Kiountouzis, E.: The insider threat to information systems and the effectiveness of ISO17799. Computers & Security 24, 472–484 (2005)
6. Dhillon, G., Moores, S.: Computer crimes: theorizing about the enemy within. Computers & Security 20, 715–723 (2001)
7. Mitnick, K.: The Art of Deception. Indianapolis. John Wiley Inc., Indiana (2002)
8. Schneier, B.: Beyond Fears. Copernicus Book ed., New York (2003)
9. Caralli, R.A.: The Critical Success Factor Method: Establishing a Foundation for Enterprise Security Management, Report CMU/SEI-2004-TR-010 (2004)
10. Dojkovski, S., Lichtenstein, S., Warren, M.J.: Fostering Information Security Culture in Small and Medium Size Enterprises: An Interpretive Study in Australia. In: Proceedings of the Fifteenth European Conference on Information Systems, St. Gallen, Switzerland, pp. 1560–1571 (2007)

Advanced Features in Bayesian Reputation Systems

Audun Jøsang[1] and Walter Quattrociocchi[2]

[1] University of Oslo - UNIK Graduate Center
josang@unik.no
[2] Institute of Cognitive Sciences and Technologies (ISTC), Italian National Research Council
walter.quattrociocchi@istc.cnr.it

Abstract. Bayesian reputation systems are quite flexible and can relatively easily be adapted to different types of applications and environments. The purpose of this paper is to provide a concise overview of the rich set of features that characterizes Bayesian reputation systems. In particular we demonstrate the importance of base rates during bootstrapping, for handling rating scarcity and for expressing long term trends.

1 Introduction

Reputation systems are used to collect and analyse information about the performance of service entities with the purpose of computing reputation scores for service objects and service entities. A fundamental assumption of reputation systems is that reputation scores can help predict the future performance of the respective entities and thereby reduce uncertainty of relying parties during the decision making processes [5]. The idea is that transactions with reputable parties are likely to result in more favourable outcomes than transactions with disreputable parties.

In the case of centralised reputation systems, ratings are collected centrally and the computed reputation scores are published online. In the case of distributed reputation systems, relying parties must discover and collect ratings from other members in the community who have had prior experience with the service entity. The relying party must then analyse the collected information to derive a private reputation score. Two fundamental elements of reputation systems are:

1. *Communication protocols* that allow participants to provide ratings about service entities to the reputation centre, as well as to obtain reputation scores of potential entities from the reputation system.
2. *A reputation computation engine* used by the reputation system to derive reputation scores for each participant, based on received ratings, and possibly also on other information.

This paper focuses on the reputation computation engines, and in particular on Bayesian computational engines. Binomial and multinomial Bayesian reputation systems have been proposed and studied e.g. in [1,3,4,6].

Many different reputation systems, including computation engines, have been proposed in the literature, and we do not intend to provide a survey or comparison in this

S. Fischer-Hübner et al. (Eds.): TrustBus 2009, LNCS 5695, pp. 105–114, 2009.

paper, but simply refer to [2]. The purpose of this paper is concisely describe the advanced features of Bayesian reputation systems, some of which have been described previously and some of which are presented here.

2   Mathematics of Bayesian Reputation Systems

2.1   Computing Reputation Scores

Binomial reputation systems allow ratings to be expressed with two values, as either positive (e.g. *Good*) or negative (e.g. *Bad*). Multinomial reputation systems allow the possibility of providing ratings in different discrete levels such as e.g. *mediocre - bad - average - good - excellent*.

Binomial Reputation Scores. Binomial Bayesian reputation systems apply to the binary state space {Bad, Good} which reflect a corresponding performance of a service entity. The Beta distributions is a continuous distribution functions over a binary state space indexed by the two parameters α and β. The beta PDF denoted by $\text{Beta}(p \,|\, \alpha, \beta)$ can be expressed using the gamma function Γ as:

$$\text{Beta}(p \,|\, \alpha, \beta) = \frac{\Gamma(\alpha + \beta)}{\Gamma(\alpha)\Gamma(\beta)} p^{\alpha-1}(1 - p)^{\beta-1} \tag{1}$$

where $0 \leq p \leq 1$ and $\alpha, \beta > 0$, with the restriction that the probability variable $p \neq 0$ if $\alpha < 1$, and $p \neq 1$ if $\beta < 1$. The probability expectation value of the Beta distribution is given by:

$$\text{E}(p) = \alpha/(\alpha + \beta). \tag{2}$$

Binomial reputation is computed by statistical updating of the Beta PDF. More specifically, the *a posteriori* (i.e. the updated) reputation is continuously computed by combining the *a priori* (i.e. previous) reputation with every new rating. It is the expectation value of Eq.(2) that is used to represent the reputation score. The Beta distribution itself only provides the underlying statistical foundation, and is otherwise not used in the reputation system.

Before receiving any ratings, the *a priori* distribution is the Beta PDF with $\alpha = Wa$ and $\beta = W(1-a)$ where W denotes the non-informative prior weight and a denotes the base rate of the outcome "Good". The default base rate is $a = 0.5$. Normally $W = 2$, which with the default base rate produces a uniform *a priori* distribution. Then after observing r "Good" and s "Bad" outcomes, the *a posteriori* distribution is the Beta PDF with $\alpha = r + Wa$ and $\beta = s + W(1 - a)$. By using Eq.(2) the reputation score S is:

$$S = (r + Wa)/(r + s + W). \tag{3}$$

This score should be interpreted as the probability that the next experience with the service entity will be "Good".

Multinomial Reputation Scores. Multinomial Bayesian reputation systems allow ratings to be provided over k different levels which can be considered as a set of k disjoint elements. Let this set be denoted as $\Lambda = \{L_1, \ldots L_k\}$, and assume that ratings are provided as votes on the elements of Λ. This leads to a Dirichlet probability density function over the k-component random probability variable $\vec{p}(L_i)$, $i = 1 \ldots k$ with sample space $[0, 1]^k$, subject to the simple additivity requirement $\sum_{i=1}^{k} \vec{p}(L_i) = 1$.

The Dirichlet distribution with prior captures a sequence of observations of the k possible outcomes with k positive real rating parameters $\vec{r}(L_i)$, $i = 1 \ldots k$, each corresponding to one of the possible levels. In order to have a compact notation we define a vector $\vec{p} = \{\vec{p}(L_i) \mid 1 \leq i \leq k\}$ to denote the k-component probability variable, and a vector $\vec{r} = \{r_i \mid 1 \leq i \leq k\}$ to denote the k-component rating variable.

In order to distinguish between the *a priori* default base rate, and the *a posteriori* ratings, the Dirichlet distribution must be expressed with prior information represented as a base rate vector $\vec{a}$ over the state space.

$$\text{Dirichlet}(\vec{p} \mid \vec{r}, \vec{a}) = \frac{\Gamma\left(\sum_{i=1}^{k}(\vec{r}(L_i) + W\vec{a}(L_i))\right)}{\prod_{i=1}^{k} \Gamma(\vec{r}(L_i) + W\vec{a}(L_i))} \prod_{i=1}^{k} \vec{p}(L_i)^{(\vec{r}(L_i) + W\vec{a}(L_i) - 1)} \,,$$

$$\text{where} \begin{cases} \sum\limits_{i=1}^{k} \vec{p}(L_i) = 1 \\[2mm] \vec{p}(L_i) \geq 0, \forall i \end{cases} \text{and} \begin{cases} \sum\limits_{i=1}^{k} \vec{a}(L_i) = 1 \\[2mm] \vec{a}(L_i) > 0, \forall i \,. \end{cases} \tag{4}$$

It can be seen that Eq.(4) simply is a generalisation of Eq.(1). Similarly to the binomial case, the multinomial reputation score $\vec{S}$ is the vector of probability expectation values of the k random probability variables expressed as:

$$\vec{S}(L_i) = \mathrm{E}(\vec{p}(L_i) \mid \vec{r}, \vec{a}) = \frac{\vec{r}(L_i) + W\vec{a}(L_i)}{W + \sum_{i=1}^{k} \vec{r}(L_i)} \,. \tag{5}$$

The non-informative prior weight W will normally be set to $W = 2$ when a uniform distribution over binary state spaces is assumed. Selecting a larger value for W would result in new observations having less influence. over the Dirichlet distribution, and can in fact represent specific *a priori* information provided by a domain expert or by another reputation system.

2.2 Collecting Ratings

Assume k different discrete rating levels. This translates into having a state space of cardinality k. For binomial reputation systems $k = 2$ and the rating levels are "Bad" and "Good". For multinomial reputation system $k > 2$ and any corresponding set of suitable rating levels can be used. Let the rating level be indexed by i. The aggregate ratings for a particular agent y are stored as a cumulative vector, expressed as:

$$\vec{R}_y = (\vec{R}_y(L_i) \mid i = 1 \ldots k) \,. \tag{6}$$

The simplest way of updating a rating vector as a result of a new rating is by adding the newly received rating vector $\vec{r}$ to the previously stored vector $\vec{R}$. The case when old ratings are aged is described in Sec.2.3.

Each new discrete rating of agent y by an agent x takes the form of a trivial vector $\vec{r}_y^x$ where only one element has value 1, and all other vector elements have value 0. The index i of the vector element with value 1 refers to the specific rating level.

2.3   Aggregating Ratings with Aging

Ratings may be aggregated by simple addition of the components (vector addition).

Agents (and in particular human agents) may change their behaviour over time, so it is desirable to give relatively greater weight to more recent ratings. This can be achieved by introducing a longevity factor $\lambda \in [0, 1]$, which controls the rapidity with which old ratings are aged and discounted as a function of time. With $\lambda = 0$, ratings are completely forgotten after a single time period. With $\lambda = 1$, ratings are never forgotten.

Let new ratings be collected in discrete time periods. Let the sum of the ratings of a particular agent y in period t be denoted by the vector $\vec{r}_{y,t}$. More specifically, it is the sum of all ratings $\vec{r}_y^x$ of agent y by other agents x during that period, expressed by:

$$\vec{r}_{y,t} = \sum_{x \in M_{y,t}} \vec{r}_y^x \tag{7}$$

where $M_{y,t}$ is the set of all agents who rated agent y during period t.

Let the total accumulated ratings (with aging) of agent y after the time period t be denoted by $\vec{R}_{y,t}$. Then the new accumulated rating after time period $t + 1$ can be expressed as:

$$\vec{R}_{y,(t+1)} = \lambda \cdot \vec{R}_{y,t} + \vec{r}_{y,(t+1)}, \text{ where } 0 \leq \lambda \leq 1 . \tag{8}$$

Eq.(8) represents a recursive updating algorithm that can be executed once every period for all agents, or alternatively in a discrete fashion for each agent for example after each rating. Assuming that new ratings are received between time t and time $t + n$ periods, then the new rating can be computed as:

$$\vec{R}_{y,(t+n)} = \lambda^n \cdot \vec{R}_{y,t} + \vec{r}_{y,(t+n)} , \quad 0 \leq \lambda \leq 1. \tag{9}$$

2.4   Convergence Values for Reputation Scores

The recursive algorithm of Eq.(8) makes it possible to compute convergence values for the rating vectors, as well as for reputation scores. Assuming that a particular agent receives the same ratings every period, then Eq.(8) defines a geometric series. We use the well known result of geometric series:

$$\sum_{j=0}^{\infty} \lambda^j = \frac{1}{1 - \lambda} \quad \text{for } -1 < \lambda < 1 . \tag{10}$$

Let $\vec{e}_y$ represent a constant rating vector of agent y for each period. The Total accumulated rating vector after an infinite number of periods is then expressed as:

$$\vec{R}_{y,\infty} = \frac{\vec{e}_y}{1 - \lambda}, \text{ where } 0 \leq \lambda < 1 . \tag{11}$$

Eq.(11) shows that the longevity factor λ determines the convergence values for the accumulated rating vector according to Eq.(8). In general it will be impossible for components of the accumulated rating vector to reach infinity, which makes it impossible for the score vector components to cover the whole range $[0, 1]$. However, entities that provide maximum quality services over a long time period wold naturally expect to get the highest possible reputation score. An intuitive interpretation of this expectation is that each long standing entity should have its own personal base rate which is determined as a function of the entity's total history, or at least a large part of it. This approach is used in the next section to include individual base rates.

2.5   Individual Base Rates

A base rate normally expresses the average in a population or domain. Here we will compute individual base rates from a "population" consisting of individual performances over a series of time periods. The individual base rate for entity y at time t will be denoted as $\vec{a}_{y,t}$. It will be based on individual evidence vectors denoted as $\vec{Q}_{y,t}$.

Let $\vec{a}$ denote the community base rate as usual. Then the individual base rate for entity y at time t can be computed similarly to Eq.(5) as:

$$\vec{a}_{y,t}(L_i) = \frac{\vec{Q}_{y,t}(L_i) + W\vec{a}(L_i)}{W + \sum_{i=1}^{k} \vec{Q}_{y,t}(L_i)} \ . \tag{12}$$

Reputation scores can be computed as normal with Eq.(5), except that the community base rate $\vec{a}$ is replaced with the individual base rate $\vec{a}_{y,t}$ of Eq.(12). It can be noted that the individual base rate $\vec{a}_{y,t}$ is partly a function of the community base rate $\vec{a}$, which thereby constitutes a two-level base rate model.

The components of the reputation score vector computed with Eq.(5) based on the individual base rate of Eq.(12) can theoretically be arbitrarily close to 0 or 1 with any longevity factor and any community base rate.

The simplest alternative to consider is to let the individual base rate for each entity be a function of the entity's total history. A second similar alternative is to let the individual base rate be computed as a function of an entity's performance over a very long sliding time window. A third alternative is to define an additional high longevity factor for base rates that is much closer to 1 than the common longevity factor λ. The formalisms for these three alternatives are briefly described below.

Total History Base Rate. The total evidence vector $\vec{Q}_{y,t}$ for entity y used to compute the individual base rate at time period t is expressed as:

$$\vec{Q}_{y,t} = \sum_{j=1}^{t} \vec{R}_{y,j} \tag{13}$$

Sliding Time Window Base Rate. The evidence vector $\vec{Q}_{y,t}$ for computing an entity y's individual base rate at time period t is expressed as:

$$\vec{Q}_{y,t} = \sum_{j=u}^{t} \vec{R}_{y,j} \quad \text{where Window Size} = (t - u) \,. \tag{14}$$

The Window Size would normally be a constant, but could also be dynamic. In case e.g. $u = 1$ the Window Size would be increasing and be equal to t, which also would make this alternative equivalent to the total history alternative described above.

High Longevity Factor Base Rate. Let λ denote the normal longevity factor. A high longevity factor λ_H can be defined where $\lambda_H > \lambda$. The evidence vector $\vec{Q}_{y,t}$ for computing an entity y's individual base rate at time period t is computed as:

$$\vec{Q}_{y,t} = \lambda_H \cdot \vec{Q}_{y,(t-1)} + \vec{r}_{y,t}, \text{ where } \lambda < \lambda_H \leq 1 \,. \tag{15}$$

In case $\lambda_H = 1$ this alternative would be equivalent to the total history alternative described above. The high longevity factor makes ratings age much slower than the regular longevity factor.

2.6 Reputation Representation

Reputation can be represented in different forms. We will here illustrate reputation as *multinomial probability scores*, and as *point estimates*. Each form will be described in turn below.

Multinomial Probability Representation. The most natural is to define the reputation score as a function of the probability expectation values of each element in the state space. The expectation value for each rating level can be computed with Eq.(5).

Let $\vec{R}$ represent a target agent's aggregate ratings. Then the vector $\vec{S}$ defined by:

$$\vec{S}_y : \left(\vec{S}_y(L_i) = \frac{\vec{R}_y^*(L_i) + W\vec{a}(L_i)}{W + \sum_{j=1}^{k} \vec{R}_y^*(L_j)} ; | \ i = 1 \dots k \right) \,. \tag{16}$$

is the corresponding multinomial probability reputation score. As already stated, $W = 2$ is the value of choice, but a larger value for the constant W can be chosen if a reduced influence of new evidence over the base rate is required.

The reputation score $\vec{S}$ can be interpreted like a multinomial probability measure as an indication of how a particular agent is expected to behave in future transactions. It can easily be verified that

$$\sum_{i=1}^{k} S(L_i) = 1 \,. \tag{17}$$

The multinomial reputation score can for example be visualised as columns, which would clearly indicate if ratings are polarised. Assume for example 5 levels:

$$\text{Discrete rating levels:} \begin{cases} L_1 : \text{Mediocre,} \\ L_2 : \text{Bad,} \\ L_3 : \text{Average,} \\ L_4 : \text{Good,} \\ L_5 : \text{Excellent.} \end{cases} \tag{18}$$

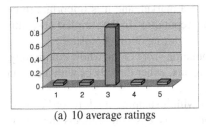
(a) 10 average ratings

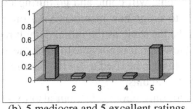
(b) 5 mediocre and 5 excellent ratings

Fig. 1. Illustrating score difference resulting from average and polarised ratings

We assume a default base rate distribution. Before any ratings have been received, the multinomial probability reputation score will be equal to $1/5$ for all levels. Let us assume that 10 ratings are received. In the first case, 10 *average* ratings are received, which translates into the multinomial probability reputation score of Fig.1.a. In the second case, 5 mediocre and 5 excellent ratings are received, which translates into the multinomial probability reputation score of Fig.1.b.

With a binomial reputation system, the difference between these two rating scenarios would not have been visible.

Point Estimate Representation. While informative, the multinomial probability representation can require considerable space to be displayed on a computer screen. A more compact form can be to express the reputation score as a single value in some predefined interval. This can be done by assigning a point value ν to each rating level i, and computing the normalised weighted point estimate score σ.

Assume e.g. k different rating levels with point values evenly distributed in the range $[0,1]$, so that $\nu(L_i) = \frac{i-1}{k-1}$. The point estimate reputation score is then:

$$\sigma = \sum_{i=1}^{k} \nu(L_i) S(L_i) . \tag{19}$$

However, this point estimate removes information, so that for example the difference between the average ratings and the polarised ratings of Fig.1.a and Fig.1.b is no longer visible. The point estimates of the reputation scores of Fig.1.a and Fig.1.b are both 0.5, although the ratings in fact are quite different. A point estimate in the range $[0,1]$ can be mapped to any range, such as 1-5 stars, a percentage or a probability.

2.7 Dynamic Community Base Rates

Bootstrapping a reputation system to a stable and conservative state is important. In the framework described above, the base rate distribution $\vec{a}$ will define initial default reputation for all agents. The base rate can for example be evenly distributed, or biased towards either a negative or a positive reputation. This must be defined by those who set up the reputation system in a specific market or community.

Agents will come and go during the lifetime of a market, and it is important to be able to assign new members a reasonable base rate reputation. In the simplest case, this can be the same as the initial default reputation used during during bootstrap.

However, it is possible to track the average reputation score of the whole community, and this can be used to set the base rate for new agents, either directly or with a certain additional bias.

Not only new agents, but also existing agents with a standing track record can get the dynamic base rate. After all, a dynamic community base rate reflects the whole community, and should therefore be applied to all the members of that community. The aggregate reputation vector for the whole community at time t can be computed as:

$$\vec{R}_{M,t} = \sum_{y_j \in M} \vec{R}_{y,t} \tag{20}$$

This vector then needs to be normalised to a base rate vector as follows:

Definition 1 (Community Base Rate). *Let $\vec{R}_{M,t}$ be an aggregate reputation vector for a whole community, and let $\vec{S}_{M,t}$ be the corresponding multinomial probability reputation vector which can be computed with Eq.(16). The community base rate as a function of existing reputations at time $t + 1$ is then simply expressed as the community score at time t:*

$$\vec{a}_{M,(t+1)} = \vec{S}_{M,t}. \tag{21}$$

The base rate vector of Eq.(21) can be given to every new agent that joins the community. In addition, the community base rate vector can be used for every agent every time their reputation score is computed. In this way, the base rate will dynamically reflect the quality of the market at any one time.

If desirable, the base rate for new agents can be biased in either negative or positive direction in order to make it harder or easier to enter the market.

When base rates are a function of the community reputation, the expressions for convergence values with constant ratings can no longer be defined with Eq.(11), and will instead converge towards the average score from all the ratings.

2.8   Continuous Ratings

It is common that the subject matter to be rated is measured on a continuous scale, such as time, throughput or relative ranking, to name a few examples. Even when it is natural to provide discrete ratings, it may be difficult to express that something is strictly good or average, so that combinations of discrete ratings, such as *"average-to-good"* would better reflect the rater's opinion. Such ratings can then be considered continuous. To handle this, it is possible to use a fuzzy membership function to convert a continuous rating into a binomial or multinomial rating. For example with five rating levels the sliding window function can be illustrated as in Fig.2. The continuous q-value determines the r-values for that level.

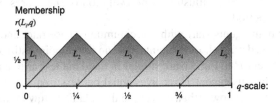

Fig. 2. Fuzzy triangular membership functions

3 Simple Scenario Simulation

A simple scenario can be used to illustrate the performance of a multinomial reputation system that uses some of the features described above. Let us assume that agent A and agent B receive the following ratings over 70 rounds or time periods.

Table 1. Sequence of ratings

Sequence	Agent A	Agent B
Periods 1 - 10	10 × L1 ratings in each period	1 × L1 rating in each period
Periods 11-20	10 × L2 ratings in each period	1 × L2 rating in each period
Periods 21-30	10 × L3 ratings in each period	1 × L3 rating in each period
Periods 31-40	10 × L4 ratings in each period	1 × L4 rating in each period
Periods 41-70	30 × L5 ratings in each period	3 × L5 ratings in each period

The longevity of ratings is set to $\lambda = 0.9$ and the individual base rate is computed with the high longevity approach described in Sec.2.5 with high longevity factor for the base rate set to $\lambda_H = 0.999$. For simplicity in this example the community base rate is assumed to be fixed during the 70 rounds, expressed by $a(L1) = a(L2) = a(L3) =$

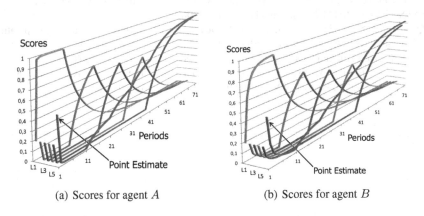

    (a) Scores for agent A (b) Scores for agent B

Fig. 3. Score evolution for agents A and B

$a(L4) = a(L5) = 0.2$. Fig.3 illustrates the evolution of the scores of Agent A and Agent B during the period.

The scores for both agents start with the community base rate, and then vary as a function of the received ratings. Both agents have an initial point estimate of 0.5.

The scores for Agent B in Fig.3.b are similar in trend but less articulated than that of agent A in Fig.3.a, because agent B receives equal but less frequent ratings. The final score of agent B is visibly lower than 1 because the relatively low number of ratings is insufficient for driving the individual base rate very close to 1. Thanks to the community base rate, all new agents in a community will have a meaningful initial score. In case of rating scarcity, an agents score will initially be determined by the community base rate, with the individual base rate dominating as soon as some ratings have been received.

4   Conclusion

Bayesian reputation systems have a solid basis in classical statistics which make them both sound and simple to adapt to various contexts. Bayesian reputation is compatible with opinions of subjective logic, thereby allowing computational trust to be combined with reputation models. This paper has shown the great flexibility of binomial and multinomial Bayesian reputation systems.

References

1. Jøsang, A., Ismail, R.: The Beta Reputation System. In: Proceedings of the 15th Bled Electronic Commerce Conference (June 2002)
2. Jøsang, A., Ismail, R., Boyd, C.: A Survey of Trust and Reputation Systems for Online Service Provision. Decision Support Systems 43(2), 618–644 (2007)
3. Jøsang, A., Haller, J.: Dirichlet Reputation Systems. In: The Proceedings of the International Conference on Availability, Reliability and Security (ARES 2007), Vienna, Austria (April 2007)
4. Jøsang, A., Luo, X., Chen, X.: Continuous Ratings in Discrete Bayesian Reputation Systems. In: The Proceedings of the Joint iTrust and PST Conferences on Privacy, Trust Management and Security (IFIPTM 2008), Trondheim (June 2008)
5. Quattrociocchi, W., Paolucci, M., Conte, R.: Dealing with Uncertainty: Simulating Reputation in an Ideal Marketplace. In: Proceedings of the 2008 Trust Workshop, at the 7th Int. Joint Conference on Autonomous Agents & Multiagent Systems, AAMAS (2008)
6. Withby, A., Jøsang, A., Indulska, J.: Filtering Out Unfair Ratings in Bayesian Reputation Systems. The Icfain Journal of Management Research 4(2), 48–64 (2005)

An MDA-Based Environment for Generating Access Control Policies

Heiko Klarl[1,2], Florian Marmé[1,3], Christian Wolff[2], Christian Emig[1,3],
and Sebastian Abeck[3]

[1] iC Consult GmbH, Keltenring 14, 82041 Oberhaching, Germany
[2] Media Computing, University of Regensburg, Germany
[3] Cooperation & Management, University of Karlsruhe (TH), Germany

Abstract. Identity management and access control are essential in the enterprise IT landscape in order to control access to applications and to fulfil laws or regulations. The global competition of enterprises leads to short development cycles and fast changes of IT applications, which requires also an error-free and quick adaption of its security. The model-driven development of access control policies promises to cope with this situation. This work introduces an mda-based environment for generating access control policies. A comprehensive overview is given on the organisational aspects, describing details of roles, artefacts and tools involved. On this basis the four phases of a model-driven development process for access control policies and their organisational aspects are presented.

Keywords: Model-driven Security, Access Control Policies, Identity Management, Model-driven Development Process.

1 Introduction

In modern enterprises business processes are extensively supported by IT systems. In order to cope with competitors and to react to demands of the global markets, adoptions of new business requirements have to be handled quickly. This leads to concerns for the companies' IT systems, business processes and their security architecture [1]. On the one hand, functional business requirements have to be implemented very fast. In order to fulfil those demands, *business process management* (BPM) [2] and *model-driven approaches* [3,4,5] have developed over the last years and have proven their benefits within software engineering. On the other hand, securing IT systems, especially the access control aspect, is still heavily based on documents without a formal and standardised structure, at the same time exposing a gap between the business and the IT perspective: In addition, there is a lack of adequate tools supporting the business side in expressing their security needs. Thus, the IT department, which has to implement the business's requirements, has to adjust both views. Typically, this is based on a rather unstructured communication process with many phases of human interaction which is error-prone, in the worst case resulting in an insufficiently secured IT landscape. We propose a model-driven development process of access

S. Fischer-Hübner et al. (Eds.): TrustBus 2009, LNCS 5695, pp. 115–126, 2009.

control policies as an improvement of the current situation: Modelling access control policies starts from a business perspective, when early business-focused models of the business process are enriched with access control statements. After this starting point a continuous refinement and transformation phase begins, leading to access control policies for a specific security product. In this paper, we give a comprehensive overview of this model-driven development process for access control policies. The different phases of the development process are described in detail and a mapping of roles, artefacts and tools to the corresponding phases is shown. The paper is organised as follows: In Section 2 the background and related work are analysed. Organisational aspects like roles, artefacts and tools are presented in Section 3, while the four phases of the development process and its relation to organisational aspects are shown in Section 4. The paper concludes with a summary and an outlook on future work in Section 5.

2   Background and Related Work

Before we discuss related work, a short overview of the work on which this paper is built upon is given, touching the fields of identity management, access control and model-driven security in the context of service-oriented architecture and business process modelling. In [6,7] *Web Services Access Control Markup Language* (WSACML) has been introduced, an access control meta-model for service-oriented architecture. WSACML describes policies at the *platform independent* level, which means that they are specified with detailed technical resource descriptions while *platform specific* details and notations for specific security products are not covered. Based on this work we have developed the WSACML2PSSP transformation tool [7], which allows the generation of platform specific security policies out of WSACML policies for commercial products e.g. *CA SiteMinder*. In order to cover access control from a business point of view as well, we describe how business processes can be enriched with security artefacts to express access control requirements [8]. In a prototypical implementation, the *UML activity diagram* has been extended with a UML2 profile for identity management. To attach access control statements to the business process, this extension introduces *DraftedPermission* and *Policy* elements. We have also applied this extension concept to the *Business Process Modeling Notation* (BPMN), adapting a BPMN modelling tool to use our extensions within graphical modelling. As the business process model is a computation independent model from a business point of view, we showed in [9] how this model could be transformed to a platform independent model, fitting the WSACML meta-model. In a broader perspective, these developments allow for the generation of platform specific security policies out of computation independent secured business process models utilising the WSACML meta-model at the platform independent level. While these studies strongly focus on specific aspects of access control, secure business process modelling, and model-driven techniques, a more general view describing the development process of access control policies as a whole is still missing. Especially the organisation of the development process and its environment like roles, artefacts of the single phases and the utilisation of tools is still not adequately shown in a comprehensive view.

As far as related work is concerned, the management of model-driven security is taken into focus in [10]. The authors make use of model-driven security for service-oriented architectures in order to cope with the steady change of applications and with the error-prone administration of security polices, introducing the *OpenPMF* framework. Some technical details of the framework are shown, but no concept of a model-driven development process for security policies is presented. In addition, there is no discussion of organisational aspects which are necessary to generate security policies in a model-driven way. Rees et al. introduce *PFIRES*, a policy framework for interpreting risk in e-business security in [11]. This framework is dedicated to high level policy management and it describes a policy life-cycle which is aligned with the software development process. The paper gives an overview on policy management and its phases from a global perspective, but it does not address a specific implementation scenario, where access control policies are developed to secure e.g. a business process. In [12], Rodríguez et al. present *M-BPSec*, a method for security requirements elicitation for business processes. Their four-phase method is decoupled from the software development process of functional components. As the method ends with the transformation of a *secure business process* into *analysis-classes* and use case diagrams, the creation of platform specific security policies is beyond the scope of this approach and there is no description of artefacts, tools, and roles covering organisational aspects. In [13] Nagaratnam et al. describe a method for business-driven application security. They introduce different roles involved in the software development process, as well as the tools used and show how an application may be brought from the analysis phase to operation: The integration of security requirements starts with the modelling of *security intentions* within business process models, which are understandable from a business perspective. Specific security requirements may be specified later on, e.g. in a UML class diagram. In contrast to our approach, the authors do not propagate a full model-driven development process for access control policies. Limiting the business view to modelling *security intentions* neglects the fact that many security requirements are driven by business needs which means that the business should have knowledge of them. The suggested use of tools is focused on a single vendor and does not comprise tools that specifically support the development of security policies.

3 Organisational Aspects – Roles, Tools and Artefacts

The model-driven development of access control policies is not just a simple sequence of single steps which have to be processed, it is also a complex process which involves different *roles, tools* and *artefacts*. Roles organise employees according to their responsibility in the enterprise. A variety of tools is utilised to support the development process. Artefacts of different kind are used as input data or are created as output within single steps of the development process. This section gives an overview on these aspects before the model-driven development process for access control policies is introduced in the following section.

3.1   Roles Involved in the Development Process

The following roles in the development process are discussed below:

- Process Owner
- Business Analyst
- Security Architect
- Security Developer
- Security Administrator

The *process owner* possesses the business process and is often represented by an organisational unit, not necessarily by a single person. From a business point of view he is in charge of the business process. His interest is to support his business by utilising the business process, therefore he is the source for improvement requests to satisfy business requirements. The process owner has a deep knowledge of all business-related aspects regarding the business process and he knows which laws or regulations have to be followed. He is able to clarify who is allowed to use the business process, a precondition for formulating *access control requirements*.

The *business analyst* is the interface between business-related and IT departments. He is experienced in *business process modelling* (BPM) and knows which business requirements can be successfully realised with the help of the IT. A deep understanding of the business domain with its requirements and characteristics enables him to link business and IT views of the problems involved.

The *security architect* has expertise in IT security architectures, especially in identity management and the modelling of access control policies. He is able to understand the non-formalised *DraftedPermission* elements and resolves them into formalised *Policy* elements. After that he will check whether all *Policy* elements are attached to the business process in a reasonable way and, if necessary, he will fix misconceptions and modelling errors.

The *security developer* is a security expert focusing on the implementation of platform specific access control policies. The security developer is responsible for generating WSACML policies out of *Policy* elements with the help of the PE2WSACML transformation tool (see sec. 3.3 for the discussion of tools involved in our approach). He has to resolve warnings and errors which are thrown during the transformation process and has to link the generated WSACML policies to service operations within the company's service-oriented architecture. In order to use the access control policies in a commercial product, the security developer creates product specific access control policies with the help of the WSACML2PSSP transformation tool.

The *security administrator* is in charge of the security infrastructure's operation, i.e. he is monitoring the systems, installing product updates, deploying and updating access control policies as well as solving problems with the security infrastructure. He has to ensure that new deployments of policies will not cause problems in the production environment and that the import of these updates will be successfully distributed in the company's security infrastructure.

3.2 Artefacts in the Development Process

The *DraftedPermission* element contains access control statements in a non-formalised and possibly incomplete manner. It enables the business site to describe their desired access control behaviour in prose which has to be refactored into *Policy* elements later. In order to use the *DraftedPermission* element within business process modelling, we have extended the *Unified Modeling Language* (UML) activity diagram and the *Business Process Modeling Notation* (BPMN). The *DraftedPermission* element has been introduced in [8], and further information can be found in [9].

The *Policy* element contains *formalised* access control statements. Attributes for describing their compliance and security status ease the handling of them. *Policy* elements are reusable, i.e. it is intended to reuse formerly defined policies when access control requirements reappear in another business scenario. The *Policy* element has been proposed in [8,9].

WSACML policies are based on an access control meta-model for web service-oriented architectures which has been introduced in [6]. WSACML describes access control policies at a *platform independent level*, i.e. they are specified with detailed technical resource descriptions: For example, the service operation to be protected is specified, but *platform specific details* on security issues and notations for security products are not covered.

Platform specific security policies are policies for a certain product, e.g. for a commercial off the shelf product. They describe access control requirements in the product's vocabulary. Platform specific security policies can be in a proprietary or standardised format like XACML; but as of 2009 most commercial products are not fully standard compliant.

The *security-enriched business process model* is described in an extended BPMN notation, supporting the annotation of security relevant information. The security-enriched business process model has its position at the beginning of the development process for access control policies which means that some work on securing the process has already been completed while other steps are still missing. The model has (formal) *Policy* elements attached to it, but also *DraftedPermission* elements containing security requirements written in prose which have to be resolved in a later phase. The business process model is enriched with access control statements but needs manual refinement for completely supporting a model-driven generation of access control policies.

The *secured business process model* in BPMN notation contains formalised *Policy* elements only. It is created out of the security-enriched business process model after all *DraftedPermission* elements are resolved into *Policy* elements. The business process model itself is the *platform independent* starting point for a model-driven development process resulting in the generation of platform specific access control policies for a commercial product.

3.3   Tools and Repositories Supporting the Development Process

Based on the process model sketched above we have developed a number of modelling and transformation tools which support the mda-based creation of access control policies. At the same time, relevant artefacts are stored in repositories which are used in the policy transformation process. Both, tools and repositories are described below.

BPMN modelling tools support the modelling of business processes. The tools provide all BPMN elements, check whether they are assembled in a correct way or support the graphical arrangement of model elements. In order to use a BPMN modelling tool for modelling access control requirements within the business process, the tool has to support an extension mechanism to include new elements like *DraftedPermission* or *Policy*.

A *business object repository* stores enterprise-wide entities like *order, customer* or *contract* which are used to describe input or output data for different activities. Each department within the enterprise has a different view on those entities. For example, the sales department defines a customer as a person who has already ordered a product, whereas the marketing department defines a customer as a person that should be convinced to place an order. As potentially contradictory views can cause difficulties in the modelling of business processes, the representation of the business object should be stored in a *business object repository* which includes all aspects of the entity within the enterprise. We developed it as a directory which supports the search for existing business objects and its attributes to utilise and interpret them in business process modelling.

The *vocabulary repository* was designed in order to support the creation of access control policies. The formal description of policies ensures syntactic correctness, but the wrong usage of attributes, e.g. the usage of non-existent attributes will lead to semantically invalid policies. To overcome this weakness, the vocabulary repository contains all attributes which may be used. These are for example *business roles, environment attributes*, names of existing *services* and *service operations*. When a policy has to be created, all attributes used can be looked up in the vocabulary repository. In addition, during transformations of policies all attributes are checked as well.

The *policy repository* contains formal security *Policy* elements which are already used in modelled business processes. The computation independent policies are stored in an XML representation we have proposed in [9]. We designed the policy repository to support the reuse of policies within the business process model in case of identical security requirements. As some access control policies reoccur frequently in different business processes, the reuse of existing policies not only saves work but also contributes to increased security as the policies stored in the policy repository have been reviewed by security experts beforehand. The policy repository is searchable so that policies fitting the user's requirements can be looked up. Meta-data fields describe the policy's content as well as security and compliance aspects.

The *WSACML policy repository* stores platform independent WSACML policies. For every policy to be stored in the repository, the tool checks whether the policy should be created or whether existing one should be updated. WSACML policies are platform independent but already linked to service operations, for example. The WSACML repository gives an overall view on access control statements for a certain service operation, as only WSACML policies are linked to entities of the IT systems architecture.

The *PE2WSACML transformation tool* extracts *Policy elements* (PE) out of a *secured business process model* and transforms them into *WSACML policies*. During the transformation process it utilises the *vocabulary repository* in order to check whether all attributes used within the policies exist and are used in a correct way. Failures that are detected during this check are displayed as warnings and error messages and have to be corrected in the *secured business process model* afterwards, before rerunning the transformation.

Platform independent WSACML policies have to be transformed to platform specific policies by the *WSACML2PSSP transformation tool* in order to be used by a commercial security product. This tool handles the meta-model of WSACML as well as the meta-models of all supported security products. Transformation rules between WSACML and the target product describe in which way the content of WSACML policies is mapped to the elements of the product's platform specific policies. This approach allows the generation of arbitrary platform specific policies as only the mapping rules to the new meta-model have

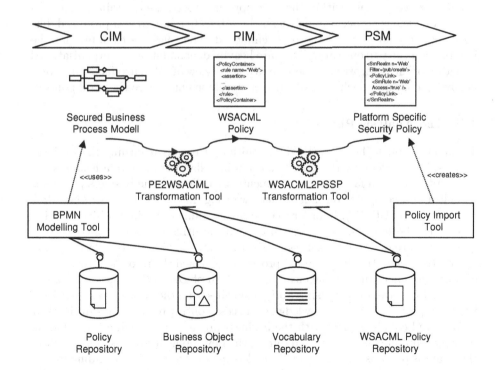

Fig. 1. Architecture Overview

to be reengineered. A specific example for this mapping has been given for *CA SiteMinder* in [7].

The *policy import tool* is a generic name for the mechanism to import platform specific security policies in a certain security product. Depending on the product the import of new or updated policies works in different ways. Some tools provide an interface allowing the import of policies by loading them into the product. Other products need a customised policy import tool, developed with the product's specific *application programming interface* (API). A policy import tool in the context of *CA SiteMinder* is used in [7].

Fig. 1 shows the relationship between transformation steps, repositories and modelling and transformation tools.

4   Model-Driven Development of Access Control Policies

In analogy with the software development process, the model-driven development process for access control policies has four phases. It starts with the modelling of the business process and its access control requirements and ends with the deployment of platform specific security policies within the IT security architecture of the enterprise. Focusing on the model-driven development of access control policies, functional aspects within the different phases are not shown in detail below. For every phase within the development process we describe specific activities and the roles performing them, the artefacts required and produced, like documents or models, and the tools employed. The roles are examples for the job function the persons carry. They are heavily dependant on the organisational structure of the enterprise. Table 1 gives an overview of roles, artefacts, and tools involved in our approach to model-driven development of access control policies.

4.1   The Analysis Phase

The analysis phase begins with the definition of details regarding the business process. This is done by the *process owners* in collaboration with a *business analyst*. As soon as all facts and requirements are collected, the business process is modelled in a computation independent way, e.g. in the *Business Process Modeling Notation* (BPMN). In order to ease the handling of business objects during modelling, the *business object repository* can be utilised. As access control requirements are driven by business needs, the team should try to collect them in this early stage of the development process and attach them to the business process model. This can be done either in the form of *DraftedPermission* elements (see sec. 3.2 above) or by reusing *Policy* elements from the *policy repository*. Utilising the process owners' knowledge on access control restrictions within their domain and coupling them with the business process model will ensure that all security requirements are covered during the development process. The result of the analysis phase is a *security-enriched business process model* including formal as well as non-formal access control requirements specified from a business point of view.

Table 1. Roles, Tools and Artefacts within the Development Process

		Phases			
		Ana.	Des.	Impl.	Depl.
Roles	Process Owners	x			
	Business Analyst	x			
	Security Architect		x		
	Security Developer		x	x	
	Security Administrator				x
Artefacts	DraftedPermission Elements	x	x		
	Policy Elements	x	x		
	WSACML Policies		x	x	
	Platform Specific Security Policies			x	x
	Security-enriched Business Process Model	x	x		
	Secured Business Process Model		x		
Tools	BPMN Modelling Tool	x	x		
	Business Object Repository	x	x		
	Policy Repository	x	x		
	Vocabulary Repository		x		
	WSACML Policy Repository		x		
	PE2WSACML Transformation Tool		x		
	WSACML2PSSP Transformation Tool			x	
	Policy Import Tool				x

4.2 The Design Phase

In the design phase, the output of the analysis phase (i.e., a *computation independent model* (CIM)) is the basis for the development of the *platform independent model* (PIM). Tasks defined in the business process model have to be mapped to existing service operations or to service operations that have to be created. As the functional development process goes beyond the scope of this paper, the necessary steps will not be described; for further information on this procedure we refer to [14]. From a security point of view *DraftedPermission* elements within the business process model have to be transformed to formalised *Policy* elements. This will be done by a *security architect*. At this point all *DraftedPermission* elements have to be resolved and the business process is designed from an IT perspective. The resulting artefact is the *secured business process model* and all *Policy* elements are stored in the *policy repository*. As a next step, the generation of platform independent *WSACML policies* can be done by the *security developer* using the *PE2WSACML transformation tool*, which reads policies from the *secured business process model* and transforms them into *WSACML policies* which are stored in the *WSACML policy repository*, at the same time unifying all *WSACML policies* linked to the same service operation. During the transformation process the attributes used within the policies are validated using the *vocabulary repository* and the *business object repository* to ensure that only valid attributes and values are used. Warnings and errors thrown by the transformation tool have to be corrected by the *security developer*. As a last step the manual mapping of the business process task names to service operations has to be done which assigns the *WSACML policy* to a specific service operation.

4.3   The Implementation Phase

As companies employ security products from a broad number of vendors, *platform specific security policies* e.g. for *CA SiteMinder* or *IBM Tivoli Access Manager* must be generated. The *WSACML2PSSP transformation tool* operated by the *security developer* uses *WSACML policies* as input and generates platform specific security policies. The transformation runs automatically and there is no need for manual rework or adaption. All plausibility checks on the attributes used within the policies have already been done in the design phase. The *WSACML2PSSP transformation tool* uses mapping rules to map the meta-model of WSACML to the meta-model of the platform specific policies. Parallel to the product specific policy generation, the implementation of functional components like services, the portal frontend or the database layer is done by developers.

4.4   The Deployment Phase

Finally, the *platform specific security policies* are delivered to the *security administrator* for deployment. All artefacts which have no direct relation to the system's security like the implemented services or the contents of are portal are handled separately. With the help of the *policy import tool*, the generated *platform specific security policies* are imported into the security product. In general, new policies are imported directly whereas existing but changed policies are only updated. The security product will audit this changes within the policies for ensuring traceability.

5   Conclusion and Further Work

In this paper, we have described a model-driven development process for access control policies which is organised in four phases just like the traditional software development process (analysis, design, implementation, deployment). While we have described the development and application of the tools used in this process to concrete scenarios in previous work, we have focused on the overall structure of the access control policy development process and the tools' role as well as their interaction with the enterprise security infrastructure here. The mda-based approach results in a unified process for developing access control policies which helps bridging communication gaps between business and IT perspectives. At the same time, this streamlined development model may also make security development more efficient. A real business scenario for applying the proposed development process of access control policies is the opening of a current account in the banking domain. The business department models the business process and adds additional access control information. Refining them results in the secured business process model, from which all necessary information can be extracted, so that WSACML policies and later product specific security policies for e.g. CA SiteMinder can be generated. A comprehensive version of this scenario is currently in progress and will be published in future work. Further work will be done on the integration of enterprise-wide compliance regulations within the development of access control policies as well as on methods to improve and measure the business process's security quality during its life cycle.

References

1. Neubauer, T., Klemen, M., Biffl, S.: Secure business process management: A roadmap. In: Proceedings of the 1st International Conference on Availability, Reliability and Security, pp. 457–464. IEEE Computer Society, Los Alamitos (2006)
2. Weske, M.: Business Process Management – Concepts, Languages, Architectures. Springer, Berlin (2007)
3. Object Management Group, Inc.: Model Driven Architecture (MDA) (July 2001)
4. Object Management Group, Inc.: MDA Guide – Version 1.0.1 (June 2003)
5. Frankel, D.S.: Model Driven Architecture: Applying MDA to Enterprise Computing. Wiley, Indianapolis (2003)
6. Emig, C., Brandt, F., Abeck, S., Biermann, J., Klarl, H.: An access control metamodel for web service-oriented architecture. In: Proceedings of the International Conference on Software Engineering Advances, IEEE Computer Society, Los Alamitos (2007)
7. Emig, C., Kreuzer, S., Abeck, S., Biermann, J., Klarl, H.: Model-driven development of access control policies for web services. In: Khoshgoftaar, T. (ed.) Proceedings of the 9th IASTED International Conference Software Engineering and Applications, Orlando, Florida, USA, pp. 165–171. IASTED (November 2008)
8. Klarl, H., Wolff, C., Emig, C.: Abbildung von Zugriffskontrollaussagen in Geschäftsprozessmodellen. In: Modellierung 2008 – Workshop Verhaltensmodellierung: Best Practices und neue Erkenntnisse, Berlin (March 2008)
9. Klarl, H., Wolff, C., Emig, C.: Identity management in business process modelling: A model-driven approach. In: 9. Internationale Tagung Wirtschaftsinformatik – Business Services: Konzepte, Technologien, Anwendungen, Band 1, Vienna, Austria, Österreichische Computer Gesellschaft (February 2009), pp. 161–170 (2009)
10. Lang, U., Schreiner, R.: Model driven security management: Making security management manageable in complex distributed systems. In: Modeling Security Workshop in Association with MODELS 2008, Toulouse, France (2008)
11. Rees, J., Bandyopadhyay, S., Spafford, E.H.: PFIRES: a policy framework for information security. Communicaiton of the ACM 46(7), 101–106 (2003)
12. Rodríguez, A., Fernández-Medina, E., Piattini, M.: M-BPSec: A method for security requirement elicitation from a UML 2.0 business process specification. In: Hainaut, J.-L., Rundensteiner, E.A., Kirchberg, M., Bertolotto, M., Brochhausen, M., Chen, Y.-P.P., Cherfi, S.S.-S., Doerr, M., Han, H., Hartmann, S., Parsons, J., Poels, G., Rolland, C., Trujillo, J., Yu, E., Zimányie, E. (eds.) ER Workshops 2007. LNCS, vol. 4802, pp. 106–115. Springer, Heidelberg (2007)

13. Nagaratnam, N., Nadalin, A., Hondo, M., McIntosh, M., Austel, P.: Business-driven application security: From modeling to managing secure applications. IBM Systems Journal 44(4), 847–867 (2005)
14. Emig, C., Weisser, J., Abeck, S.: Development of SOA-based software systems - an evolutionary programming approach. In: Proceedings of the International Conference on Internet and Web Applications and Services. IEEE Computer Society, Los Alamitos (2006)

An Extended Role-Based Access Control Model for Delegating Obligations

Meriam Ben-Ghorbel-Talbi[1,2], Frédéric Cuppens[1], Nora Cuppens-Boulahia[1], and Adel Bouhoula[2]

[1] Institut TELECOM/Telecom Bretagne, 2 rue de la Châtaigneraie,
35576 Cesson Sévigné Cedex, France
{meriam.benghorbel,frederic.cuppens,nora.cuppens}@telecom-bretagne.eu
[2] SUP'COM Tunis, Route de Raoued Km 3.5, 2083 Ariana, Tunisie
bouhoula@planet.tn

Abstract. The main aim of access control models is to provide means to simplify the management of the security policy, which is a fastidious and error-prone task. Supporting delegation is considered as an important mean to decentralize the administration and therefore to allow security policy to be more flexible and easier to manipulate. Our main contribution is the proposition of a unified model to the administration and delegation of obligations. Managing such delegations implies more requirements than managing traditional privileges delegation. In fact, delegating obligations may include two interpretations: the delegation of the obligation and the delegation of the responsibility related to this obligation. Therefore, it is important to deal with these two notions separately. Moreover, since delegating an obligation involves the delegation of sanctions, then the consent of the user who receives this delegation may be required in some cases. We address in this paper these requirements and we propose a formalism to deal with them.

1 Introduction

Delegation is the process whereby a user without any specific administrative prerogatives obtains the ability to grant some authorizations. In the field of access control, it is important to have a system that allows delegation, in order to simplify the management of the security policy and manage collaborative work securely, especially with the increase of shared information and distributed systems. In our recent work [1,2], we proposed a unified model based on the OrBAC formalism (Organization Based Access Control) to deal with administration and delegation. We showed that our model provides means to specify many delegation requirements such as multi-grained delegation (i.e. role and permission delegation), transfer, multi-step delegation (propagation of the delegated rights), agent-acted delegation (delegation by a third party), temporary and multiple delegation. We also showed that it is possible to deal with revocation schemes such as cascade revocation (i.e. the revocation of the whole delegation chain) and strong revocation (i.e. the revocation of all other delegations associated to

S. Fischer-Hübner et al. (Eds.): TrustBus 2009, LNCS 5695, pp. 127–137, 2009.

a given user). Since, obligations [3,4,5] are one main means to control the security policy, in particular usage control [6,7], it is also important to support this aspect. In this paper we are focused on the administration and the delegation of obligations. We will show what are the main differences between managing obligation delegation and permission delegation, namely the notion of responsibility and consent, and suggest a formalism to manage these requirements. The issue of obligation delegation was previously sketched in [8,9,10], but, to our best knowledge, this is the first that a complete formalism to deal with obligation delegation is defined.

This paper, is organized as follows. In section 2 we give an overview of the OrBAC model. In section 3 we present the basic principles of its administration model AdOrBAC and we show how to extend this model to deal with the administration of obligations. Then, in section 4 we discuss some delegation features, such as the notion of responsibility, the bilateral agreement and the propagation of obligations. Section 6 presents related work. Finally, concluding remarks and future work are made in section 7.

2   System Description

In our work we are based on the OrBAC formalism [11]. This model provides means to specify the security policy at the organization level that is independently of the implementation of this policy. Thus, instead of modelling the policy by using the concrete concepts of subject, action and object, the OrBAC model suggests reasoning with the roles that subjects, actions or objects play in the organization. The role of a subject is simply called a role, whereas the role of an action is called an activity and the role of an object is called a view. The concept of view is different from the concept of class. A class is a taxonomical concept used to structure the object descriptions, i.e. a class groups objects that have similar characteristics. By contrast, a view is an organizational concept used to structure the policy specification, i.e. a view groups objects on which the same security rules apply. Moreover, the concept of context [12] is explicitly introduced in OrBAC. This means that, the security rules do not apply statically but their activation may depend on contextual conditions (examples of context may be Night, Working-Hours or Urgency). Contexts are classified into five kinds: the *Temporal* context that depends on the time at which the subject is requesting for an access to the system, the *Spatial* context that depends on the subject location, the *User-declared* context that depends on the subject objective (or purpose), the *Prerequisite* context that depends on characteristics that join the subject, the action and the object and the *Provisional* context that depends on previous actions the subject has performed in the system.

In OrBAC, there are eight basic sets of entities: Org (a set of organizations), S (a set of subjects), A (a set of actions), O (a set of objects), R (a set of roles), $\mathcal{A}$ (a set of activities), V (a set of views) and C (a set of contexts). In the following we give the basic OrBAC built-in predicates:

- **Empower** is a predicate over domains $OrgxSxR$. If org is an organization, s a subject and r a role, $Empower(org,s,r)$ means that org empowers s in r.
- **Use** is a predicate over domains $OrgxOxV$. If org is an organization, o is an object and v is a view, then $Use(org,o,v)$ means that org uses o in view v.
- **Consider** is a predicate over domains $OrgxAxA$. If org is an organization, α is an action and a is an activity, then $Consider(org,\alpha,a)$ means that org considers that action α implements activity a.
- **Hold** is a predicate over domains $OrgxSxAxOxC$. If org is an organization, s a subject, α an action, o an object and c a context, $Hold(org,s,\alpha,o,c)$ means that within organization org, context c holds between s, α and o.
- **Permission** and **Prohibition** are predicates over domains $OrgxR_sxA_axV_ox$ C, where $R_s= R \cup S$, $A_a= \mathcal{A} \cup A$ and $V_o= V \cup O$. More precisely, if org is an organization, g is a role or a subject, t is a view or an object, p is an activity or an action and c is a context, then $Permission(org,g,p,t,c)$ (resp.$Prohibition(org,$ $g,p,t,c)$) means that in organization org, grantee g is granted permission (resp. prohibition) to perform privilege p on target t in context c.
- **Obligation** and **Dispensation** are predicates over domains $OrgxR_sxR_sxA_ax$ V_oxCxC. More precisely, if org is an organization, g_1 and g_2 are roles or subjects, t is a view or an object, p is an activity or an action and c_1, c_2 are contexts, then $Obligation(org,r_1,r_2,a,v,c_1,c_2)$ (resp. $Dispensation(org,r_1,r_2,a,v,c_1,c_2)$) means that in organization org, g_2 is obliged to g_1 (resp. dispensed) to perform p on t when context c_1 is activated and before context c_2 is activated. The meaning of these different attributes is further explained in section 3. Notice that rules used in this paper are considered as production rules.

3 Administration of Obligations

The OrBAC model is associated with a self administrated model called AdOr-BAC [13,14]. This model is based on an object-oriented approach, thus we do not manipulate privileges directly (i.e. *Permission*, *Prohibition*, *Obligation* and *Dispensation*), but we use objects having a specific semantics and belonging to specific views, called administrative views. Each object has an identifier that uniquely identifies the object and a set of attributes to describe the object. The view **Licence** is used to specify and manage users' privileges. Therefore, objects belonging to this view may have four types: licence, ban, duty, exempt; and according to this type the existence of an object in this view is interpreted as a *Permission*, a *Prohibition*, an *Obligation* or a *Dispensation*, respectively. The view **Role_assignment** is used to manage the assignment of subject to roles, and objects in this view are interpreted as an *Empower*. Since, in this paper we are focused on the administration of obligations, we will only describe duty objects that belong to the *Licence* view. These objects have the following attributes: *Type*: the object type (duty), *Auth*: organization in which the duty applies, *Obligator*: subject in favor of whom the duty is contracted, *Obligatee*: subject to which the obligation is assigned, *Task*: action that must be executed, *Target*: object on which the duty applies, *Context*: specific conditions that must be satisfied to activate the obligation and *Context_Violation*: specific conditions that represent the obligation deadline, this means that the obligatee must perform the obligation before this deadline, otherwise the obligation is considered violated and sanctions must be imposed on the obligatee. The existence of a valid duty in view *Licence* is interpreted as an obligation by the following rule:

$Obligation(Auth, R_1, R_2, P, T, Ctx, CtxV)$:-
$\quad Use(Org, D, licence), Type(D, duty), Auth(D, Auth),$
$\quad Obligator(D, R_1), Obligatee(D, R_2), Task(D, P),$
$\quad Target(D, T), Context(D, Ctx), Context\_Violation(D, CtxV).$

When the attribute obligatee is a role, we need an additional rule to derive obligations to subjects:

$Obligation(Auth, Subj_1, Subj_2, Act, Obj, Ctx, CtxV)$:-
$\quad Obligation(Auth, Subj_1, R, Act, Obj, Ctx, CtxV),$
$\quad Use(Auth, R, role), Empower(Auth, Sub_2, R).$

There are two other similar rules to respectively interpret duties when the attribute privilege is an activity and the attribute target is a view.

We define another rule to derive actual obligations (using predicate *Is-obliged*) for some subject, action and object when the obligation context is active:

$Is\_obliged(Sub, Act, Obj, CtxV)$:-
$\quad Obligation(Org, Ob, Sub, Act, Obj, C, CtxV), Hold(Org, Sub, Act, Obj, C).$

When the violation context is active and the obligation is not fulfilled by the obligatee, we need to derive a violation for this user. For this purpose, we introduce the two following predicates:

- **Violation** is a predicate over domains *SxSxAxO*. If s and s' are subjects, a is an action and o is an object, then *Violation(s,s',a,o)* means that subject s' has violated the obligation to perform action a on object o requested by subject s. When the predicate *Violation* is derived, a sanction must be imposed. This generally corresponds to the activation of new security rules (e.g. prohibitions or obligations).
- **Fulfilled** is a predicate over domains *SxSxAxO*. If s and s' are subjects, a is an action and o is an object, then *Fulfilled(s,s',a,o)* means that s' has fulfilled the obligation requested by s to perform a on o. When the predicate *Fulfilled* is derived the actual obligation (*Is_obliged*) is removed from the policy.

Now, we can define the following rule to derive violations when the violation context is active and the obligation is not fulfilled:

$Violation(S_1, S_2, Act, Obj)$:-
$\quad Is\_obliged(S_1, S_2, Act, Obj, CtxV), Hold(Org, S_2, Act, Obj, CtxV).$

4   Delegation of Obligations

The management of delegation is based on the AdOrBAC model. The delegation model is an extension of the administration model, using specific views called delegation views. There are two sub-views: **Licence_delegation** and **Licence_transfer** defined to manage the delegation and the transfer of obligations. Objects belonging to these views (i.e. duties) have the same attributes and semantics as duty objects belonging to the *Licence* view. They also have an additional attribute called *grantor*: subject who delegates the duty. This attribute is important to revoke the delegation and to recover the grantor initial duties when the transfer is revoked. Do not confuse attribute *grantor* with attribute *obligator*, the grantor is the subject who delegates his/her obligation and the obligator is the subject in favor of whom the duty is contracted. *Licence_delegation* and *Licence_transfer* views may also be used to delegate and transfer permissions (using licence objects). Moreover, there are other delegation views such as *role_delegation*, *role_transfer*, *grant_option* that may be used to deal with role delegation, role transfer, mutli-step delegation and agent-acted delegation, respectively. We have also proposed to deal with revocation features, such as cascade and strong revocation. We will not give more details about these aspects here but, we argue that thanks to the OrBAC facilities, namely the use of contexts and the object-oriented approach, it is possible to express administration requirements, including delegation and revocation requirements, in a single model (for further details see [1,2]). In this paper, we show how to manage obligation in our model and how to deal with features related to the delegation of obligations, such as the delegation with or without responsibility, the delegation with bilateral agreement, i.e. the obligatees consent is required to share the obligation or the responsibility.

Shared obligation with full responsibility. To share obligations, users may use view *Licence_delegation*. Since it is a sub-view of view *Licence* then inserting a duty in this view will derive an obligation for the obligatee. Note that we distinguish between obligation and responsibility. It is important to deal with these two notions because there is a difference between the delegation of an obligation to do some tasks and the delegation of the responsibility related to this obligation. As mentioned in [8], "in real life, the notion of obligation appears to include both interpretations, e.g. someone else may pay a traffic-offence fine for you, but may not go to jail for you". For this purpose, we define two kinds of shared obligations: with full and with limited responsibility. In the first case, the grantor delegates his/her obligation and also the responsibility of this obligation to the obligatee. This means that, the grantor and the obligatee are obliged to the same obligator. For instance, in a conference program committee the PC chair obligates a reviewer *Frederic* to review some article (*paper*01) after a given event activation (*begin_review*) and before a given deadline (*end_review*):

$Obligation(conf, pcChair, frederic, review, paper01, begin\_review, end\_review).$

where contexts *begin_review* and *end_review* are temporal contexts that represent the dates of the beginning and the end of the review process.

    Frederic delegates the obligation to review his article to another reviewer, say *Meriam*. For this purpose, he may insert a duty into the *Licence_delegation* view as follows: *Type*: Duty, *Auth*: Conf, *Grantor*: Frederic, *Obligator*:

PcChair, *Obligatee*: Meriam, *Task*: Review, *Target*: Paper01, *Context*: Immediate, *Context_Violation*: End_review.

So, the following obligation is created for *Meriam*:

Obligation(conf, pcChair, meriam, review, paper01, immediate, end_review).

where context *immediate* is activated immediately after the delegated obligation is created by *Frederic*.

In this case, *Meriam* (the obligatee) and *Frederic* (the grantor) are obliged to the PC chair (the obligator) and have the same responsibilities.

Shared obligation with limited responsibility. In this case the obligatee shares the obligation with the grantor, but does not share the responsibility with him/her. This means that he/she is obliged to the grantor and not to the original obligator. To explain this, let us consider a situation where, in organization *Supcom*, the professor *Adel* is obliged, in the context *exam_period*, to send back his students notes to the head of department before a given deadline D:

Obligation(supcom, head_dpt, adel, sendback, students_notes, exam_period, D).

Adel delegates this obligation with limited responsibility to his assistant, say *Meriam*. This means that, if the obligation is not fulfilled, then only *Adel* (the grantor) will be responsible to the head of department (the original obligator), and *Meriam* (the obligatee) will be responsible only to *Adel*:

Obligation(supcom, adel, meriam, sendback, students_notes, exam_period, D).

Note that, in our model, the difference between the delegation with full and with limited responsibility is the obligator attribute of the delegated duty. Indeed, in the context of limited responsibility the obligator is the grantor of the obligation. The management of these delegation is further discussed in section 5.

Transfer of Obligation. As we stated earlier, the obligation transfer is performed using view *Licence_transfer*. We define the following rule to deal with duties in this view:

Dispensation(Auth, Ob, Sub, Act, Obj, Ctx, CtxV):-
    Use(Org, D, licence_transfer), Type(D, duty), Auth(D, Auth),
    Grantor(D, Sub), Obligator(D, Ob), Task(D, Act),
    Target(D, Obj), Context(D, Ctx), Context_violation(D, CtxV).

According to this rule, inserting a duty in view *Licence_transfer* will derive a dispensation to the grantor. Obviously, it will also derive an obligation to the obligatee just like the delegation of obligation since, *Licence_transfer* is a subview of *Licence_delegation*. Notice that in the case of transfer it is not allowed to transfer a limited responsibility like in delegation. In fact, when the grantor transfers his/her obligation then he/she is neither obliged nor responsible of this obligation. Therefore, it is important to transfer the obligation with full responsibility to maintain the policy consistency.

Fulfillment and propagation. In the case of shared obligation, the obligation is considered fulfilled if either the grantor or the obligatee performs the task. For this purpose, we define the following rule:

$Fulfilled(S_1, S_2, A, O)$:-
$\quad Fulfilled(S_3, S_4, A, O), Use(Org, D, licence\_delegation),$
$\quad Type(D, duty), Obligator(D, S_3), Obligatee(D, S_4), Grantor(D, S_2),$
$\quad Task(D, A), Target(D, O), Is\_obliged(S_1, S_2, A, O).$

This rule means that if a shared obligation is fulfilled by an obligatee S_4, then we derive a fulfillment to the grantor S_2, if he/she still has the concrete obligation. Note that obligator S_3 and grantor S_2 may be the same user, i.e. in the case of delegation with limited responsibility. Otherwise, in the case of full responsibility, S_3 and S_1 are the same user. Conversely, we define another rule to derive a fulfillment to the obligatee, if the grantor fulfills the obligation. But, in this case it is important to check that there is no other similar[1] obligations delegated by another user to this obligatee:

$Fulfilled(S_1, S_2, A, O)$:-
$\quad Fulfilled(S_1, S_3, A, O), Use(Org, D, licence\_delegation),$
$\quad Type(D, duty), Obligator(D, S_1), Obligatee(D, S_2), Grantor(D, S_3),$
$\quad Task(D, A), Target(D, O), Is\_obliged(S_1, S_2, A, O),$
$\quad \neg(Use(Org, D', licence\_delegation), Type(D', duty),$
$\quad Obligator(D', S_1), Obligatee(D', S_2), Grantor(D', S_4), \neg(S_4 = S_3),$
$\quad Task(D', A), Target(D', O), Is\_obliged(S_1, S_4, A, O)).$

This rule means that, if there is a shared obligation fulfilled by grantor S_3, then a fulfillment is derived to obligatee S_2 if these conditions are satisfied: (1) S_2 still has the concrete obligation and, (2) there is no similar active obligation[2] delegated to S_2 by a different grantor S_4. To explain this let us turn back to the conference program committee example. We assume that the obligation to review *paper01* is also assigned to the reviewer *Nora*, which also delegates it to *Meriam*. Therefore, when *Frederic* performs the review of this paper, we should not derive a fulfillment for *Meriam* since the delegated obligation by *Nora* is still active. Note that in this case the delegation is necessary with full responsibility. Otherwise, grantor S_3 and obligator S_1 are the same user and similarly for grantor S_4 and obligator S_1. But, in our defined rule, S_3 and S_4 must be different users.

Delegation consent. In our model, we distinguish between two forms of delegation: bilateral agreement delegation (with obligatee's consent) and unilateral agreement (without consent request). In fact, according to the relationships between the grantor and the obligatee, the consent of this latter may be required or not to perform the delegation of obligation. We consider that there are two basic types of relationships: power relationships where one user is a subservient to another user and peer relationships where neither user is subservient to other user. To manage users communication [15], we define two speech acts as follows:

$Question(Sender, Receiver, Request(Action, Object)).$
$Answer(Sender, Receiver, Request(Action, Object)).$

---

[1] We consider that obligations are similar if they concern the same obligator, obligatee, task and target.

[2] By active obligation we mean that there is a concrete obligation.

where *Action* may be a delegation action (i.e. delegate, transfer, revoke), *Object* may be a delegation duty and *Answer* may be a *Positive_Answer* or a *Negative_Answer*. Therefore, a grantor may request the consent of another user (the obligatee) when he/she wants to delegate (transfer or revoke) to him/her a given obligation. We consider that in the case of power relationships the grantor is allowed to delegate his/her obligations without the consent of the obligatee. Otherwise, the grantor is obliged to request the obligatee's consent and the delegation is allowed only if a positive response is received. More details about the management of the delegation policy are presented in the following section. Note that, the consent request may also be used in the case of delegation (transfer or revocation) of permissions and roles. In addition, we may use these speech acts to request a right by delegation, this means that a user may request another user to delegate (transfer or revoke) to him/her a given permission or role.

5   Delegation Policy Management

In our model, to manage the delegation policy, i.e. which users are allowed to delegate (transfer or revoke) their obligations, the administrator should specify which user is permitted to have an access to the delegation views (i.e. insert or delete objects from these views). Moreover, thanks to the use of contexts, different conditions can be specified to restrict the delegation rights. For instance, we may specify that users are allowed to delegate their obligations without the consent of the obligatee, in the case of power relationships[3]:

$Permission(Org, default\_role, delegate, licence\_delegation, power\_relationships)$.

where context *power_relationships* holds if there is a power relationships between the grantor and the obligatee, for instance a hierarchical relationship:

$Hold(Org, U, delegate, D, power\_relationships)$:-
    $Use(Org, D, licence\_delegation), Type(D, duty), Grantor(D, U), Obligatee(D, U')$,
    $Empower(Org, U, R), Empower(Org, U', R'), Sub\_role(Org, R', R)$.

We may also define that users are allowed to delegate their obligations (either in power or peer relationships) if the obligatee's consent is received:

$Permission(org, default\_role, delegate, licence\_delegation, consent\_deleg)$.

where context *consent_deleg* is defined as follows:

$Hold(Org, U, delegate, D, consent\_deleg)$:-
    $Use(D, licence\_delegation), Type(D, duty), Grantor(D, U)$,
    $Obligatee(D, U'), Question(U, U', request(delegate, D))$,
    $Positive\_Answer(U', U, request(delegate, D))$.

Other contexts may be defined to manage the right to delegate obligations with full or with limited responsibility. For instance, context *limited_respons*:

$Hold(Org, U, delegate, D, limited\_respons)$:-
    $Use(D, licence\_delegation), Type(D, duty)$,
    $Grantor(D, U), Obligator(D, U)$.

$Permission(org, default\_role, delegate, licence\_delegation, limited\_respons)$.

---

[3] *default_Role* is a role in which all authorized users are empowered.

This permission means that users are allowed to delegate their obligations in the context *limited_respons*, i.e. the obligator is the grantor of the obligation.

6   Related Work

Contrary to the delegation of roles and permissions that have been largely discussed in existing models, delegation of obligations are relatively neglected especially in role-based delegation models. This is due to the fact that obligations and their management are not widely addressed in role-based models. We give in this section some of the works present in the literature that are related to the delegation of obligations. In [8] authors propose four different forms of delegation, namely transfer, sharing, splitting and outsourcing, but they only discuss these classifications and do not specify a model to manage delegation. As in our model, they consider that in the case of transfer the grantor is no longer obliged to perform the obligation. In shared obligation the obligatee shares also the responsibility of the obligation, this is equivalent to the delegation with full responsibility in our case. A split obligation occurs when the action required is split into two (or more) parts, this is not addressed in our paper, since we have only considered obligations on atomic actions. Finally, outsourced obligation occurs when the grantor of the obligation is also the obligator of this obligation, this is equivalent to the delegation with limited responsibility in our model. [9] only considers the sharing of obligations with full responsibility and the transfer of obligations. Three forms of delegation are defined: delegation by command, through a joint action and by institutional context. The first form is equivalent, in our model, to the delegation in the context of power relationships. Delegation through a joint action corresponds to the delegation in the case of peer relationships when the bilateral agreement is required, and finally, the delegation by institutional context is equivalent to the agent-based delegation in our model. In [10] authors propose to deal with the delegation of obligation using the Alloy specification language. In this work only the transfer of obligations is supported and authors consider that the obligator must review that the obligatee carried the delegated task out satisfactorily before the deadline. In other words, the grantor is considered as the obligator of the obligation he/she delegates. These works do not propose a sufficient means to deal with all the delegation requirements presented in this paper. Moreover, unlike our model, they do not explicitly show how the delegation policy is managed, i.e. how to specify who is allowed to delegate obligations, which obligations can be delegated and in which conditions. Thanks to the use of the OrBAC formalism (e.g. organizational approach and contexts), our proposed model is more comprehensive and it provides means to manage fine-grained delegation.

7   Conclusion

Our main aim in this paper was to study the issue of the delegation of obligations and to identify the related requirements. Due to space limitation, we have proposed to deal with some of these requirements, such as the sharing and the transfer of obligations, the notion of responsibility, the delegation with consent, the propagation and the fulfillment of obligations. We also gave some examples to show how the delegation policy can be managed using contexts. Many more features still remain to be discussed. One of these features is to consider obligations on non-atomic actions and manage the delegation of sub-obligations (splitting obligation). We may also specify that the violation context of the delegated obligation is consistent with the task delay, this means that we must be able to express such constraint: the grantor is not allowed to delegate an obligation to review a paper within a short delay, e.g. one day. Another feature is to allow the grantor to specify the sanction in the case of delegation with limited responsibility (i.e. he/she is the obligator), but in this case we must be able to control these sanctions. Moreover, we propose to further study the users communication protocol, so that users may negotiate the delegation that they receive. For instance, the obligatee may negotiate the sanction or the responsibility of the obligation he/she receives by delegation. Finally, we plan to propose a conflict management strategy to deal with the policy consistency such as in [16].

Acknowledgments. This work is partially funded by the FLUOR project (ANR-07-SESU-005-01).

References

1. Ben-Ghorbel, M., Cuppens, F., Cuppens-Boulahia, N., Bouhoula, A.: Managing Delegation in Access Control Models. In: ADCOM (2007)
2. Ben-Ghorbel-Talbi, M., Cuppens, F., Cuppens-Boulahia, N., Bouhoula, A.: Revocation schemes for delegation licences. In: Chen, L., Ryan, M.D., Wang, G. (eds.) ICICS 2008. LNCS, vol. 5308, pp. 190–205. Springer, Heidelberg (2008)
3. Bettini, C., Jajodia, S., Wang, X., Wijesekera, D.: Obligation Monitoring in Policy Management. In: POLICY (2002)
4. Cuppens, F., Cuppens-Boulahia, N., Sans, T.: Nomad: a Security Model with Non Atomic Actions and Deadlines. In: CSFW (2005)
5. Gama, P., Ferreira, P.: Obligation Policies: An Enforcement Platform. In: POLICY (2005)
6. Park, J., Sandhu, R.: The UCON$_{ABC}$ Usage Control Model. TISSEC 7(1) (2004)
7. Pretschner, A., Hilty, M., Basin, D.: Distributed Usage Control. Communications of the ACM (2006)
8. Cole, J., Derrick, J., Milosevic, Z., Raymond, K.: Author obliged to submit paper before 4 july: Policies in an enterprise specification. In: Sloman, M., Lobo, J., Lupu, E.C. (eds.) POLICY 2001. LNCS, vol. 1995, p. 1. Springer, Heidelberg (2001)
9. Pacheco, O., Santos, F.: Delegation in a role-based organization. In: Lomuscio, A., Nute, D. (eds.) DEON 2004. LNCS, vol. 3065, pp. 209–227. Springer, Heidelberg (2004)
10. Schaad, A., Moffett, J.D.: Delegation of Obligations. In: POLICY (2002)
11. Abou-El-Kalam, A., Benferhat, S., Miège, A., Baida, R.E., Cuppens, F., Saurel, C., Balbiani, P., Deswarte, Y., Trouessin, G.: Organization Based Access Control. In: POLICY (2003)

12. Cuppens, F., Cuppens, N.: Modeling Contextual Security Policies. IJIS 7 (2008)
13. Cuppens, F., Miège, A.: Administration Model for Or-BAC. CSSE 19(3) (2004)
14. Cuppens, F., Cuppens-Boulahia, N., Coma, C.: Multi-Granular Licences to Decentralize Security Administration. In: SSS/WRAS (2007)
15. Kagal, L., Finin, T.: Modeling Conversation Policies using Permissions and Obligations. JAAMAS 14(2) (2007)
16. Cuppens, F., Cuppens-Boulahia, N., Ben-Ghorbel, M.: High Level Conflict Management Strategies in Advanced Access Control Models. ENTCS 186 (2007)

The OPL Access Control Policy Language*

Christopher Alm[1], Ruben Wolf[2], and Joachim Posegga[3]

[1] Steria Mummert Consulting AG, Germany
christopher.alm@steria-mummert.de
[2] Fraunhofer SIT, Darmstadt, Germany
ruben.wolf@sit.fraunhofer.de
[3] Institute of IT Security and Security Law, Passau, Germany
itsec@uni-passau.de

Abstract. Existing policy languages suffer from a limited ability of directly and elegantly expressing high-level access control principles such as history-based separation of duty [22], binding of duty [26], context constraints [24], Chinese wall properties [10], and obligations [20]. It is often difficult to extend a language in order to retrofit these features once required or it is necessary to use complicated and complex language constructs to express such concepts. The latter, however, is cumbersome and error-prone for humans dealing with policy administration.

We present the flexible policy language *OPL* that can represent a wide range of access control principles in XML directly, by providing dedicated language constructs for each supported principle. It can be easily extended with further principles if necessary. OPL is based on a module concept, and it can easily cope with the language complexity that usually comes with a growing expressiveness. OPL is suitable to be used in an enterprise environment, since it combines the required expressiveness with the simplicity necessary for an appropriate administration.

1 Introduction

Role-based access control (RBAC) is a well-understood concept and many RBAC-based systems and models have been proposed [15,16]. Although RBAC facilitates permission management, in particular in enterprise domains, existing RBAC systems and models have to be carefully analysed whether they keep their promises: RBAC as a security mechanism for efficient permission management might provide considerable advantages, but systems implemented on the top of a RBAC security mechanism, i.e. the real access control management implementation, do not necessarily match this. However, if management systems lack suitable administrative support—by means of functionality and usability—they might even have negative impacts on the effective security level of the underlying security mechanism[11].

---

* This work was supported by the German Ministry of Education and Research (BMBF) as part of the project ORKA (http://www.orka-projekt.de).

S. Fischer-Hübner et al. (Eds.): TrustBus 2009, LNCS 5695, pp. 138–148, 2009.

In order to assess the suitability of an actual role-based management system, we suggest to review the characteristics of policy specification and administration with respect to complexity and expressiveness:

Firstly, *complexity* can be examined by the compactness of permission specifications, e.g. whether a specific access control concept requires 10 or 100 lines within the access control policy. Additionally, the degree of complexity may also be analyzed by usability and administrative comfort. This includes, e.g., all functions of a management system supporting administrators and efforts to reduce administrative errors that result in insecure systems. Secondly, *expressiveness* of access control systems can be considered with respect to their extensibility, e.g. the ability to enrich the applied policy language with new authorization constraints. Expressiveness may also be estimated in respect to the number of supported access control primitives and the ability to express high-level access control concepts—such as Chinese wall [10] or history-based separation of duty constraints [22]—elegantly and directly without complicated and lengthy low-level language constructs.

Our observation is that existing solutions in RBAC do not address the competing issues of complexity vs. expressiveness very well: They can not offer the expressiveness required by organizations without being complicated and confronting the administration of high-level access control principle with too much complexity. We address this issue in this paper by presenting a new policy language, OPL, which has been embedded in an organizational control architecture as part of the ORKA project [1]. OPL is an abbreviation for *ORKA Policy Language*. The syntax and semantics of the language are defined in full detail in a technical report [5]. Our main contributions are the following:

– A new policy language OPL which is based on the principle of modularizing the supported access control concepts. Each concept is represented by a dedicated high-level language construct called *policy module*, which can be (re-)used and combined with other policy modules in order to create a policy (cf. Sect. 2). OPL is the policy language of the ORKA organizational control architecture developed in the ORKA research project [1]; in particular a rich tool set for OPL has been developed, which includes an administration tool, two different enforcement engines, and policy validation tools. OPL is an XML application and has a formal semantics in Object Z.
– We demonstrate how policy modules can be used to match the expressiveness required by an organization (cf. Sect. 3). OPL directly supports advanced access control principles which, to the best of our knowledge, cannot be expressed by means of dedicated high-level language constructs in any other existing policy language. Examples of such principles are history-based separation of duty or binding of duty on the task layer. We have developed a suite of policy modules which can express the policies of the ORKA case studies, in particular the one from Schaad et al. [22].
– We show that the modularization concept introduced by OPL is the right approach for coping with the complexity of highly expressive policy languages: For each application of OPL we support only what is really required by the

organization, thus we keep the application of the policy language streamlined and focused (cf. Sect. 3 and 2).

– We show how OPL can be extended with new features in Section 2.1.

2   OPL Overview

2.1   Language Structure

OPL represents each access control principle such as separation of duty or context constraints by means of a dedicated *policy module*. Such policy modules can be seen as building blocks that are combined to form a policy. The combination works as follows: During the policy engineering process the policy designer *selects* all the required policy modules and fills them with data of the specific scenario. A policy module A may depend on another policy module B; so, whenever one selects A it is necessary to select B as well. Figure 1 shows our current set of modules and their dependencies. A dependency is shown as UML generalization where specific classes depend on more general ones. It should be noted that in cases where the concept of roles is not needed, such as in Chinese wall, modules could also have been made depended from a more general root module than RBAC.

For example, *RBACCoreM* comprises basically the core component of the RBAC standard [15], *RoleHierarchyM* adds a role hierarchy, *SepDutyM* adds separation of duty, *ExoContextM* adds exogenous context constraints similar to Strembeck and Neumann's approach [24], and *WFCoreM* and its submodules add workflow related concepts such as history-based separation of duty for tasks and prerequisite constraints.

The extensibility of OPL is achieved by adding a new policy module for any newly required access control concept. The formal semantics and the XML syntax of OPL directly support this kind of extension because they are based on a dedicated extensible framework [2].

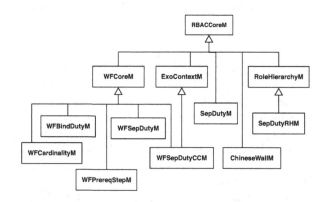

Fig. 1. Current Policy Module Hierarchy

Since each application of OPL has to include only the policy modules needed to express the required access control concepts, administration may focus on these policy modules. For each policy module a dedicated user interface may be provided, which reduces the complexity of the policy language.

2.2 Policy Model vs. Policy Objects

Before we explain OPL at a more detailed level, it is important to distinguish between the notion of the *policy model* and the notion of a *policy object*. The policy model defines the structure and the properties of a policy and the rules according to which policies are created. In contrast, a policy object is the representation of a concrete policy with real data for a concrete scenario. This is very similar to the distinction between classes and objects in object-oriented programming.

2.3 Policy Modules

As pointed out above, an OPL policy is a combination of policy modules encompassing the access control principles. This subsection describes the combination of policy modules from the perspective of OPL policy objects (i.e. the actual OPL policies) as well as from the perspective of the OPL policy model.

Policy Object Perspective. From the perspective of a policy object, a policy module consists of all the necessary static data that needs to be loaded by a policy decision point in order to be able to enforce the access control principle provided through the module. For example, with regard to RBAC, these static data comprise the users, roles, permissions, user assignment, and permission assignment. Dynamic data created by the PDP at run time, such as session data and role activations as well as context information that needs to be retrieved from the environment, is not stored in the policy object. The format or syntax of policy objects, an XML application in which the selected policy modules are concatenated (cf. Section 2.4).

Policy Model Perspective. From the perspective of a policy model, a policy module comprises the following definitions. Note that these definitions have to be made whenever introducing a new policy module.

- **Data types:** A policy module must declare all the data types out of which its data structures are constructed. These data types may be used to introduce name spaces. For example, *RBACCoreM* introduces the name space *ROLE*, from which all role names must be chosen.
- **Data structures:** A policy module defines all its data structures in terms of sets and relations. For example, *RBACCoreM* introduces the user assignment relation $UA \subseteq U \times R$.
- **Dependencies:** It needs to be specified on which other policy modules a policy module depends upon. In case of dependency of module A on module

B, it is allowed and sometimes required in A to refer to data that has been introduced by B. For example, in the separation of duty module, only those roles that have been defined in the RBAC core module are allowed to be declared as critical roles.

- **Enforcement semantics:** A policy module defines rules according to which an access decision is made. While we have developed a full formal semantics in Object Z for OPL, this paper mostly uses informal descriptions since our discussion here does not need to refer to the formal semantics (cf. Section 2.5). Furthermore, we have implemented two policy decision engines based on this semantics (cf. Section 2.6).
- **Administrative constraints:** A policy module may define rules about its data structures that must not be violated by the administration of the policy. Such rules may incorporate data from other policy modules the it depends upon. An example is static separation of duty: the policy module ensures that no user is assigned to two critical roles. Such rules are enforced automatically by the ORKA administration tool.

The combination of all defined policy modules is the OPL policy model; in terms of its formal semantics, this combination is realized through a logical conjunction.

2.4   XML Syntax

We have developed an XML DTD comprising all the data structures of the OPL policy model. In this DTD, the single policy modules are simply concatenated. By relying on this DTD, an implementation of the policy model (i.e. a policy engine) can store all its static policy data in an XML file.

For illustration consult Figures 2 and 3: They show excerpts of the DTD for user assignments and for separation of duty critical role sets. An example of a policy object in XML representation is given in Section 3.

2.5   Formal Semantics

We have developed a full formal representation of the OPL policy model (i.e. formal semantics). Since the focus of this paper is on OPL itself rather than on

```
<!ELEMENT user_assignments
    (user_assignment)*>
<!ELEMENT user_assignment EMPTY>
<!ATTLIST user_assignment
    role_id CDATA #REQUIRED
    user_id CDATA #REQUIRED>
```

Fig. 2. User Assignments

```
<!ELEMENT static_separation_of_duty
    (critical_role_sets)>
<!ELEMENT critical_role_sets
    (critical_role_set)*>
<!ELEMENT critical_role_set
    (critical_roles)>
<!ATTLIST critical_role_set
    cardinality CDATA #REQUIRED
    name CDATA #IMPLIED
    description CDATA #IMPLIED
>
<!ELEMENT critical_roles (critical_role)+>
<!ELEMENT critical_role EMPTY>
<!ATTLIST critical_role
    role_id CDATA #REQUIRED >
```

Fig. 3. Critical Role Sets

$[USER, ROLE, PERM,$
$SESSION]$

$DECISION ::= grant \mid deny$

```
__ RBACCorePolicy _____
  U : ℙ USER
  R : ℙ ROLE
  P : ℙ PERM
  UA : USER ↔ ROLE
  PA : ROLE ↔ PERM
  _____
  UA ⊆ U × R
  PA ⊆ R × P
```

```
__ RBACCoreM _____
  _____
  Policy : ↓RBACCorePolicy_©
  S : ℙ SESSION
  SR : S ↔ Policy.R
  SU : S → Policy.U
  _____
  Policy ∈ ↓RBACCorePolicy
  ∀ s : S • SR(|{s}|) ⊆ Policy.UA(|{SU(s)}|)

  __ CheckAccess _____
  s? : SESSION
  p? : PERM
  d! : DECISION
  _____
  d! = grant ⇒ ∃ r : ROLE; p : PERM •
    (s?, r) ∈ SR ∧ (r, p) ∈ Policy.PA
    ∧ p ∈ Policy.P
```

Fig. 4. RBAC Core Module (Object Z)

the formalism behind, we only briefly sketch the formal semantics. Generally, the formal semantics is useful for two reasons: First, it gives a a precise definition of the policy model without ambiguities. This turned out to be very useful for resolving misinterpretations, conflicts, and confusion during the implementation of the OPL engines. Second, a major part of the ORKA project is focused on using formal reasoning techniques for policy validation, so a formal semantics for the underlying policy model is inevitable.

The formal semantics of OPL is expressed in the Object Z [23] formal specification language. Figure 4 shows the definition of the RBAC core policy module. Since RBAC is a widely known model, this Object Z specification should be to some extend self-explaining and we explain only the basic features.

The formal semantics covers all the items listed in Section 2.3 such as data structures, data types, dependencies, enforcement semantics, and administrative constraints. At the beginning, the used data types such as *ROLE* are introduced. The class *RBACCorePolicy* contains the data structures of the policy (above the short line) as well as the administrative constraints as class invariants (below the short line). The enforcement semantics is given by the class *RBACCoreM* by the definition of the operation *CheckAccess*. Dependencies are not available here since *RBACCoreM* does not depend on any other modules. They would be shown as a list of parent classes in both classes.

It is obvious from the formal semantics that our policy model clearly separates information stored in the policy (cf. *RBACCorePolicy* class) from dynamic information such as role activation necessary for the policy enforcement (cf. *RBACCoreM* class). With regard to the definition of a policy language, this is a clear advantage of our policy model over traditional RBAC models and their extensions [15,9,24]. It is only necessary to encode the data structures of the policy (cf. *RBACCorePolicy* class) by means of the DTD (cf. Section 2.4) for defining a policy language in our approach.

2.6   Implementation

OPL is the policy language of the organizational control architecture developed by the ORKA project [1]; we developed a prototype implementation of the complete architecture, and a rich tool set for OPL, including an administration tool and two policy engines.

The administration tool developed by Mustafa et al. [21] makes use of an encoding of the administrative constraints of our policy model in the USE tool. Thereby it is automatically ensured that an administrator does not violate any administrative constraints (i.e. structural properties) of OPL. For example, it is impossible to create a policy with inconsistent static separation of duty constraints. Furthermore, the administration tool provides a graphical user interface to give administrators easy access to all OPL features (i.e. policy modules). We have also implemented two policy engines:

- Our **Java native engine** is a straightforward implementation of the OPL policy model in Java. It supports all policy modules shown in Figure 1 and it can be connected to context providers such as the workflow management system via a sophisticated context information framework.
- An **XACML engine:** in order to bring OPL tools, advantages, and solutions to the XACML world, we have developed a translator from OPL to XACML. We discovered constraints which can only be expressed in XACML by making use of lengthy rule sets with complex XACML targets that need to be dovetailed with each other. An Example is HDSoDTPCC, as shown in Section 3, where we needed to duplicate critical task sets in XACML that need to be synchronized with each other. However, it would be beyond the scope of this paper to go into the details of this translation. It will be treated in a follow-up paper.

We conducted a performance test to compare our OPL Java native enforcement engine with the SUN XACML reference implementation [25] where both enforce a congruent policy. In all test scenarios, the OPL engine was significantly faster. Full details and precise results will be documented in a subsequent paper.

3   Policy Modules and Their Application

We exemplify our approach with the banking scenario described by Schaad et al. [22] and explain how to specify real-world requirements representing advanced access control principles with our modularization approach. We selected two requirements from the loan origination process for this (cf. Table 3 of [22]) that include separation of duty constraints as well as operational or workflow-based constraints. We show their realization in OPL by module selection and combination; note that we show only fragments of the policy necessary to implement the respective requirements. A comprehensive example, i.e. a model of the full banking scenario in OPL, is available in a technical report [5].

Requirement 1: No person may be assigned to the two exclusive roles pre/post processor. First, both roles are declared using module `module_rbac_core_policy`. Second, we use the `module_sep_duty_policy` module to specify a static separation of duty constraint between both clerk roles (cf. Fig. 5).

Requirement 7: If the customer is an industrial customer, then a clerk may perform tasks 1 to 9 or 10, but not both for the same customer. This requirement represents an operational separation of duty constraint or a special kind of dynamic separation of duty property that requires contextual information about the execution path of a workflow and the specific case (customer) that was manipulated. For the realization we use two OPL modules (cf. Fig. 6). First, the context constraint `industrial` is specified with the module `module_exo_context_policy`. A context constraint can be specified using any context function available in the system represented by its function name and its necessary parameters. In our example, a customer information provider returns the type of the given customer as a string. Second, we use the formerly declared context constraint in the module `module_wf_sep_duty_cc` to specify a

```
<module_rbac_core_policy>
 <roles>
  <role role_id="clerk_pre"/>
  <role role_id="clerk_pre"/>
 <roles>
<module_rbac_core_policy>

<module_sep_duty_policy>
<static_separation_of_duty>
 <critical_role_sets>
  <critical_role_set
    cardinality="2">
   <critical_roles>
    <critical_role
      role_id="clerk_pre"/>
    <critical_role
      role_id="clerk_post"/>
   </critical_roles>
  </critical_role_set>
 </critical_role_sets>
</static_separation_of_duty>
</module_sep_duty_policy>
```

```
<module_exo_context_policy>
 <context_constraint cc_id="is_industrial">
  <context_function_id id="equals"/>
  <context_function_parameters>
   <parameter value="cust_info_provider.get_type(cust-id)"
     type="context" />
   <parameter value="industrial" type="string" />
  </context_function_parameters>
 </context_constraint>
</module_exo_context_policy>

<module_wf_sep_duty_cc_policy>
 <hdsodtpcc>
  <hdsodtpcc_partitioning cc_id="is_industrial">
   <hdsodtpcc_partition>
    <cc_partition_task task_id="1_input_cust_data"/>
    <cc_partition_task task_id="2_customer_ident"/>
    <cc_partition_task task_id="3_check_cred_worthin"/>
    <cc_partition_task task_id="4_check_rating"/>
    <cc_partition_task task_id="5_bank_signs_form"/>
    <cc_partition_task task_id="6_choose_bundled_prod"/>
    <cc_partition_task task_id="7_price_bundled_prod"/>
    <cc_partition_task task_id="8_print_opening_form"/>
    <cc_partition_task task_id="9_customer_signs_form"/>
   </hdsodtpcc_partition>
   <hdsodtpcc_partition>
    <cc_partition_task task_id="10_bank_signs_form"/>
   </hdsodtpcc_partition>
  </hdsodtpcc_partitioning>
 </hdsodtpcc>
</module_wf_sep_duty_cc_policy>
```

Fig. 5. Requirement 1 in OPL

Fig. 6. Requirement 7 in OPL

history-based separation of duty constraint with task partitionings depending on a context constraint (HDSoDTPCC); i.e. this constraint applies only if the context constraint is_industrial evaluates to true. Informally, this history-based separation of duty constraint has the semantics that once a user executed a task which is included in some partition, the user is bound to this partition in the future; i.e.: he or she is only allowed to perform tasks that are also included in the same partition. However, the user is allowed to perform tasks that are not included in any partition of the partitioning. Note that this constraint works on a per workflow-instance basis. Our experience has shown that this new kind of constraint has a potential to implement many of today's business requirements.

   The examples above show that OPL as policy language provides a direct and elegant matter to specify advanced access control requirements.

4   Related Work

Numerous access control policy languages and models have been proposed in the literature; we outline a few of them that are particularly significant w.r.t. our approach: OASIS XACML[20] is rule-based policy mark-up language that can mostly simulate the ANSI RBAC standard using the role-based profile[6]. XACML supports authorization constraints such as mutual exclusion, history, and dynamic conditions. By default, XACML cannot express important organizational principles such as delegation or workflow-aware policies. XACML can be extended with respect to its expressiveness, however, logical quantification is missing in order to express constraints in a direct and elegant way. The flexibility and expressiveness results in verbosity and complexity[18]. The Ponder policy framework[13,12] provides a strongly-typed and rule-based language. With respect to expressiveness, the language uses OCL for constraints. It supports time-, history-, and object-based constraints. Ponder has a notion of roles, delegation, and obligation. It is barely compatible with the ANSI RBAC standard. Approaches for formal semantics and policy reasoning[7,17,19] may reduce administrative complexity. Dynamic constraints like history-based constraints cannot be validated. The X-GTRBAC policy framework[9,8] defines a semi-formal, XML-based policy specification language which is compatible with the RBAC standard and supports static, dynamic and temporal constraints. With respect to complexity, the standard model may be extended by a decentralized administration model with support for administrative domains. With respect to policy validation, the X-GTRBAC framework supports consistency checks but no inference rules. The Adage authorization toolkit[27] provides a semi-formal language. With respect to expressiveness, the language supports static and dynamic constraints (e.g. operational, object-based and history-based) and various security models such as Chinese Wall or Bell La-Padula. Workflow-based constraints are not supported. The Adage language has a somewhat fixed expressiveness and cannot easily extended. The language is not compatible with the RBAC standard although it is similar. It has no formal semantics, there is no approach to reduce administrative complexity by means of policy validation and resolving conflicting policy rules. Fernandez et al. [14] provide an UML-based pattern system for classification of access control models that can help system designers to find suitable access control models. In contrast to their promising pattern approach we provide an authorization architecture comprising of a universal policy language, a formal semantics and respective engines that allows the modeling and enforcement of arbitrary access control methods and models. For our approach we decided not to use UML (or UML/OCL) due to its lack of formal semantics and human readability. More details and additional related models and languages are described in technical reports[4,3].

5   Conclusions and Future Work

This paper presented OPL, a flexible policy language which aims at bridging the gap between the expressiveness required by organizations and the simplicity needed for practical administration. This is accomplished, on the one hand, by OPL's property of representing high-level access control principles as single modules, and by the possibility of combining the modules. Through the availability of an administration tool that is directly based on this modular language structure, OPL policies can be administered more easily: during policy administration, an administrator needs to focus only on one policy module at a time. On the other hand, OPL's expressiveness and extensibility is achieved in such a way that any feature can be added as a separate and possibly new module. Furthermore, we have demonstrated that our current set of modules can already enforce important access control requirements.

As future work, we strive for extending our library of policy modules, in particular to encompass a delegation concept. Finally, a follow-up paper will address our translation from OPL to XACML.

References

1. The ORKA Project Homepage, http://www.orka-projekt.de/index-en.htm
2. Alm, C.: An Extensible Framework for Specifying and Reasoning About Complex Role-Based Access Control Models. Technical Report MIP-0901, Department of Informatics and Mathematics. University of Passau, Germany (2009)
3. Alm, C., Drouineaud, M.: Analysis of Existing Policy Languages. Technical report, ORKA Consortium (2007), http://www.orka-projekt.de/download/del-ap2.3-requirements-policy-language.pdf
4. Alm, C., Drouineaud, M., Faltin, U., Sohr, K., Wolf, R.: On Classifying Authorization Constraints Approaches. Technical report, ORKA Consortium (2006), http://www.orka-projekt.de/download/del-ap2.1-authorization-constraints.pdf
5. Alm, C., Wolf, R.: The Definition of the OPL Access Control Policy Language. Technical Report MIP-0902, Department of Informatics and Mathematics. University of Passau, Germany (2009)
6. Anderson, A.: XACML Profile for Role Based Access Control, RBAC (2004)
7. Bandara, A.: A Formal Approach to Analysis and Refinement of Policies. PhD thesis (2005)

8. Bertino, E., Bonatti, P., Ferrari, E.: TRBAC: A Temporal Role-based Access Control Model. In: Proc. of the 5th ACM Workshop on Role-Based Access Control, July 26–27, pp. 21–30. ACM Press, New York (2000)
9. Bhatti, R., et al.: X-GTRBAC: an XML-based policy specification framework and architecture for enterprise-wide access control. ACM TISSEC 8(2), 187–227 (2005)
10. Brewer, D., Nash, M.: The Chinese Wall Security Policy. In: Proc. of IEEE Symposium on Security and Privacy, pp. 206–214 (1989)
11. Chiasson, S., Biddle, R., Somayaji, A.: Even Experts Deserve Usable Security: Design guidelines for security management systems. In: Workshop on Usable IT Security Management, USM 2007 (2007)
12. Damianou, N.: A Policy Framework for Management of Distributed Systems. PhD thesis, University of London (2002)
13. Damianou, N., Dulay, N., Lupu, E.C., Sloman, M.: The Ponder Policy Specification Language. In: Sloman, M., Lobo, J., Lupu, E.C. (eds.) POLICY 2001. LNCS, vol. 1995, pp. 18–28. Springer, Heidelberg (2001)
14. Fernandez, E.B., Pernul, G., Larrondo-Petrie, M.M.: Patterns and Pattern Diagrams for Access Control. In: Furnell, S.M., Katsikas, S.K., Lioy, A. (eds.) TrustBus 2008. LNCS, vol. 5185, pp. 38–47. Springer, Heidelberg (2008)
15. Ferraiolo, D., Sandhu, R., Gavrila, S., Kuhn, D., Chandramouli, R.: Proposed NIST standard for role-based access control. ACM TISSEC 4(3) (2001)
16. Ferraiolo, D.F., Kuhn, D.R., Chandramouli, R.: Role-Based Access Control. Computer Security Series. Artech House, Boston (2003)
17. Kowalski, R., Sergot, M.: A Logic-based Calculus of Events. New Gen. Comput. 4(1), 67–95 (1986)
18. Lorch, M., et al.: First Experiences Using XACML for Access Control in Distributed Systems. In: Proc. of the ACM workshop on XML Security (2003)
19. Lupu, E.C., Sloman, M.: Conflicts in Policy-Based Distributed Systems Management. IEEE Trans. Softw. Eng. 25(6), 852–869 (1999)
20. Moses, T.: eXtensible Access Control Markup Language (XACML) Version 2.0, 2005. OASIS Standard (2005)
21. Mustafa, T., et al.: Implementing Advanced RBAC Administration Functionality with USE. In: Proc. of the 8th Int. Workshop on OCL Concepts and Tools (2008)
22. Schaad, A., Lotz, V., Sohr, K.: A Model-checking Approach to Analysing Organisational Controls. In: Proc. of 11th ACM SACMAT, pp. 139–149 (2006)
23. Smith, G.: The Object-Z Specification Language. Springer, Heidelberg (2000)
24. Strembeck, M., Neumann, G.: An Integrated Approach to Engineer and Enforce Context Constraints in RBAC Environments. ACM TISSEC 7(3) (2004)
25. Sun Microsystems, Inc., http://sunxacml.sourceforge.net/
26. Wainer, J., et al.: W-RBAC - A Workflow Security Model Incorporating Controlled Overriding of Constraints. Int. J. Cooperative Inf. Syst. 12(4), 455–485 (2003)
27. Zurko, M., Simon, R., Sanfilippo, T.: A User-Centered, Modular Authorization Service Built on an RBAC Foundation. In: Proc. of the IEEE Symposium Security and Privacy, Oakland, CA, May 1999, pp. 57–71. IEEE Computer Society Press, Los Alamitos (1999)

Operational Semantics for DKAL: Application and Analysis

Yuri Gurevich[1] and Arnab Roy[2,⋆]

[1] Microsoft Research Redmond
gurevich@microsoft.com
[2] Stanford University
arnab@cs.stanford.edu

Abstract. DKAL is a new expressive high-level authorization language. It has been successfully tried at Microsoft which led to further improvements of the language itself. One improvement is the separation of concerns between static core policies and dynamic workflow; important safety properties can be proved from the core policies alone, independently from the workflow. Another improvement is true decentralization; different principals live in different worlds exchanging information by means of communication and filtering assertions. We also present some complexity results.

1 Introduction

Preamble. Distributed Knowledge Authorization Language (DKAL) is a new high-level authorization language for distributed systems [6,7]; it is based on liberal datalog [6,3] and is considerably more expressive than other high-level authorization languages in the literature. The first practical application of DKAL was to the problem of automating source asset management (SAM) at Microsoft. We partook an active role in that endeavor. The automation problem involves more than DKAL and is still work in progress. While the trial has been successful, the application provoked improvements of DKAL that became a part of a larger revision of DKAL [7]. In this paper we present some lessons learned during the first practical application of DKAL and the improvements that we made to DKAL. In addition, we present some related theoretical results. We presume some familiarity with [6]; otherwise this paper is self-contained.

Source asset management (SAM). Large software companies have many partners, contractors and subcontractors who need to access the sources of the various software products produced by the company. The ever-growing number of such requests necessitates clear access control policies regulating who is entitled to use what sources, where, for how long, and so on. The company also needs processes in place to efficiently implement those policies. DKAL enables formulating rich and sophisticated policies that result in simpler audit and feasible automation.

⋆ The work was done in the summer of 2008 when the second author was an intern at Microsoft Research.

S. Fischer-Hübner et al. (Eds.): TrustBus 2009, LNCS 5695, pp. 149–158, 2009.

Lessons. The most important lesson that we learned working on SAM was a separation of concerns: static core policies on one side, and dynamic workflow on the other side. The workflow includes the procedural aspects of access decisions; the idea is to ensure the flexibility of the the way access decisions are made. It may be quite complex, but the policies should be succinct and easy to understand. Furthermore, the policies should guarantee important safety properties of the access decision process for any workflow. Various compliance requirements and regulations typically can be formulated as safety properties. It is desirable that the policies alone guarantee the compliance with those requirements and regulations thus eliminating the need to understand large amounts of procedural code.

The other important lesson was that in the case of automated access control regulated by clear access control policies, it is crucial for auditing purposes to properly log all human judgments. No set of policies and processes makes industrial access control deterministic. The inherent non-determinism is resolved by human judgments in making and delegating access decision. Logging these judgments is necessary for auditing purposes as it allows the auditor to understand who made what decisions and whether they had the right to do so (either originally or by delegation).

Operational semantics. As a result of the lessons learned, we improved the operational semantics of DKAL achieving true decentralization. In SecPAL [2], the precursor of DKAL, principals are distributed but their sayings are collected and processed together. In DKAL 1 [6], principals compute their own knowledge, yet some vestiges of a centralized approach remain, e.g. the global state. Now different principals live in different worlds exchanging information by means of communication and filtering assertions. Information exchange is allowed to be flexible, separating policy and workflow. Additionally, logging the right information is a natural byproduct of the way operational semantics is defined.

Complexity. We explored two communication models for defining workflows and proved that deciding reachability questions is possible in polynomial time in certain cases whereas deciding invariants is coNP-complete.

2   Related Work

Several languages have been developed in recent years to express authorization policies. The late genealogy of DKAL consists primarily of Binder, Delegation Logic and SecPAL. Binder [5] builds directly on Datalog, extending it with an import/export construct says that connects Datalog policies of different principals and makes the issuer of an imported assertion explicit. Delegation Logic [9,10] does not have explicit issuers for all assertions but it has constructs specific to authorization including ones for delegation, representation and thresholds.

SecPAL [2] has both explicit issuers and specific authorization constructs designed with distributed systems in mind. The number of constructs is deliberately kept low, but the language is expressive and captures numerous standard authorization scenarios. One important construct is *can say*: if A says B can say foo and if B says foo then A says foo. The can-say construct can be nested. The semantics is defined by means of a few deduction rules but, for execution purposes, SecPAL reduces to safe Constraint Datalog. Nesting of the can-say construct gives rise to relations whose arity depends on the nesting depth.

DKAL [6] extends SecPAL in many directions as far as expressivity is concerned. But it is quite different and builds on Liberal Datalog [6,3]. In particular DKAL allows one to freely use functions; as a result, principals can quote other principals. Contrary to SecPAL, communication in DKAL is targeted. Targeted communication plugs an information leak in SecPAL [6, §4] and improves the liability protection. The additional expressivity is achieved within the same bounds of computational complexity as that of SecPAL.

The main novelty of this paper is that we take workflow into account and deal explicitly with the runtime evolution of policies. In this connection we extend DKAL with the *from* construct. In [6], the sender directs communication to particular receivers but the receivers are passive. The from construct allows the receivers to filter incoming information. A limited policy evolution is possible in SecPAL: policy statements can be revoked but revocation is governed by static rules.

There has been work on the analysis of dynamic evolution of authorization policies in the Trust Management framework [11]. The approach there has been to specify statically what kind of policy rules can be added or removed. They analyzed reachability and invariant checking. We do that too in our framework. The richness of DKAL compared to the simpler TM language makes these questions even more interesting.

Modeling access control policies has been a scientifically very fruitful area with a considerable amount of literature, [1,4] to cite two. Since we focus on operational semantics in this paper, we skip a detailed discussion of the literature on policy modeling itself. Interested readers are referred to [6].

3   Operational Semantics

We refine the computation mechanism of DKAL, making explicit the transaction of information that was only partially explicit in [6]. Also we model situations where principals may listen only to information that they want to listen to by introducing a `from` construct.

We use the following form of DKAL's TrustApplication rule:

$$x \ \leq \ (p \text{ said } x + p \text{ tdon } x)$$

Here `tdon` alludes to "trusted on." (For experts on DKAL: we deprecate predicate `knows`$_0$ and function `said`$_0$, and we rename `tdon`$_0$ and `tdon` to `tdon` and `tdon`* respectively.)

3.1 Terminology

Every principal has an immutable, or at least stable, core policy and a dynamic policy where it can assert communication statements. We use the following notation:

Π_p Core policy of p.

Δ_p Dynamic policy of p.

$\mathcal{K}_p$ $\{x : \Pi_p \cup \Delta_p \vdash x$, no free variables in $x\}$, $\mathcal{K}_p$ is the *knowledge* of p.

3.2 Communication Rules

The main rule is COM. In simple form it says that if a principal A says an infon x to a principal B and if B is willing to accept x then x gets transmitted and B learns that A said x. In general, the rule is more complicated and involves a substitution η such that ηx is ground.

$$\frac{\begin{cases} (A \text{ to } q : x \leftarrow x_1, x_2, \cdots, x_m, \delta) \in \Pi_A \cup \Delta_A \\ (B \text{ from } p : y) \in \Pi_B \cup \Delta_B \\ \{\eta x_1, \eta x_2, \cdots, \eta x_m\} \subseteq \mathcal{K}_A, \text{Substrate}_A \models \eta\delta \\ \eta p = A, \eta q = B, \eta x = \eta y, \text{ no free variables in } \eta x \end{cases}}{\Delta_B + = A \text{ said } \eta x} \text{ (COM)}$$

The last line means that Δ_B is augmented with infon A said ηx. In practical implementations, any such communication resulting from this rule will be logged.

COM can be generalized to express common scenarios more succinctly. One such scenario is that if a principal B accepts an infon x, then it accepts infons of the form

$$z_1 \text{ tdon } z_2 \text{ tdon } \ldots \ z_k \text{ tdon } x.$$

$$\frac{\begin{cases} (A \text{ to } q : z_1 \text{ tdon } z_2 \text{ tdon } \ldots z_k \text{ tdon } x \\ \qquad \leftarrow x_1, x_2, \cdots, x_m, \delta) \in \Pi_A \cup \Delta_A \\ (B \text{ from } p : y) \in \Pi_B \cup \Delta_B \\ \{\eta x_1, \eta x_2, \cdots, \eta x_m\} \subseteq \mathcal{K}_A, \text{Substrate}_A \models \eta\delta \\ \eta p = A, \eta q = B, \eta x = \eta y, \text{ no free variables in } \eta x \text{ and } \eta z_i\text{'s} \end{cases}}{\Delta_B + = A \text{ said } \eta z_1 \text{ tdon } \eta z_2 \text{ tdon } \cdots \eta z_k \text{ tdon } \eta x} \text{ (TCOM)}$$

4 Example

Alice wants to download an article from the Chux (an allusion to Chuck's) store. Publishing house Best owns the copyright and delegates downloading permission to Chux. Chux has the policy that anybody meeting certain approval criteria can download the article. All this gives rise to the following core policies.

Π_{best} :   best to p : chux tdon p $canDownload$ article

Π_{chux} :   chux to q : q $canDownload$ article $\leftarrow$ $approve(q, \text{article})$

Π_{alice} :   alice : best tdon* alice $canDownload$ article

Alice starts the process by issuing a dynamic from assertion.

$$\text{alice asserts}\quad \text{from } r : \text{alice } canDownload \text{ article.} \qquad (1)$$

Assuming the relation $approve(alice, \text{article})$ is true, we have this evolution:

$$\text{By (1),}\quad \Delta_{alice} + = \text{ alice from } r : \text{alice } canDownload \text{ article.} \qquad (2)$$

$$\text{By (2), } \Pi_{best}, \text{TCOM}\quad \Delta_{alice} + = \text{ best said chux tdon}$$
$$\text{alice } canDownload \text{ article.} \qquad (3)$$

$$\text{By (2), COM}\quad \Delta_{alice} + = \text{ chux said alice } canDownload \text{ article.} \qquad (4)$$

$$\text{By (3,4), } \Pi_{alice}\quad \Pi_{alice} \cup \Delta_{alice} \vdash \text{ alice knows}$$
$$\text{alice } canDownload \text{ article.} \qquad (5)$$

We now add more details to the previous example. Chux lets a customer download an article if she authorizes the right amount of money for payment and has a perfect payrate. Chux trusts his accountant ac.Chux on customer's payrate.

Π_{chux} :   chux to a : a $canDownload$ $s \leftarrow a$ $authorized$ \$$k$ to chux for s,
a $hasPayRate$ Perfect, $price(s) = k$.

chux : accounts.Chux tdon a $hasPayRate$ e.

chux : a tdon a $authorized$ \$$k$ to chux for s.

chux from a : a $authorized$ \$$k$ to chux for s.

$\Pi_{ac.Chux}$:   ac.Chux to chux : a $hasPayRate$ $e \leftarrow a$ $hasPayRate$ e.

The last assertion is not a tautology. If accounts.chux knows that a has PayRate e then it says that to Chux.

Alice starts by authorizing payment to Chux for the article and then asks for the article. Chux then asks whether Alice has perfect payrate. The dynamic assertions are as follows:

alice asserts   to chux : alice $authorized$ \$40 to chux for article.

alice asserts   from r : alice $canDownload$ article.

chux asserts   from a : alice $hasPayRate$ e.

If the price of the article is \$40 and Alice has a perfect payrate, we can again infer using the operational semantics that Alice knows she can download the article.

5   Modeling Source Asset Management

In this section we explore the application of DKAL to a practical problem in large software companies, namely Source Asset Management (SAM). This encompasses formulating a policy and processes for making code access decisions.

A Project Manager in a large software company A wants a codeset to be accessed by staff at another company. In A, the codeset is owned by an Information Asset Owner (IAO) who usually delegates such access decisions to a Source Rep. The access decision takes into account the codeset, the company to access the codeset, the type of permission — read/write or read-only.

In our DKAL model, authorizations are managed by Authorization Managers (AMs) of the respective companies. AMs are automated tools modeled as principals. As far as code authorization is concerned, the AM of the company is (or represents) the company itself. The Project Manager, IAO and Source Rep are also modeled as principals. The policy of the authorization manager A-AM of A may be as follows:

$\Pi_{A\text{-}AM}$: p **tdon** q $canGet(codeset, parameters) \leftarrow assetOwner(p, codeset)$.

p **tdon** q **tdon** r $canGet(codeset, parameters) \leftarrow$

p **tdon** r $canGet(codeset, parameters)$, p is the manager of q.

p **tdon** q $canAccess(code, parameters) \leftarrow$

p is a Project Manager, r $canGet(codeset, parameters)$,

r is the AM of q, code is in codeset.

p **tdon** q **tdon** r $canAccess(code, parameters) \leftarrow$

p **tdon** q $canAccess(code, parameters)$.

The $canGet$ function specifies access permission to a set of source code files, whereas the $canAccess$ function specifies access permission to a particular source code file.

Consider a scenario where A wants to allow a vendor B an access to a codeset, and where B-AM has the policy

$\Pi_{B\text{-}AM}$: A-AM **tdon** B-AM $canGet(codeset, parameters)$.

A-AM **tdon** q $canAccess(code, parameters)$.

Suppose that Alan, Alfred, Andrew, Anthony and Alice work for A, and let Alan $\triangleright$ Alfred $\triangleright$ Andrew $\triangleright$ Anthony where $p \triangleright q$ means p is the manager of q. The role of Alice in the hierarchy will not matter. Suppose further that Alan is the IAO of *drivercodes*, a codeset that is to be given access to by B. A simplified workflow for the access decision may be as follows:

Access decision starts; Anthony goes to A-AM to request that B be given access to drivercodes.

A-AM *asserts* **from** p : B-AM $canGet($drivercodes, params1$)$.

Decision is escalated to Andrew, and then to Alfred.

Alfred *asserts* **to** *A*-AM : *B*-AM *canGet*(drivercodes, params1).

Alan *asserts* **to** *A*-AM : Alfred **tdon** *B*-AM *canGet*(drivercodes, params1).

A-AM communicates decision to *B*-AM.

A-AM *asserts* **to** *B*-AM : *B*-AM *canGet*(drivercodes, params1).

A developer Bruce in *B* needs a portion of drivercodes called gfx. Policy of Bruce is as follows:

$$\Pi_{bruce} : \quad B\text{-AM } \textbf{tdon } \text{Bruce } canAccess(code, parameters).$$

A typical workflow to acquire this code would be as follows:

Bruce asks for access to the code.

Bruce *asserts* **from** *p* : Bruce *canAccess*(gfx, params1).

In the workflow, this goes to *B*-AM. *B*-AM forwards the query along.

B-AM *asserts* **from** *p* : Bruce *canAccess*(gfx, params1).

In the workflow, query goes to *A*-AM, which again forwards the query.

A-AM *asserts* **from** *p* : Bruce *canAccess*(gfx, params1).

The workflow "chooses" who to ask about the query. It happens to be Alice. She decides to grant the code access to Bruce.

Alice *asserts* **to** *A*-AM : Bruce *canAccess*(gfx, params1).

Anthony confirms that Alice has the authority to grant access.

Anthony *asserts* **to** *A*-AM : Alice **tdon** Bruce *canAccess*(gfx, params1).

A-AM infers that Bruce can access the code and informs *B*-AM accordingly.

A-AM *asserts* **to** *B*-AM : Bruce *canAccess*(gfx, params1).

B-AM trusts *A*-AM on such statements and concludes that Bruce can access the code. *B*-AM communicates the decision to Bruce.

B-AM *asserts* **to** Bruce : Bruce *canAccess*(gfx, params1).

Bruce concludes that he can access the code.

As you can imagine, the workflow can proceed in myriad possible ways. Yet, the core policies of *A*-AM, *B*-AM and Bruce lets us state the following theorem, which holds independent of the workflow.

Theorem 1 (Safety of SAM Policy)

1. *If B-AM* **knows** *B-AM canGet(codeset, parameters)*
   then B-AM **knows** *A-AM* **said** *B-AM canGet(codeset, parameters)*
2. *If Bruce* **knows** *Bruce canAccess(code, parameters)*
   then Bruce **knows** *B-AM* **said** *Bruce canAccess(code, parameters)*

Proving invariant relations of this nature is hard in general, as we will find out in the next section.

6   Complexity Analysis of Safety Properties

6.1   Unrestricted Communication in Restricted DKAL

In this subsection we consider a restricted, yet useful fragment $DKAL^-$ of DKAL which is DKAL without variables, without $+$, canActAs, canSpeakAs, exists, tdon* and without substrate constraints in the rules. Note that attributes allow us to deal with roles even in the absence of canActAs, canSpeakAs. As opposed to canActAs and canSpeakAs, attributes take parameters. In the restricted fragment, we have three forms of infons. Firstly, there are *primitive infons* of the form $\text{Attribute}(a_1, \ldots, a_r)$ where elements a_i are regular. Secondly, we have *said infons* of the form p said x. Thirdly, we have *tdon infons* of the form p tdon x.

The communication is unrestricted in the following sense. We are interested in the consequences of the core policy of a given principal, say A, without restricting information that A can learn from other principals.

To simplify exposition, we let Σ_A be the set of said infons derived by the COM rule from Δ_A and communications to A by other principal. For example, if $(B$ to $A : x) \in \Delta_A$ and $(A$ from $B : x) \in \Delta_B$ then $(B$ said $x) \in \Sigma_A$. From the perspective of knowledge, it is sufficient to work with Σ_A, since the from and to statements by themselves do not add any knowledge for A; it is only when we combine corresponding from and to statements by the COM rule that additional knowledge is derived.

One interesting property is the reachability relation which is defined as follows: an infon I is reachable from a core policy Π_A if there exists a set Σ_A such that $\Pi_A \cup \Sigma_A \vdash A$ knows I.

Theorem 2 (Reachability)
The reachability relation for $DKAL^-$ is polynomial time computable.

Proof. Without loss of generality, we may assume that initially Σ_A is empty. We transform the total policy $\Pi_A \cup \Sigma_A$ of A in ways that preserve the reachability status of the given infon I.

Remove Some Said infons from Core Policy

1. Remove any rule $(p$ said $x) \leftarrow x_1, \ldots, x_k$ from Π_A and add the assertion $(p$ said $x)$ to Σ_A.
2. If an infon p said x occurs in the body of a rule R in Π_A, remove the infon from the body of R and and add the assertion $(p$ said $x)$ to Σ_A.

The new policy $\Pi_A^1 \cup \Sigma_A^1$ has the following property. In any core rule $y_0 \leftarrow y_1, \ldots, y_m$, every infon y_i is either primitive or a tdon infon. Obviously, $\Pi_A \cup \Sigma_A^1 \vdash A$ knows I if and only if $\Pi_A^1 \cup \Sigma_A^1 \vdash A$ knows I.

Augment tdon Rules. For any core rule p_1 tdon p_2 tdon $\ldots$ tdon p_j tdon x $\leftarrow x_1, \ldots, x_k$ where x is primitive or a said infon, do the following. Add core rules

$$p_2 \text{ tdon } p_3 \text{ tdon } \ldots \; p_j \text{ tdon } x \leftarrow p_1 \text{ tdon } p_2 \text{ tdon } \ldots \; p_j \text{ tdon } x$$
$$p_3 \text{ tdon } \ldots \; p_j \text{ tdon } x \leftarrow p_2 \text{ tdon } p_3 \text{ tdon } \ldots \; p_j \text{ tdon } x$$

$$\ldots$$

$$p_j \text{ tdon } x \leftarrow p_{j-1} \text{ tdon } p_j \text{ tdon } x$$
$$x \leftarrow p_j \text{ tdon } x$$

Also add the following assertions to Σ_A:

$$p_1 \text{ said } p_2 \text{ tdon } \ldots \; p_j \text{ tdon } x$$
$$p_2 \text{ said } p_3 \text{ tdon } \ldots \; p_j \text{ tdon } x$$

$$\ldots$$

$$p_{j-1} \text{ said } p_j \text{ tdon } x$$
$$p_j \text{ said } x$$

This way we obtain $\Pi_A^2 \cup \Sigma_A^2$. Observe that $\Pi_A \cup \Sigma_A^2 \vdash A \text{ knows } I$ if and only if $\Pi_A^2 \cup \Sigma_A^2 \vdash A \text{ knows } I$.

Any said infon $p \text{ said } x$ is reachable from any Π_A with a witness Σ_A asserting $(A \text{ from } p : x)$ and Σ_p asserting $(p \text{ to } A : x)$. So we may assume that I is primitive or a tdon infon. Recall that the DKAL derivability relation is polynomial time. Thus it suffices to prove that I is reachable from Π_A if and only if $\Pi_A^2 \cup \Sigma_A^2 \vdash A \text{ knows } I$. The if part is obvious. It remains to prove the only if part.

We claim that A cannot derive a new primitive or tdon infon as a result of learning any additional information, that is as a result of extending Σ_A^2 with any additional assertion R of said infon $p \text{ said } x$ (after using the COM rule with corresponding from and to assertions). Indeed, there are no said infons in the bodies of the rules in $\Pi_A^2 \cup \Sigma_A^2$. So adding R triggers no rule. Further, if $\Pi_A^2 \cup \Sigma_A^2 \vdash p \text{ tdon } x$ (x can be an infon of any type) then, by the second transformation above, $\Pi_A^2 \cup \Sigma_A^2 \vdash x$. So adding R does not help either. But these are the only ways that a said assertion can be helpful.

We say that $(A \text{ knows } I_1) \longrightarrow (A \text{ knows } I_2)$ is an invariant for a core policy Π_A if $\Pi_A \cup \Sigma_A \vdash A \text{ knows } I_1$ implies $\Pi_A \cup \Sigma_A \vdash A \text{ knows } I_2$ for any set Σ_A. This gives rise to a binary invariant relation $\text{Inv}(I_1, I_2)$ for $DKAL^-$.

Theorem 3 (Invariant Checking)
Computing the invariant relation for $DKAL^-$ is coNP-complete.

The proof is in [8].

6.2   Restricted Communication in Unrestricted DKAL

In this subsection we analyze the complexity of deciding classes of safety properties for unrestricted DKAL. The core policy does not have any from rules.

The workflow interacts with the DKAL inference machine through `from` assertions only. The content of `from` assertions is unrestricted within the bounds of syntactic well-formedness.

Since the `to` assertions can only be derived from the core policy, we need to look at the union of the policies of all the principals $\bigcup_\alpha \Pi_\alpha$ in order to analyze reachability and invariant checking. We assume that the number of variables in each rule in each policy is fixed a-priori and that α ranges over all principals in the system. We have the following results which are proved in [8].

Theorem 4 (Reachability Checking)
The reachability relation for DKAL is polynomial time computable.

Theorem 5 (Invariant Checking)
Computing the invariant relation for DKAL is coNP-complete.

References

1. Abadi, M., Burrows, M., Lampson, B., Plotkin, G.: A calculus for access control in distributed systems. ACM Transactions on Programming Languages and Systems 15(4), 706–734 (1993)
2. Becker, M.Y., Fournet, C., Gordon, A.D.: SecPAL: Design and Semantics of a Decetralized Authorization Language. In: 20th IEEE Computer Security Foundations Symposium (CSF), pp. 3–15 (2007)
3. Blass, A., Gurevich, Y.: Two Forms of One Useful Logic: Existential Fixed Point Logic and Liberal Datalog. Bulletin of the European Association for Theoretical Computer Science 95, 164–182 (2008)
4. Blaze, M., Feigenbaum, J., Lacy, J.: Decentralized trust management. In: Proc. 1996 IEEE Symposium on Security and Privacy, pp. 164–173 (1996)
5. DeTreville, J.: Binder, a Logic-Based Security Language. In: IEEE Symposium on Security and Privacy, pp. 105–113 (2002)
6. Gurevich, Y., Neeman, I.: DKAL: Distributed-Knowledge Authorization Language. In: 21st IEEE Computer Security Foundations Symposium (CSF 2008), pp. 149–162 (2008)
7. Gurevich, Y., Neeman, I.: DKAL 2 — A Simplified and Improved Authorization Language. Microsoft Research Tech Report MSR-TR-2009-11 (February 2009)
8. Gurevich, Y., Roy, A.: Operational Semantics for DKAL: Application and Analysis. Microsoft Research Tech Report MSR-TR-2008-184 (December 2008)
9. Li, N.: Delegation Logic: A Logic-Based Approach to Distributed Authorization, Ph.D. thesis, New York University (September 2000)
10. Li, N., Grosof, B.N., Feigenbaum, J.: Delegation Logic: A Logic-Based Approach to Distributed Authorization. ACM Trans. on Information and System Security (TISSEC) 6(1), 128–171 (2003)
11. Li, N., Winsborough, W.H., Mitchell, J.C.: Beyond Proof-of-Compliance: Safety and Availability Analysis in Trust Management. In: Proceedings of 2003 IEEE Symposium on Security and Privacy, May 2003, pp. 123–139 (2003)

$HB - MAC$: Improving the $Random - HB^{\#}$ Authentication Protocol

Panagiotis Rizomiliotis

Dep. of Inf. and Comm. Syst. Eng., University of the Aegean
Karlovassi GR-83200, Samos, Greece

Abstract. The $Random-HB^{\#}$ protocol is a significant improvement of the HB^{+} protocol introduced by Juels and Weis for the authentication of low-cost RFID tags. $Random - HB^{\#}$ improves HB^{+} in terms of both security and practicality. It is provably resistant against man-in-the-middle attacks, where the adversary can modify messages send from the reader to the tag and performs significantly better than HB^{+}, since it reduces the transmission costs and provides more practical error rates. The only problem with $Random - HB^{\#}$ is that the storage costs for the secret keys are insurmountable to low cost tags. The designers of the protocol have proposed also an enhanced variant which has less storage requirements, but it is not supported by a security proof. They call this variant just $HB^{\#}$. In this paper we propose a variant of the $Random - HB^{\#}$. The new proposal maintains the performance of the $Random - HB^{\#}$, but it requires significantly less storage for the key. To achieve that we add a lightweight message authentication code to protect the integrity of all the exchanged messages.

1 Introduction

Low-cost Radio Frequency Identification (RFID) tags will probably constitute the most pervasive device in history. Supply-chain management, inventory monitoring, payment systems, are only a few of the applications where RFID tags are used.

In most of the applications, there is much interest in deploying cryptographic mechanisms for tag authentication. In general, it is well studied how to design authentication protocols based on standard cryptographic algorithms. On the other hand, the maintenance of the cost of tags as low as possible, institutes space, as well as, peak and average power consumption limitations. (Especially for passive RFID tags which derive their power from the reader's signal). Considering that a public key algorithm like the RSA requires some tens of thousands of gate equivalents for implementation and that even symmetric encryption algorithms like block ciphers need some thousands of gate equivalents ([4]), it is clear that the implementation of one of the standard authentication schemes is too expensive for a tag in the form of Electronic Product Codes (EPC) ([3]) that can devote only hundreds of gates for security (at most 2000 gate equivalents are usually available for security).

S. Fischer-Hübner et al. (Eds.): TrustBus 2009, LNCS 5695, pp. 159–168, 2009.

In this context, the need for lightweight authentication protocols is imperative. Among the proposed solutions, one of the most prominent ones is the HB^+ protocol ([8]). The HB^+ protocol is based on the HB protocol ([7]), initially proposed for the secure identification of human beings. Due to the resemblance of the limited memory and computation capabilities between humans and low-cost tags, the HB consists a very promising starting point. HB and its variants performs only dot-product and bit exclusive-or computations. A crucial part of the protocol is the generation of random binary vectors. It is generally assumed that a noise bit can be 'cheaply' generated from physical properties like the thermal noise, diode noise, shot noise etc.

HB^+ is a symmetric key authentication protocol supported by a security proof in the so co called DET-model. In this model the attacker interacts with the honest tag up to a number of times, and then she tries to impersonate the valid tag. The security of the protocol is based on the conjectured hardness of the *Learning Parity in the presence of Noise (LPN)* problem. The attack model does not include adversaries that can manipulate messages exchanged between the reader and the tag, mounting man-in-the middle (MIM) type attacks. As was shown in [5], there is a simple MIM attack against the HB^+, that can efficiently reveal the secret key shared between the tag and the reader. Motivated by this attack several variants of the HB^+ protocol have been proposed ([2], [1], [6], [12], [14], [15]).

The $Random - HB^\#$ ([6]) protocol is one of these variants. $Random - HB^\#$ is provably secure in the DET-model, as well as in the GRS-MIM model, which includes attacks where the adversary can modify messages send from reader to the tag. The security of the protocol is based on a generalization of the LPN problem, the MHB puzzle. The $Random - HB^\#$ not only increases the security of HB^+, but it improves its efficiency, providing more practical transmission costs and error rates. Besides his undeniable advantages, $Random - HB^\#$ has a significant drawback. The necessary key sizes are prohibitively big for low-cost tags. Some practical modifications have been proposed to reduce the key size, but the proof of security does not apply.

In this paper, we propose a new HB family variant, the $HB - MAC$ protocol. Our proposal is based on the MHB puzzle, that was also used in $Random - HB^\#$, but we adopt a different approach. More precisely, we use this problem to create a lightweight authentication code. Traditionally, in HB type protocols the tag and the reader exchange blinding and challenge messages without any precaution. Our objective is to secure the new scheme by protecting the integrity of all the messages exchanged between the tag and the reader. The $HB - MAC$ has the same error rates, that is false rejection and false acceptance rates, as the $Random - HB^\#$ protocol. On the other hand, with a slight increase of the transmission costs, it needs up to 1/4 less tag memory for key storage than $Random - HB^\#$. The new protocol is not supported by a security proof, but we believe that we will be able to provide one shortly.

The paper is organized as follows. In Section 2, we describe the $Random - HB^\#$ protocol. In Section 3, we introduce the $HB - MAC$ protocol. We analyze its properties and we provide a security analysis. Finally, in Section 4, we give practical parameters for the new protocol and we compare it with the $Random - HB^{\#}$ protocol.

2   The $Random - HB^{\#}$ Protocol

In this section, we briefly describe the $Random - HB^{\#}$ protocol. We try to apply, as possible, the established notation. We use $Ber(\eta)$ to denote the Bernoulli distribution with parameter η, meaning that a bit $\nu \in Ber(\eta)$, then $Pr[\nu = 1] = \eta$ and $Pr[\nu = 0] = 1 - \eta$. A vector ν randomly chosen among all the vectors with length m, such that $\nu(i) \in Ber(\eta)$ and $\eta \in (0, 1/2)$, for $1 \leq i \leq m$, is denoted as $\nu \in_R Ber(m, \eta)$. Finally, we use $b \in_R \{0, 1\}^k$ to denote any random vector b with length k.

The $Random - HB^{\#}$ protocol is a recently proposed variant of the HB^+, a three pass protocol based on the HB protocol ([7]). The entire authentication process requires r rounds. If the tag fails at most t number of rounds, then it is authenticated. In [8], it was shown a concrete reduction of the $Learning\ Parity$ $in\ the\ presence\ of\ Noise\ (LPN)$ problem to the security of the HB^+ protocol in the so called detection-based model. LPN is conjectured to be hard. The original proof was further simplified and extended ([9], [10]).

Definition 1. $(LPN\ Problem)$ $Let\ A\ be\ a\ random\ (q \times k)\text{-}binary\ matrix,\ let\ x$ $be\ a\ random\ k\text{-}bit\ vector,\ let\ \eta \in (0, 1/2)\ be\ a\ noise\ parameter,\ and\ let\ \nu\ be\ a$ $random\ q\text{-}bit\ vector\ such\ that\ wt(\nu) \leq \eta q.\ Given\ A,\ \eta,\ and\ z = A \cdot x^t + \nu^t,\ find$ $a\ k\text{-}bit\ vector\ y^t\ such\ that\ wt(A \cdot y^t + z) \leq \eta q.$

The attack model does not include more powerful adversaries like the ones that can manipulate messages exchanged between the reader and the tag. As was shown in [5], there is a simple man-in-the-middle (MIM) attack against HB^+, that can easily reveal the secret vectors x and y.

Motivated by this MIM attack, several variants of HB^+ have been proposed ([2], [1], [6], [12],[14], [15]). One of the most interesting proposals is the $Random - HB^{\#}$ protocol ([6]), since it can provably resist such MIM attacks.

$Random - HB^{\#}$ is supported by a proof of security in the so called GRS-MIM model. The GRS-MIM model contains the MIM attacks, where the adversary is able to modify messages send from the reader to the tag. It is clear that the MIM attack presented in [5] is included.

$Random - HB^{\#}$ can be seen as a natural matrix extension of HB^+. The tag and the reader, instead of vectors, they share a two matrices X and Y with size $k_X \times m$ and $k_Y \times m$ respectively. The protocol is again a three pass one, but now the reader needs only one round instead of r to authenticate the tag (Fig. 1).

Besides the immunity to MIM attacks, the $Random - HB^{\#}$ protocol achieves two more goals. Keeping the low computational complexity of HB^+, in the same time, it reduces the extensive transmission costs of HB^+ and provides more practical error rates. The main drawback is that, in order to achieve the

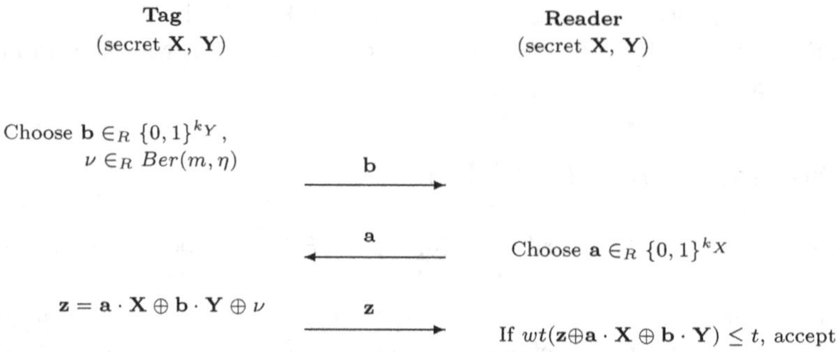

Tag		Reader
(secret **X**, **Y**)		(secret **X**, **Y**)

Choose $\mathbf{b} \in_R \{0,1\}^{k_Y}$,
$\quad \nu \in_R Ber(m, \eta)$

$\xrightarrow{\quad \mathbf{b} \quad}$

$\xleftarrow{\quad \mathbf{a} \quad}$ Choose $\mathbf{a} \in_R \{0,1\}^{k_X}$

$\mathbf{z} = \mathbf{a} \cdot \mathbf{X} \oplus \mathbf{b} \cdot \mathbf{Y} \oplus \nu \qquad \xrightarrow{\quad \mathbf{z} \quad}$

If $wt(\mathbf{z} \oplus \mathbf{a} \cdot \mathbf{X} \oplus \mathbf{b} \cdot \mathbf{Y}) \le t$, accept

Fig. 1. The $Random - HB^{\#}$ protocol

aforementioned objectives, $Random - HB^{\#}$ needs more memory bits for the secret keys, which makes it rather impractical for low-cost RFID tags.

Memory cost. To store the secret matrices the tag needs $(k_X \cdot m + k_Y \cdot m)$ bits.

Transmission cost. The $Random - HB^{\#}$ requires $(k_Y + k_X + m)$ bits to be transfered in total.

Error Rates. The false rejection rate of the protocol,

$$P_{FR} = \sum_{i=t+1}^{m} \binom{m}{i} \tag{1}$$

and false acceptance rate,

$$P_{FA} = \sum_{i=0}^{t} \binom{m}{i} 2^{-m}. \tag{2}$$

Security of $Random - HB^{\#}$. The HB# is provably secure under both the DET model and the GRS-MIM models. That is, it is secure against passive eavesdroppers and adversaries that can actively query a legitimate tag, as well as against attackers that can modify the messages send by the reader to the tag. To prove the security of the scheme, a natural matrix-based extension of the LPN problem was introduced and its hardness was proved in [6]. The extended problem is called *MHB puzzle* (because its proof is based on the theory of weakly verifiable puzzles) and it is defined as follows.

Definition 2. *(MHB puzzle)[[6]] Let $\eta \in (0, 1/2)$ and m and q be polynomials in k. On input the security parameter 1^k, the generator G draws a random secret $(k \times m)$-binary matrix X, q random vectors $(a_1, \cdots, a_q)$ of length k, computes for $1 \le i \le q$ the set of answers $z_i = a_i \cdot X + \nu_i$, where each bit of ν_i is 1 with probability η, and draws a random vector a of length k constituting the challenge* *to the adversary. It outputs $\{(\boldsymbol{a_i}, \boldsymbol{z_i})\}_{1 \leq i \leq q}$ and $\boldsymbol{a}$. The solver returns a vector $\boldsymbol{z}$. The secret check information is $\boldsymbol{X}$, and the verifier V accepts if, and only if, $\boldsymbol{z} = \boldsymbol{a} \cdot \boldsymbol{X}$.*

Lemma 1 ([6]). *Assume the hardness of the LPN problem. Then, the MHB puzzle is $(1 - \frac{1}{2})$-hard.*

In [6], a concrete reduction of the MHB puzzle to the security of the $Random - HB^{\#}$ protocol is provided. We are going to use the MHB puzzle in our proposal as well. The choice of parameters was evaluated in [13].

3 $HB - MAC$: A New Variant of the HB Protocol

In this section, we propose a new variant of the HB protocol, using some of the virtues of the $Random - HB^{\#}$ protocol. The new scheme appears in Fig. 2.

The reader shares a different secret $k \times m$ binary matrix $\boldsymbol{M}$ with each tag. Initially, the tag generates a random vector $\boldsymbol{b}$ with length k and a vector $\boldsymbol{\nu_1}$ with length m, such that each bit of $\boldsymbol{\nu_1}$ follows the Bernoulli distribution $Ber(\eta)$, i.e. $Pr[\boldsymbol{\nu_1}(i) = 1] = \eta$ and $Pr[\boldsymbol{\nu_1}(i) = 0] = 1 - \eta$, for $1 \leq i \leq m$. The tag sends $\boldsymbol{b}$ and $\boldsymbol{msg_1} = \boldsymbol{b} \cdot \boldsymbol{M} \oplus \boldsymbol{\nu_1}$ to the reader. The reader, among all the tags under his jurisdiction, finds one such that for the corresponding matrix $\boldsymbol{M}$, it holds $wt(\boldsymbol{msg_1} \oplus \boldsymbol{b} \cdot \boldsymbol{M}) \leq t$, for some value t. This step is used for the identification of the tag.

Upon identification of the tag, the reader generates a random vector $\boldsymbol{a}$ with length k and a vector $\boldsymbol{\nu_2} \in Ber(m, \eta)$. Then, the reader transmits $\boldsymbol{a}$ and $\boldsymbol{msg_2} = \boldsymbol{a} \cdot \boldsymbol{M} \oplus \boldsymbol{\nu_2}$. If the identification fails, the reader computes a random vector $\boldsymbol{c}$ with length m and transmits $\boldsymbol{a}$ and $\boldsymbol{msg_2} = \boldsymbol{c}$.

The tag checks the condition $wt(\boldsymbol{msg_2} \oplus \boldsymbol{a} \cdot \boldsymbol{M}) \leq t$. If the condition is true, then the tag generates $\boldsymbol{\nu_3} \in Ber(m, n)$ and sends $\boldsymbol{msg_3} = (\boldsymbol{a} \oplus \boldsymbol{b}) \cdot \boldsymbol{M} \oplus \boldsymbol{\nu_3}$.

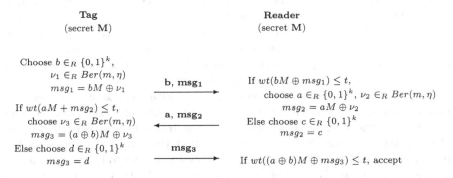

Fig. 2. The $HB - MAC$ protocol

Otherwise, it generates and sends a random message $msg_3 \in_R \{0,1\}^m$. As a last step, the reader authenticates the tag, if $\mathrm{wt}(msg_3 \oplus (b \oplus a) \cdot M) \leq t$.

Memory cost. The tag requires $k \cdot m$ bits for M.

Transmission cost. The tag sends $k + 2 \cdot m$ bits and the reader $k + m$ bits, and in total $2 \cdot k + 3 \cdot m$ bits are transfered.

Error Rates. The false rejection can occur if any of the three conditions

$$\mathrm{wt}(\nu_i) \leq t,$$

for $i = 1, 2, 3$, fails. That is, the false rejection rate of the protocol equals,

$$P_{FR} = 3 \cdot \sum_{i=t+1}^{m} \binom{m}{i} \eta^i (1 - \eta)^{m-i}. \tag{3}$$

Similarly, we have a false acceptance if all conditions $\mathrm{wt}(\nu_i) \leq t$, for $i = 1, 2, 3$, are falsely satisfied, i.e.

$$P_{FA} = \left(\sum_{i=0}^{t} \binom{m}{i} 2^{-m} \right)^3. \tag{4}$$

Leaving aside the generation of the random and noise vectors the computation on the tag required by the $HB-MAC$ is limited to dot-product and exclusive-or bit operations, like most of the HB variants. It easy to verify that the computational requirements are almost the same as the $Random - HB^{\#}$ protocol.

3.1   Security Analysis

There are two main design decisions that diversify $HB - MAC$ from the other HB-type authentication protocols. Firstly, almost all the proposed protocols, including HB^+ and $Random - HB^{\#}$, try to complete identification and authentication of the tag at the same time. In $HB - MAC$, we separate the two procedures. The first pair of messages, i.e. b and $b \cdot M + \nu$, send by the tag, is used for the identification of the tag by the reader, while the rest of the protocol is used for authentication. Of course any eavesdropper can trivially replay the first pair of messages and achieve its identification from the reader as a legitimate tag, but that has no impact on the security of the protocol, since the attacker has to pass the authentication phase that follows.

The second crucial design decision had to do with the use of a message authentication code to guarantee the integrity of the messages exchanged. It is no surprise that the most powerful attacks against HB^+ (as well as against many of its variants) are active attacks, meaning that the attacker is able to either modify or chose the challenge message send by the reader to the tag, since this message (as well as the blinding message send by the tag) has no protection against malicious modifications. In order to deal with this inherent weakness of the HB-family protocols, the designers of $Random - HB^{\#}$ have successfully applied the idea of using matrices as shared secrets. The pitfall is that, in order to resist active attacks, especially the man-in-the middle attack presented in [5], the sizes of the matrices have to be insurmountable big, making the protocol unsuitable for low cost RFID tags. (In [6], a more practical version of the protocol is also proposed, that we will discuss in the next section). In $HB - MAC$, we follow a different path. We increase the resistance against active attacks by adding a message authentication code to each message exchanged between the tag and the reader.

A well studied message authentication scheme is the following: the two communicating entities secretly chose the same hash function, which they apply to the messages, and the resultant hash values are encrypted before transmission. When the one-time pad is used for the encryption, the construction is unconditionally secure ([11]).

Let $h_M(x) = x \cdot M$, where M is a $k \times m$ matrix and x a vector with length k. The family of hash functions $\{h_M : \forall\ M\ k \times m\ matrix\}$ is a universal family of hash functions ([11]). The message

$$msg = h_M(x) \oplus \nu \tag{5}$$

is used as the message authentication code (MAC) of x. For a random vector ν, the scheme is unconditionally secure ([11]). In our case, $\nu \in Ber(m, \eta)$, $\eta \in (0, 1/2)$, and the security of the scheme is based on the hardness of the MHB puzzle.

In the security analysis of both HB^+ and $Random - HB^{\#}$, the attackers are divided in three categories:

Passive attacker. The attacker can only eavesdrop the communication between a legitimate tag and the reader. From each execution of the protocol, an eavesdropper can store three pairs of messages and their MAC. In order to impersonate a legitimate tag, the attacker has to compute two new such pairs. Of course she can just replay the first pair, and pass the identification phase. For the authentication phase, she has to efficiently compute a MAC value of $a \oplus b$.

Active attacker. The attacker that can query a legitimate tag. Due to the message authentication code, the attacker can query the tag only for messages that she knows their MAC value. The power of the attacker is also limited by the use of the blinding message message b, as it was initially proposed in [8], for the HB^+ protocol.

Man-in-the-middle type attacker. The attacker can modify the message send from the reader to the honest tag. Similarly to the above analysis for the passive attackers, a MIM attacker that wants to modify a message send by the reader to the tag needs to know the MAC of the derived message.

It is clear from the above that in all three attack models, the feasibility of the attack depends on the capability of the attacker to compute the MAC value $x \cdot M \oplus \nu$ for a given message x. We distinguish three cases.

1. *The attacker guesses the MAC value.* Since each message can have at most $\sum_{i=0}^{t} \binom{m}{i}$ different MAC values, the probability of guessing the correct one is $\sum_{i=0}^{t} \binom{m}{i} \cdot 2^{-m}$.

2. *The attacker replays an old MAC-value.* In that case we assume that the attacker has stored D different messages $\boldsymbol{x}$ and a corresponding MAC value, by eavesdropping previous executions of the protocol. The total number of stored bits is $D \cdot (k+m)$. The probability a given message to be among the stored ones is $D/2^k$.

3. *The attacker computes $\boldsymbol{x} \cdot \boldsymbol{M}$.* The attacker eavesdrops pairs of messages $\boldsymbol{x}^{(i)}$ and the corresponding MAC values $\boldsymbol{x}^{(i)} \cdot \boldsymbol{M} \oplus \boldsymbol{\nu}^{(i)}$ and computes $\boldsymbol{x} \cdot \boldsymbol{M}$ for a given message $\boldsymbol{x}$. This is the MHB puzzle and from [6], the success probability is negligibly close (in k) to $\frac{1}{2^m}$, assuming the hardness of the LPN problem.

Note 1. When any of the conditions $\mathrm{wt}(\boldsymbol{\nu_i}) \leq t$, for $i = 1, 2, 3$, fails, it means that either the reader or the tag are not legitimate, with very high probability (depending on the value of P_{FR}). We have decided not to interrupt the protocol, in order to avoid any leakage of information that such an action could cause.

4   Parameter Values and a Practical Proposal

Four parameters must be considered when the $HB - MAC$ protocol is implemented. Namely, the number of rows k and columns m of the secret matrix $\boldsymbol{M}$, the noise level η and the threshold t. We have that $\eta \in (0, 1/2)$. Following the notation in [6], the threshold t is defined as $t = um$, where $u \in (\eta, 1/2)$.

The first thing that we must have in mind, when we choose the parameters, is the performance of the tag. More precisely, for low cost tags where the authentication is a necessary but not sufficient feature, false rejection rate higher than 1% is totally unacceptable. From (3), we have that the false rejection rate depends on m, t and η.

From the security analysis we have that the overall security of the protocol depends on k and m. For 80-bit security, we choose $k, m \geq 160$. Generally, by choosing twice the bits of the aimed security satisfy all the three cases of computing the MAC of a message. (Probably, we could choose smaller values, but intuitively we need twice the size of security to cover sophsitcated attacks based on the birthday paradox).

Using the same noise levels as in [6], we present some practical characteristics of the protocol in Fig. 3. Also, in Fig. 3, we have the corresponding characteristics of $Random - HB^{\#}$. We do not present any parameters for the HB^{+}, since we know already from [6] that its performance is inferior than the performance of $Random - HB^{\#}$. From Fig. 3, it is clear that the performance of the two protocols

	$HB^{\#}$							
k_X	k_Y	m	η	t	P_{FR}	P_{FA}	$Trans.(bits)$	$Storage(bits)$
80	512	1164	0.25	405	2^{-45}	2^{-83}	1,756	689,088
80	512	441	0.125	113	2^{-45}	2^{-83}	1,033	261,072
	$HB - MAC$							
	k	m	η	t	P_{FR}	P_{FA}	$Trans.(bits)$	$Storage(bits)$
	160	1164	0.25	405	2^{-43}	2^{-249}	2,808	186,240
	160	441	0.125	113	2^{-43}	2^{-249}	1,362	70,560

Fig. 3. Practical parameters for $HB - MAC$ and $Random - HB^{\#}$ protocols

is almost the same. The only difference is that the $HB - MAC$, by slightly increasing the transmission costs, has significantly less storage costs (almost four times less).

In [6], a more practical variant of $Random - HB^{\#}$ was proposed, called $HB^{\#}$. More precisely, motivated by the message authentication schemes introduced in [11], it was proposed the use of a special class of matrices, namely the Toeplitz matrices. A $k \times m$ Toeplitz matrix is a matrix that can be fully described by its first column and first row. That is only $k + m - 1$ bits have to be stored.

In this variant, the tag needs to store only $(k_X + k_Y + 2 \cdot m - 2)$ bits instead of $(k_X \cdot m + k_Y \cdot m)$ bits for the two secret matrices X and Y. Of course this idea for storage cost reduction applies in our protocol as well, reducing the storage cost from $k \cdot m$ bits to $k + m - 1$. The security of the Toeplitz based version needs further investigation for both $Random - HB^{\#}$ and $HB - MAC$.

Note 2. The attack that was recently proposed against the $Random - HB^{\#}$ protocol ([13]) applies also against the $HB - MAC$, but both protocols can be easily protected by increasing the size of the shared secrets. For the comparison of their performance, we have decided to keep the values of the parameters as they appear in [6].

5 Conclusion

In this paper, we introduced a new HB family variant, the $HB - MAC$ protocol. Our proposal is based on the MHB puzzle. We use this problem to create a lightweight authentication code. Our objective was to secure the new scheme by protecting the integrity of all the messages exchanged between the tag and the reader. The $HB - MAC$ has practically the same error rates, that is false rejection and false acceptance rates, as the $Random - HB^{\#}$ protocol. On the other hand, with a slight increase of the transmission costs, it needs up to 1/4 less tag memory for key storage than $Random - HB^{\#}$.

We believe that the adoption of lightweight message authentication codes, as in the case of $HB - MAC$, will lead the HB family protocols to new design directions.

References

1. Bringer, J., Chabanne, H., Dottax, E.: HB^{++}: a Lightweight Authentication Protocol Secure against Some Attacks. In: IEEE International Conference on Pervasive Sevices, Workshop on Security, Privacy and Trust in Pervasive and Ubiquitous Computing - SecPerU (2006)
2. Duc, D.N., Kim, K.: Securing HB^+ against GRS Man-in-the- Middle Attack. In: Proceedings of the Symposium on Cryptography and Information Security, SCIS 2007 (2007)
3. EPCGLOBAL, http://www.epcglobalinc.org/
4. Feldhofer, M., Dominikus, S., Wolkerstorfer, J.: Strong authentication for RFID systems using the AES algorithm. In: Joye, M., Quisquater, J.-J. (eds.) CHES 2004. LNCS, vol. 3156, pp. 357–370. Springer, Heidelberg (2004)
5. Gilbert, H., Robshaw, M., Silbert, H.: An Active Attack against HB^+-a Provable Secure Lightweighted Authentication Protocol. Cryptology ePrint Archive, Report 2005/237 (2005) http://eprint.iacr.org
6. Gilbert, H., Robshaw, M.J.B., Seurin, Y.: $HB^{\#}$: Increasing the security and efficiency of HB^+. In: Smart, N.P. (ed.) EUROCRYPT 2008. LNCS, vol. 4965, pp. 361–378. Springer, Heidelberg (2008)
7. Hopper, N.J., Blum, M.: Secure human identification protocols. In: Boyd, C. (ed.) ASIACRYPT 2001. LNCS, vol. 2248, pp. 52–66. Springer, Heidelberg (2001)
8. Juels, A., Weis, S.A.: Authenticating Pervasive Devices with Human Protocols. In: Proceedings of Crypto 2005. LNCS, vol. 3126, pp. 293–308. Springer, Heidelberg (2005)
9. Katz, J., Shin, J.S.: Parallel and concurrent security of the HB and HB$^+$ protocols. In: Vaudenay, S. (ed.) EUROCRYPT 2006. LNCS, vol. 4004, pp. 73–87. Springer, Heidelberg (2006)
10. Katz, J., Smith, A.: Analyzing the HB and HB^+ Protocols in the Large Error Case, http://eprint.iacr.org/2006/326.pdf
11. Krawczyk, H.: LFSR-based hashing and authentication. In: Desmedt, Y.G. (ed.) CRYPTO 1994. LNCS, vol. 839, pp. 129–139. Springer, Heidelberg (1994)
12. Munilla, J., Peinado, A.: HP-MP: A Further Step in the HB-family of Lightweight authentication protocols. Computer Networks 51, 2262–2267 (2007)
13. Ouafi, K., Overbeck, R., Vaudenay, S.: On the security of hB# against a man-in-the-middle attack. In: Pieprzyk, J. (ed.) ASIACRYPT 2008. LNCS, vol. 5350, pp. 108–124. Springer, Heidelberg (2008)
14. Piramuthu, S.: HB and Related Lightweight Authentication Protocols for Secure RFID Tag/Reader Authentication. In: CollECTeR Europe Conference, Basel, Switzerland, June 9-10 (2006)
15. Piramuthu, S., Tu, Y.: Modified HB Authentication Protocol. In: Western European Workshop on Research in Cryptology, Germany (July 2007)

Author Index